Chri
Merry Christmas,
May your talents soar
beside your castle
at the sea!
Love, Mom & Dad

Seascape Gardening

From New England to the Carolinas

Seascape Gardening

ANNE HALPIN
Photography by **ROGER FOLEY**

 Storey Publishing

The mission of Storey Publishing is to serve our customers by publishing practical information that encourages personal independence in harmony with the environment.

Edited by Carleen Madigan Perkins
Cover design by Kent Lew
Text design by Kent Lew and Vicky Vaughn
Production by Vicky Vaughn and
    Jennifer Jepson Smith
Indexed by Christine R. Lindemer,
    Boston Road Communications
Illustrations copyright © Janet Fredericks

Printed in China by Regent Publishing Services
10 9 8 7 6 5 4 3 2 1

Text copyright © 2006 by Anne Halpin
Cover and interior photographs copyright © Roger Foley
    with the exception of those listed on page 215

The information in this book is true and complete to the best of our knowledge. All recommendations are made without guarantee on the part of the author or Storey Publishing. The author and publisher disclaim any liability in connection with the use of this information. For additional information please contact Storey Publishing, 210 MASS MoCA Way, North Adams, MA 01247.

Storey books are available for special premium and promotional uses and for customized editions. For further information, please call 1-800-793-9396.

LIBRARY OF CONGRESS CATALOGING-IN-PUBLICATION DATA

Halpin, Anne Moyer.
    Seascape gardening / by Anne Halpin ; photographs by Roger Foley.
        p. cm.
    Includes index.
    ISBN-13: 978-1-58017-533-1; ISBN-10: 1-58017-533-3 (jacketed hardcover : alk. paper)
    ISBN-13: 978-1-58017-531-1; ISBN-10: 1-58017-531-7 (pbk. : alk. paper)
    1. Seaside gardening. 2. Seaside gardening—Atlantic Coast (U.S.) I. Title.

SB460.H35 2006
635.9'0914'6—dc22
                                                                2005021732

For all the intrepid gardeners who nurture plants near the sea

Contents

CHAPTER 1

Coastal Conditions

WHO DOESN'T LOVE THE SEASHORE? The sparkling water, the soft summer breezes, and the rhythmic crashing of waves on the beach have a way of drawing the tension right out of us. The climate at the seashore is so congenial because it is modified by the ocean. Look at the USDA Hardiness Zone Map (see page 216) and you will notice that coastal areas are designated as warmer zones than places not far inland. In summer and early autumn, the seaside is indeed a pleasant place.

ABOVE: Purple wands of anise hyssop (*Agastache* sp.) and pink cosmos sway in the coastal breezes in this seaside garden.

RIGHT: A quiet cove at sunset along the dramatic, rocky shoreline of Massachusetts becomes a very different place when storm winds blow.

But for plants, as for year-round residents, the seashore can be a tough place to live. There is a lot of wind, for one thing; at the beach it blows almost constantly, carrying with it abrasive sand and drying salt. The soil is sandy — almost entirely sand close to the beach — and sand is a harsh growing medium for plants. Sand is low in the nutrients plants need to grow, and it is usually dry, because rainwater passes through it quickly, ending up in the water table far below.

Autumn weather is mild along the coast, because the sea cools more slowly than do the landmasses inland. But in spring the weather is cool because the ocean warms more slowly than land, and spring weather can be unpredictable at the seashore, with chilly rains and late cold snaps alternating with spells of mild, sunny conditions. Fall brings hurricanes; winter offers the coastal storms called nor'easters that can be as devastating as hurricanes. Plants can be flattened by the strong storm winds, trees can be uprooted, and high tides can wash over the dunes and flood gardens with icy saltwater.

To survive at the seashore without help from humans, a plant has to be able to stand up to winds and abrasive blasting from wind-driven sand and salt. It can demand little in the way of nourishment from the soil, and it must be able to survive with little water or to send its roots deep underground to tap into the nearest aquifer. In addition, the plant has to endure the salty fogs that settle over it when the wind is still. But plants can, and do, survive at the shore. When you grow plants adapted to seashore conditions, and create sheltered places for other kinds of plants, seaside gardens can be dazzling and full of color from spring well into fall, or even winter in the southernmost regions.

To succeed with a garden at the seashore, you first have to understand the sort of environment you're dealing with. That's where we'll begin.

Goldenrod is one tough plant — it grows happily among rocks near the water's edge and withstands salt spray and wind.

A Snapshot of the Seashore, from North to South

THE COASTLINE IS CONSTANTLY changing in response to climatic cycles. During the ice ages, the polar ice caps expanded and glaciers formed, locking up more water, so the overall sea level dropped. More land was exposed and the beaches were broader. During warmer periods, the polar ice caps shrank, glaciers melted and retreated farther and farther north, and the sea level rose. In our own time, global warming is widely believed to be causing shrinkage of the polar ice and a corresponding rise in sea level. As the shoreline moves, coastal plants and animals move along with it.

Rivers also influence the coastline. Bays, estuaries, and salt marshes all formed as a result of the action of rivers. Rivers flowing into the sea carry with them sediments and dissolved materials that are deposited on the ocean floor when the river meets the sea. The sediments build up over time — they cover the continental shelf, which was created as sea level rose after the last ice age and now underlies the fairly shallow water close to the coast.

Ocean waves and currents help to shape the coastline too. The waves pound away relentlessly. Waves in winter are bigger and stronger than summer waves, which are gentler. Winter waves tend to erode and wear down beaches, while in summer the beach can be naturally replenished when the waves are less intense.

THE ROCKY NORTH

The Atlantic seacoast looks different depending on where you are. The northernmost part of the coast, from Maine south to Connecticut, is the edge of the North American continent itself; it is rocky, with wooded bluffs and stony shores. There are high cliffs and headlands, rocky bluffs that were once part of ancient mountains, ledges and caves, bays and coves. The coastline changes continuously, but these rocky shores have changed little

Along the coast of the northeastern United States, rocky ledges and bluffs drop right to the edge of the sea, and where beaches do exist, they are usually stony.

From Cape Cod southward, Atlantic beaches are sandy and lined with dunes, an ecosystem undergoing a continual process of change as beaches are eroded and rebuilt.

since ancient times. Rock seems hard and permanent to us, but it is slowly, constantly weathering. Waves wear away at the base of rocky cliffs, rainwater seeps into cracks and causes fractures when it freezes, and eventually pieces of the rock break off and fall. The rock pieces break into smaller stones, and eventually are ground into sand. In the Northeast, the coastline drops steeply toward the ocean and the strong tides and high-energy wave action carry away any sand that forms — there's no place for it to collect. Instead of being flat and sandy, many of the beaches there are covered with stones.

There are islands, capes, and peninsulas in the Northeast, surrounded by bays and coves. Around some of the edges of these bodies of water are marshes. Long Island Sound, which lies between Long Island and Connecticut, protects both southern Connecticut and northern Long Island from the effects of the ocean.

From Massachusetts to Long Island, the seashore was formed by debris left behind by glaciers as they retreated after the last ice age. As you travel down the coast, from Cape Cod southward, you can find salt marshes and sandy beaches. From Long Island to South Carolina, the seashore is lined mostly with beaches and dunes. These beaches are in a process of continuous change; they shrink, then are replenished in response to natural seasonal cycles

and the effect of storms. As the beach and dunes reestablish themselves, their position is often a bit farther landward than their previous position. Human interventions — bulkheads, jetties, and other coastal structures — also alter the coastline. These structures cause sand to erode in one place and deposit in another.

SANDY SHORES

From Long Island south to Virginia Beach, in northern Virginia, the Atlantic coastline is a low, flat plain. The Delmarva Peninsula, made up of Delaware and parts of Maryland and Virginia, lies between the ocean and the Chesapeake Bay. The Delaware Bay turns southern New Jersey into a sort of peninsula, too. A string of low-lying, sandy barrier islands runs along this stretch of the coast, with bays separating them from the mainland.

Barrier islands are created by the action of waves and currents that deposit sand that builds up high enough to rise out of the ocean. The islands begin as sandbars that get bigger and bigger and then act as buffers for the mainland coast, dissipating the force of surging ocean waves during storms and absorbing the energy generated by tides and ocean currents to ameliorate the impact of floods and winds. The Atlantic barrier islands are not isolated entities but are connected to one another by common winds, water currents, and, in

Freshwater rivers deposit sediment where they flow into the salty sea, and estuaries form around the junction of river and ocean.

turn, the movement of sand along the coast. What happens to one of the barrier islands affects the rest. The seaward sides of the barrier islands are lined with dunes. The back sides have salt marshes and, in some cases, more dunes.

Beaches and barrier islands are ephemeral, in geological terms. They change all the time, from year to year and even day by day. The chain of barrier islands ends with North Carolina's Outer Banks. Farther south is Cape Hatteras, the most northerly of a series of capes that extends into South Carolina. At Cape Hatteras, the warm Gulf Stream flowing north meets cold offshore currents flowing south, and the climate can be stormy. The North Carolina coast represents the limit of the growing range for a variety of plants. Some, such as palms, can grow no farther north. For others, like beach heather, North Carolina is the southern limit of their range.

THE LOW COUNTRY

The coast of South Carolina is generally calmer than that of North Carolina. A number of islands, called sea islands, lie off the coast. These islands are wider than the Outer Banks and the barrier islands farther north. Dunes lie along the oceanfront, with flatlands and swales around them. Farther into the interior of the islands the natural vegetation is pine and oak woodlands. The western boundary of the sea islands and the eastern edge of the mainland are dotted with marshes, with creeks cutting through them. The Ashley and Cooper Rivers run into the ocean and deposit sediment at their mouths.

RIVERS, ESTUARIES, AND BAYS

Rivers affect the ocean wherever they empty into it. They deposit sediment into the sea that can change the coastline. Estuaries, salt marshes, and bays all can form because of the action of rivers. Estuaries, which are really tidal rivers, are a unique environment, a mix of freshwater and saltwater. The freshwater flowing into an estuary from a river is lighter and less dense than saltwater and tends to float on top of the saltwater where it flows into the bay.

Salinity varies in an estuary. Closer to the river, the water is brackish, lower in salt. Approaching the bay, the water becomes increasingly salty. Sea creatures living in estuaries must adapt to fluctuating salt levels caused by tidal currents and flooding caused by storms.

Bays are parts of the ocean protected by arms of land extending into the sea. The tide rises and falls in a bay as it does in the ocean, but large waves do not break onto the shoreline as they do on ocean beaches. Although waterfront conditions on the bay are often less severe than those on the oceanfront, storms can still cause damage.

THE COMPOSITION OF SAND

The composition of beach sand varies along the length of the coast. Northern and mid-Atlantic beaches contain a high percentage of quartz particles, which offer little in the way of mineral nutrients for plants. The sand provides a medium in which plants can anchor their roots, but it offers little else for them. Farther down the coast, in South Carolina, the sand contains calcium carbonate, which comes from the decomposition of seashells. But no matter what its composition, beach sand doesn't stay in one place — it blows around almost constantly. Over time, entire dunes can move and re-form.

Changes in the Land

On eastern Long Island, Montauk daisies (*Nipponanthemum nipponicum*) bloom lavishly in October. Tolerant of salt and wind, these are growing right on the dunes.

Not all seashore places are the same. Although this book deals with only the temperate parts of the Atlantic coast of the United States (the subtropical climates of Florida and the Deep South are a very different environment), there's a lot of variation from one end to the other, and sometimes even within a five-mile stretch. The rocky coast of Maine is a whole lot different from the Outer Banks of North Carolina. The back side of the primary dune is different from the plain a mile behind it.

BARRIER BEACHES AND PRIMARY DUNES

Beaches form when ocean waves and currents deposit sand, or rock weathers over time, on an unobstructed coastline. An important thing to remember about beaches is that they change all the time. The sand is constantly on the move. Along the Atlantic Coast, winter storms tear away at the beach and the dunes. In summer, the ocean is quieter and the beach rebuilds. As described on pages 11 to 13, the beach surface may be sandy or stony (in which case it is called shingle).

Dunes are simply mounds of sand that form where something stops the flow of wind inland from off the sea, in turn causing the wind to drop the sand it is carrying to the lee side of the obstruction. The obstruction need not be large—it could be as small as a clump of grass or a piece of driftwood. Sand begins to pile up around the obstruction as the wind dumps more of it, always to the lee side. Over time, a dune is built. Then pioneer plants, notably American beach grass (*Ammophila breviligulata*) and sea oats (*Uniola paniculata*), begin to colonize the dune and hold the sand in place. American beach grass is adept at stabilizing moving sand because its rhizomes grow both horizontally and vertically, providing good anchorage. We usually think of dunes in relation to barrier beaches, but dunes can be found in other places where there's a lot of wind and enough sand for it to blow around. Near the coast, dunes can form along shores at the back of barrier islands as well as at the front, and along the shores of the mainland, too. The dunes develop when the wind blowing across the beach picks up sand and carries it along until it meets with plants, fences, or other impediments that slow it down enough to cause it to drop the sand.

Dunes protect the land behind them from the ravages of the sea. Naturally formed dunes have breaks in them through which ocean surges can flow and release their considerable energy. Where these gaps don't exist, such as in artificially constructed dunes or hard structures like seawalls, wave energy doesn't dissipate and the waves are more likely to erode the

Only the most resilient plants can survive in sand dunes, even secondary dunes set back from the beach. Most dune plants are low growing, and the few trees that can adapt, like these pines, will not be tall.

beach and cut away at the dunes. Eventually the sea will break through somewhere.

Even naturally occurring dunes change. The wind that forms the dunes can also destroy them. The breakdown process often starts when the dunes are disturbed by people or animals walking on them, vehicles driving over them, natural vegetation being damaged or removed during construction, recreational activities, or storms or other forces of nature.

Sometimes referred to as the "pioneer zone," the beach and primary dunes are the toughest places for plants to grow. The primary dunes are those closest to the sea. Not many plants can survive on the beach on a long-term basis, and almost none of the ones that can are woody. You won't find trees growing on the barrier beaches of the Atlantic Coast, at least not on their own. In fact, the first plants of any kind are found from the high-tide line into the dunes. It's almost always windy at the beach, with abrasive sand and drying salt carried on the breezes and gusts. Sand can be carried in the air when the wind blows 12 to 15 miles per hour or faster — a very common occurrence. The system of dunes above the high-tide line on the beach protects the flatlands behind them. But occasionally a storm will send the tide surging into the dunes, flooding inland areas.

Plants play a critical role in the ecosystem of beach and dune. American beach

Bluffs, being raised above the highest wind and salt concentrations, can support a greater variety of plants than can dune environments.

grass, for example, helps to stabilize the dunes on which it grows along the Middle Atlantic beaches. Farther south, sea oats are an important dune stabilizer. The plants' leaves trap sand being blown inland and slow the speed of the wind as it passes over the tops of the dunes. The wide-ranging roots of the grass plants help to keep the sand in place on the dunes and prevent them from eroding.

Many communities actively plant beach grass to protect their dunes. Some put up snow fencing, which also reduces the degree of erosion on primary dunes.

COASTAL BLUFFS

When you think about the rocky coast of Maine, you're thinking of coastal bluffs. Ocean bluffs are found farther down the coastline as well, such as in Montauk, at the very eastern tip of Long Island. But they are most closely associated with New England. The bluffs are raised above sea level — in some places by more than 100 feet — and don't get hit with as much salt spray as barrier beaches and primary dunes. The northern shore of Long Island has coastal sound bluffs — sandy bluffs that border Long Island Sound, which separates Long Island from Connecticut.

Long Island's bluffs are sandy, but along the northern Atlantic coast the underlying rock contains less quartz, and the soil that results is less sandy and more moist. Where the bluffs are wooded the soil contains more organic matter and nutrients than beach sand. In some parts of New England, the woods come almost to the edges of bays. Flooding from high tides isn't an issue on the bluffs. These environments are altogether more congenial places for plants — and easier places to garden — than beachside locations. Still, they are not without challenges. The soil on

Dunes form where beach grass and other barrier plants obstruct the wind blowing inland from the ocean and cause it to drop the sand it carries.

Behind the dunes lies a somewhat protected "scrub zone." It can support a good variety of plants, though it is sometimes inundated with seawater.

Much of the seaside landscape in South Carolina — often called the Low Country — is dominated by low-lying saltwater marshes.

New England bluffs is rocky. Fogs rolling in off the ocean bring moisture, but they also carry salt, which is drying to plants. And the wind can be severe.

COASTAL PLAINS

A coastal plain, sometimes referred to as the "scrub zone" (which for our purpose here is not quite the same as the broader coastal plain defined by geologists), we will consider to be the flat landmass that lies behind primary dunes or coastal bluffs. The coastal plain gets some protection from salt spray and wind from the dunes or bluffs, and the soil, while sandy, generally has at least a thin layer of organic matter on top. But storms can still send saltwater flooding inland, and strong winds blow. Planting or building windbreaks makes the coastal plain a better place for gardening.

In some places there are depressions in the coastal plain, between the primary and secondary dunes, called swales. A variety of plants grows naturally in these low pockets — bearberry (*Arctostaphylos uva-ursi*), bayberry (*Myrica pensylvanica*), beach plum (*Prunus maritima*), and eastern red cedar (*Juniperus virginiana*), for instance. If the water table is close enough to the surface, ponds may form in these depressions; if the ocean does not flood into them, these ponds can contain freshwater. When seawater mixes in they become brackish, and marsh habitats — supporting plants like cordgrass (*Spartina pectinata*) and sea lavender (*Limonium carolinianum*) — may develop around their edges.

The size of our coastal plain varies a great deal. In Maine there really is no coastal plain, but in North Carolina it extends inland for about 150 miles.

BARRIER ISLANDS AND SALT MARSHES

Barrier islands are narrow islands separated from the mainland by saltwater bays or lagoons. They lie parallel to the coastline, close to sea level, and are subject to plenty of wind and salt spray. Storms can bring saltwater flooding to barrier islands, and in severe storms the sea can cross the entire island to meet the lagoon. The soil is mostly sand, with perhaps a thin layer of organic matter on top. Even with regular rainfall, plants must have deep roots and be able to tolerate drought if they are going to survive.

Barrier islands may have secondary dunes behind the coastal plain, on the north or west side (depending on which part of the coast they are near). The lee (landward) side of secondary dunes can be home to an assortment of plants in different microclimates.

The two big limiting factors for plants growing on barrier beaches are how exposed they are to the briny sea breezes and how far above sea level they sit. At lower elevations, plants must endure occasional flooding, but they are also closer to the water table, so more moisture is available on a regular basis.

Farther up the back of a dune, the surface of the sand becomes hot and dry in summer. Only plants that have deep roots can access the water table. The only other plants that can grow here without human intervention are desert plants that can survive for long periods without water.

Salt Spray and Gale-force Winds

Wind is a constant at the seashore, and plants must be able to bend before it without breaking. Ornamental grasses are flexible enough to sway and dance in the breeze.

THE WEATHER AT THE SEASHORE IS often dramatic, and it can change quickly. But no matter where you live along the coast, your plants will have to contend with wind, salt, sand, and intense sun. It's important to choose plants that can handle the stressful conditions, of course. But gardeners can take steps to moderate the climate in their garden, to give plants a more hospitable environment and to broaden the range of plants likely to thrive in it.

Plants native to seashores have developed special adaptations that enable them to withstand the environmental stresses. Many are especially strong structurally, with sturdy but flexible trunks and branches able to withstand strong winds. Some plants (grasses, for instance) bend and sway before the wind so their stems do not snap. Deep root systems provide good anchors against the wind, and can travel far underground to tap into natural water sources. Some plants, such as beach plum, are smaller when they grow near the beach and grow larger in more protected locations farther back. See "How Plants Protect Themselves" (page 19) for more on plants' protective measures.

Here are some of the major challenges the seashore environment presents, and how to work with them in the garden. When you understand what combination of conditions exists right on your property,

you can figure out which plants are good candidates for your landscape and garden, and how you can modify the existing conditions to better suit their needs.

WIND

It's usually windy at the seashore. The wind is sometimes continuous, at other times intermittent, but it doesn't ever stop for long. Its speed can vary from a gentle breeze to a stiff gale to hurricane force of 80 miles per hour and up. The direction of the prevailing wind can change with the seasons. On Long Island, where I live, summer winds loaded with salt blow out of the south or south-southwest, and winter brings the fierce storms called nor'easters, which are driven by icy northeast winds. If the southwest corner of a beachfront property, or the northeast corner of a property fronting on Long Island Sound or a north-facing bay, is exposed, the wind will just bulldoze right through and chew up the landscape. Not all of the East Coast is subject to nor'easters, but they can occur in places as far apart and as different in climate as Maine and the Outer Banks of North Carolina.

It is especially important to understand wind direction if you live right along the beach. If the beach lies perpendicular to the direction of the prevailing winds, as in much of North Carolina, your property will be hit with stronger winds that will carry more salt across the beach and farther inland than if you live where the beach lies parallel to the prevailing winds, as is the case in much of South Carolina. There will be heavier salt spray on a perpendicularly positioned beach, too.

Wind affects seashore gardens in a number of ways. Strong winds can do plenty of damage in and of themselves. But at the seashore, the wind carries sand and salt with it, which causes even more trouble. Windblown sand is abrasive, scouring leaves and blasting stems. Salt blown onto leaves is very drying, drawing out moisture and sometimes causing burning of the foliage. The closer you are to the beach, the more extreme will be the effects that are produced by the wind.

Trees along a driveway or road, and the dunes at the back of the beach, can funnel wind like tall buildings in cities do. The wind can speed along these avenues faster than it blows over surrounding areas. These channeled winds can be very destructive to plants. If you have this problem on your property, you may need to either move some of the affected plants to different locations or install additional windbreaks.

If you are building a house or making other improvements on a property that has significant wind exposure, be very wary of removing the existing native vegetation. Remove as few plants as you possibly can, and replant the area as soon as the construction project is complete.

The best defense against the wind is a good windbreak. For waterfront properties, a windbreak is essential if you want to be able to grow any plants other than the toughest native species. See chapter 3 for information on creating a windbreak for your garden.

SALT

Salt gets into seashore gardens both from the air and from floodwaters. Windborne salt can cause serious damage to plants over time, and here's how: As waves break upon the shore, they throw droplets of seawater into the air. The saltwater droplets then travel inland on the wind, and some

HOW PLANTS PROTECT THEMSELVES

Seashore plants have developed a variety of adaptations that enable them to withstand salt spray, sand blasting, drying winds, and intense sun. Many plants, such as bayberry (*Myrica pensylvanica*) and yaupon holly (*Ilex vomitoria*), have tough, leathery leaves that resist damage from salt and dry out more slowly than thin leaves.

Some plants, such as sea grape and southern magnolia (*Magnolia virginiana*), have smooth, glossy leaves that repel saltwater. Others, like wax myrtle (*Myrica cerifera*) and most blue-toned conifers, have a waxy protective coating on their leaves that fends off salt and slows the evaporation of moisture.

Still other plants, such as sea buckthorn (*Hippophäe rhamnoides*) and Russian olive (*Elaeagnus angustifolius*), have very narrow or small leaves that offer less surface area to be battered by wind-blown sand and salt, and also less space for salt to cling to. Other leaves curl their edges inward to reduce transpiration and conserve moisture. Gray and silver leaves such as those of artemisias are covered with fine hairs that hold salt off the leaf surface and also reflect back some of the fierce sunlight, keeping the plants' internal temperature from rising to damaging levels. In addition, these leaf hairs protect the stomates, the pores from which leaves excrete moisture and gases.

Some plants conserve moisture by opening their stomates at night, when it's cooler, and closing them during the hot daytime, when evaporation is greatest.

Some plants, such as seashore elder (*Iva imbricata*) and glassworts (*Salicornia* spp.), are succulent and can store water in their stems or leaves. Some plants have even developed special glands that filter salt from the water the plants take in to fuel their growth (photosynthesis requires freshwater) and expel it from the plant. Some species of *Limonium* (sea lavender) contain these salt glands, as do salt hay and smooth cordgrass.

Some plants have more than one of these special adaptations.

The narrow, feathery foliage of tamarisk is especially salt tolerant. Here, its fall color catches the evening sun.

of the water evaporates along the way, making the salt more concentrated. Eventually the salt drops down to land on the plants (or anything else) below. Unless washed away by rain or a spray from a hose or sprinkler, the salt builds up on the plants, with the heaviest accumulation on the side of the plant nearest the sea. Growth on that side of the plant slows down, as the salt draws moisture from the leaves and interferes with transpiration and the normal growth processes of the plant tissues. The side of the plant facing away from the sea develops less of a salty cover, and continues to grow more or less normally. After a while, the lopsided growth produces a plant that appears to lean away from the water — the windswept look that is so typical of trees, especially, growing near the beach.

A hedge or other windbreak between the sea and the garden can protect plants from the worst effects of wind and salt spray. See chapter 3 for information on how to create a windbreak for your garden. When planning a beachfront garden, it's a good idea to put the most salt-tolerant plants in the most exposed spots.

Salt spray is most damaging to plants within 1,000 feet of the shoreline, and to new growth and tender young leaves early in the growing season. Salt-damaged leaves will turn brown and may die off if the damage is severe enough. Luckily for Atlantic shore gardeners, the worst storms come in late summer and fall, when the current year's growth has matured and gotten tougher. Surprisingly, in some cases salt appears actually to be *good* for plants. Some gardeners swear that salt spray rids their roses and hollies of insect infestations, and helps to control fungal diseases. Salt spray has also been reported to benefit lilacs and zinnias, which are notoriously prone to mildew.

Salt can also land on plants when fog envelops the garden when the air is still. Fog-borne salt just sits on the plants until the mist clears and rain or the gardener washes it off.

Salt can also come into contact with plants through water. This can happen in a couple of ways. First, during a storm, high tides can flood the beach and flow through gaps in the dunes or, in extreme circumstances, pour right over them, flooding inland areas beyond. Even the best-protected gardens can experience occasional storm-surge flooding if they are located near thc beach in low-lying areas. The second way saltwater can get into the garden is during times of drought, when the water table drops so low that saltwater gets into the groundwater. Saltwater infiltration is becoming especially problematic as unrelenting development in seashore towns puts more and more pressure on finite water supplies.

When groundwater becomes salty, plants draw up the saltwater through their roots. But too much salt begins to pull moisture out of the leaves, in a process called exosmosis. The plants start to wilt, and eventually they'll die from lack of water. The gardener's natural response is to water the drooping plants. But if the water coming from the hose or sprinkler is salty, watering only exacerbates the problem.

Plants native to the seashore have developed varying degrees of tolerance to salt, and some other kinds of plants are naturally tolerant, too. See "Salt-Tolerant Plants" (right) for listings of plants and their level of salt tolerance.

Some plants will withstand occasional saltwater flooding without undue harm, especially if the flooding occurs while the plants are dormant. See "Plants That Tolerate Flooding," (page 22). Still, it is far better for plants not to have to cope with saltwater around their roots. If drought and resulting saltwater infiltration are an ongoing or increasingly frequent problem where you live, you would be wise to rely on salt-tolerant plants for your property, especially when choosing trees and shrubs. This is particularly true if you get your water from a well rather than from a municipal source. Grow intolerant flowers, herbs, and vegetables in containers, where you can control the water source.

SALT-TOLERANT PLANTS

Plants with High Salt Tolerance	Plants with Moderate Salt Tolerance*
Agave spp., century plant (drought tolerant)	*Acer rubrum*, red maple
Arundo donax, giant reed	*Agapanthus* spp., lily of the Nile
Chamaecyparis obtusa, Hinoki falsecypress	*Ageratum houstonianum*, flossflower
×*Cupressocyparis leylandii*, Leyland cypress	*Artemisia* 'Silver King'
Euonymus fortunei, wintercreeper	*Asclepias tuberosa*, butterfly weed
Gaillardia, blanketflower	*Begonia semperflorens*, wax begonia
Hedera helix, English ivy	*Calendula officinalis*, pot marigold
Ilex vomitoria, yaupon holly (drought tolerant)	*Canna* spp., canna
Ipomoea pes-caprae, beach morning glory	*Catharanthus roseus*, Madagascar periwinkle
Juniperus conferta, shore juniper (drought tolerant)	*Centaurea cyanus*, bachelor's button
Juniperus horizontalis, creeping juniper (drought tolerant)	*Cosmos* spp., cosmos
	Cycas revoluta, sago palm
Juniperus virginiana, eastern red cedar (drought tolerant); may show some burning when very exposed; best used along with other plants	*Helianthus annuus*, sunflower
	Hemerocallis spp., daylily
	Ilex cornuta, Chinese holly
Lantana camara, lantana	*Juniperus chinensis*, Chinese juniper
Liriope spicata, lilyturf	*Ligustrum* spp., privet
Magnolia grandiflora, southern magnolia	*Liriope muscari*, lilyturf
Myrica cerifera, wax myrtle	*Lobularia maritima*, sweet alyssum
Nerium oleander, oleander	*Mahonia aquifolium*, holly grape
Ophiopogon japonicus, mondo grass	*Nyssa sylvatica*, tupelo
Panicum amarulum, bitter panic grass	*Ophiopogon japonicus*, mondo grass
Parthenocissus quinquefolia, Virginia creeper	*Pentas lanceolata*, star-cluster
Pittosporum tobira, Japanese pittosporum	*Persea borbonica*, redbay
Portulaca grandiflora, rose moss (drought tolerant)	*Phlox drummondii*, annual phlox
Quercus virginiana, live oak	*Podocarpus macrophyllus*, yew pine
Schizachyrium scoparium, bluestem	*Pyracantha coccinea*, firethorn
Tamarix ramosissima, tamarisk, salt cedar	*Rosmarinus officinalis*, rosemary
Trachelospermum jasminoides, Confederate jasmine	*Salvia* spp., sage
Thymus spp., thyme	*Santolina chamaecyparissus*, lavender cotton
Uniola paniculata, sea oats	*Sedum acre*, goldmoss sedum
Viburnum tinus, laurustinus	*Senecio cineraria*, dusty miller
	Serenoa repens, saw palmetto
	Thuja orientalis, arborvitae
	Verbena spp., verbena
	Vitex agnus-castus, chastetree

*These plants do best when planted in sheltered areas behind windbreaks.

Sedum is hardy and drought tolerant. It can also withstand occasional saltwater flooding, especially during winter dormancy.

If parts of your property flood regularly and are poorly drained (if, for instance, your land is marshy or near an estuary or wetland), think long and hard before you put in garden beds and borders there. Examine existing vegetation for clues. If you find the groundsel bush (*Baccharis halimifolia*) in residence, for example, there is likely saltwater, too. This shrub is native to coastal wetlands and can tolerate a high degree of salt around its roots.

If you nonetheless want to explore landscape possibilities, first consult your local building codes for ordinances that specify what homeowners may or may not do to wetlands and estuaries on their property, or parts of the property adjoining natural wetlands. Wetlands are important wildlife habitats and water-recharge areas, and are closely regulated in many coastal communities, even when they are located on private property. If you are allowed to plant in your wet spots, work with an experienced, well-qualified environmental engineer, landscape architect, or garden designer to plan the garden.

SAND

Sand is a helpful ingredient in soil; its large particles and loose texture help to lighten and aerate heavy, fine-textured clay soils into which it is incorporated. But as a main component of soil, sand leaves a lot to be desired. The beach sand found along the East Coast is made up almost entirely of quartz particles, which contain few of the nutrients plants need to grow. It has no organic matter to nourish beneficial soil microbes. The problem of poor nutritional value is compounded by the sand's inability to hold water.

Water is one of the main vehicles for transporting nutrients from soil to plants via their roots. Water powers plants' growth processes, and fine-textured beach sand repels water at first. Watering it is like trying to moisten peat moss or talcum powder. But when the sand does become wet, the moisture drains through it quickly, and plant roots have little time to absorb what they need. On top of that, the constant winds cause plants to lose what moisture they do have through rapid transpiration from their leaves. Salt deposited on leaves also draws out moisture. Without frequent watering in summer, seaside gardens can be full of stressed-out plants.

There are a few ways to reduce the amount of water a seaside garden is likely to swallow. Using drought-tolerant plants is one option. Working lots of organic matter into the soil is another (see chapter 3). Laying mulch after the garden has been planted also helps conserve soil moisture (see chapter 4). Many seaside homeowners install automatic watering systems for lawns and gardens. Overhead sprinklers, although less efficient than underground

Beach sand is a difficult growing medium for plants; it contains few nutrients for them and practically no organic matter, and moisture passes quickly through it.

systems, can be beneficial at the shore because they help rinse salt deposits from plant leaves. But any watering system should be carefully calibrated to provide thorough, deep watering and not just a quick daily spritz.

One additional problem with beach sand is that the carbonate in the seawater and the lack of humic acid formed by decaying plant material usually means the pH is alkaline, which makes some nutrients unavailable to plants even when they are present in the root zone. You can't, however, automatically assume that your soil is alkaline if you live at the shore. Seacoast soils away from the beach can be acidic. My own garden is about 1,000 yards from a bay and the soil is quite acid. Trailing arbutus, wintergreen, and huckleberry bushes grow wild in my backyard along with pine and oak trees — remnants of the pine/oak woodland that once covered this area. A soil test is always a good idea for seashore gardens.

Another problem with sand is that it blows around so easily. Carried on a strong wind, sand particles can scour leaves, bury young plants, and blanket lawns. It flies into woodlands; piles up against walls, fences, and rocks; and gets into equipment and machinery. Windbreaks will help trap blowing sand and keep it out of the garden.

STRONG SUN

Sunlight near the sea is especially intense because it bounces off the water and reflects off the light-colored sand. The beating sun heats up the sand on the beach — as you know if you've ever tried to walk barefoot on the beach up near the dunes in July. The sand can be 50 degrees hotter than the air temperature. The same effect, to a lesser degree, occurs away from the beach. Mulching the garden will help moderate soil temperatures for plants.

The strong sun near the sea can heat sandy soil to lethal levels for plants. Mulching the garden can help moderate soil temperatures.

Seeking Shelter

IF YOU OWN BEACHFRONT PROPERTY, you won't want to garden on the beach or the primary dunes. Primary dunes are off-limits for planting in many communities because they are so important in protecting the land behind them from flooding and erosion during storms. The ecosystem is too delicate to support landscaping even if you were permitted to install any. And not much grows on the dunes, anyway.

But the somewhat sheltered land *behind* the dunes — on the coastal plain, in swales, atop bluffs — offers plenty of opportunity for gardening, and the ecosystem is more stable in these places.

If you can plant on the lee side of the dunes, put in drought- and salt-tolerant ground covers to stabilize them. Bearberry and shore juniper are two of the best. It might be tempting to use beach grass, too, but beach grass does better on the windward side of the dunes (as explained in the entry on beach grass in chapter 5). Vines are also helpful for stabilizing dunes. Virginia creeper (*Parthenocissus quinquefolia*) and muscadine grape (*Vitis rotundifolia*) both do well behind the dunes and may creep right over the top.

If you live in an exposed location, plant windbreaks or hedges as described in chapter 3 to create sheltered areas for gardening, and also be sure to take advantage of the protected area that exists behind your house. You'll have the greatest choice of plants for gardens in these sheltered places. If your house is higher than one story, you can even include some shade trees in the landscape if you site them behind the house.

If you live along a rocky coastline where the soil is thin, consider a rock garden. You might be able to make some of the natural outcrops part of your garden by tucking plants into soil-filled pockets and crevices in the rock.

The dunes are essential for protecting the shoreline, and they provide shelter for beachfront gardens planted behind them. Planting drought- and salt-tolerant plants on the lee side of dunes helps stabilize the sand.

CHAPTER 2

Planning and Design

O<small>NCE YOU HAVE A GOOD UNDERSTANDING OF THE GROWING</small> conditions available on your seashore property, you can start to plan your garden. You'll probably want to start by thinking about what kinds of plants you'd like to grow — this is the most enjoyable part of garden design for many of us. But those decisions should also fit with your lifestyle and the kind of house you have. And you also need to find the best places on your property for the plants you want to grow. Depending upon your location and the kind of garden you want, you may need to modify the environment to create more congenial growing conditions for your plants.

ABOVE: A straight path, a mortared brick wall with pillars framing a view, and topiary standards in elegant urns give this seaside garden a serene, formal look.

RIGHT: This informal perennial garden blends loose drifts of yellow-orange black-eyed Susan (*Rudbeckia hirta*), red and yellow daylilies (*Hemerocallis* cvs.), lavender mallows (*Malva* sp.), and deep red coreopsis.

Finding the Best Site

A sheltered spot behind the house can accommodate tropicals like canna, coleus, and sweet potato vine, whose leaves would be battered by wind in an exposed beachfront location.

ALL GARDENERS WITHIN A FEW MILES of the sea have to contend with wind and salt to some degree, but specific conditions vary widely. Salt, wind, and sand are most intense on waterfront properties, and oceanfront properties have the toughest conditions of all. If your house is on an ocean beach, you will be able to grow a variety of salt-tolerant plants in the lee of the dunes. Ornamental plants with less resistance to salt and wind will need to be behind a windbreak or shelterbelt. Hedges or informal screens of plants can provide a secondary line of protection or, farther away from the water, they may be all the protection necessary. See "Creating Sheltered Places" on page 41 for information on windbreaks and hedges.

The area behind your house can also be a good place for plants, as can low spots over which the wind passes easily. If your house is more than one story high, the protected area behind it will be higher too, and you may be able to include some trees in the garden to create shade and add structure to the landscape. Take advantage of any protected spots you can find. But be wary of planting along the sides of the house, where salty winds can whip by and prove very damaging to plants.

It's important to know the direction from which the prevailing winds blow on your property, both in summer and in winter. Even if you only use your seashore house in summer, the plants are there year-round. To create a sheltered spot, you need to have something sizable — whether it be plants or structures — between the garden and the wind. For example, on eastern Long Island, where I live, the prevailing winds blow out of the north to northeast in winter and from the south-southwest (right off the ocean) in summer, so windbreaks should be placed on those sides of properties to protect garden plantings from wind damage.

Another strategy for seaside gardeners is to grow plants in containers, especially on decks and patios and around swimming pools. In the event of a storm, the containers can be moved under cover, or replanted afterward if they are too big to move.

Most salt-tolerant plants are sun lovers used to growing in somewhat exposed locations. But a sheltered position in full sun will afford you the broadest choice of shrubs, perennials, annuals, and ornamental grasses, including some without a lot of tolerance to salt. Roses, too, need plenty of sun to thrive. Southern gardeners will have more choices, because many plants that prefer full sun in the North need some shade in the afternoon in torrid southern landscapes, especially in seaside areas where the sun is especially intense. (The plant profiles in chapter 5 contain information about each plant's degree of salt tolerance and sun/shade requirements.)

This garden on the lee side of a seaside house is full of color from dahlias, coreopsis, cosmos, and geraniums in a lively mix of pinks, reds, and yellows.

What Kind of Garden?

When you've got potential garden sites figured out, you can turn your attention to how you want the garden to look and what you might like to grow there. Here is where your lifestyle figures in. For instance, if your seashore house is a second home that you use only in summer, you will probably want to showcase shrubs and flowers that bloom in summer. If you use the house primarily on weekends, you might opt for a low-maintenance landscape of shrubs, ornamental grasses, and ground covers, especially if you will be taking care of the garden yourself. Weekenders who want more demanding plants, such as perennials and annuals that need deadheading, can hire a local nursery or landscaping company to maintain the garden.

If your seaside house is your permanent home, you will want to think about providing interest in your landscape year round. The structural elements of the garden — trees and shrubs, fences and walls, paths and driveways, arbors and trellises — play a more prominent role in winter, when the summer flowers have died back. Evergreens offer year-round color and structure.

If you enjoy watching birds, plan to include in your landscape some plants they can use for food, cover, and nesting sites. Find likely spots for feeders and a birdbath. You can also plant a garden to attract butterflies or hummingbirds. Using environmentally friendly techniques and materials in your garden will make it especially supportive of wildlife.

The garden profiles in chapter 4 provide some fine examples of successful seaside gardens up and down the East Coast. Perhaps they will inspire you as you set out to create your own little piece of paradise. If you study the photos, you will find a variety of ingenious solutions to the challenges posed by seaside sites. Let these examples point you toward paths you might take in your own thinking about the kind of garden you want to create.

An Indian bench backed by tall rosemary plants that are overwintered in a greenhouse strikes an exotic note in a Long Island garden.

WHAT'S YOUR STYLE?

Garden designs are as diverse as the people who create them, and you will derive the greatest satisfaction from your garden when it expresses your own personal sense of style. The best gardens are the ones that express the personalities of their owners. In figuring out what kind of garden you want, you don't need to be a slave to the rules of garden design.

That said, you do need to investigate whether your community has ordinances governing things like setbacks and hedge heights, whether you can have a meadow if you want one or if a mowed lawn is mandated, and whether there are utility casements and rights-of-way on your property that must be maintained. Also, it takes time and experience to learn how to work with plants to express your style and create different effects. You can certainly rely on established design traditions to guide you. If you are new to gardening, or new to gardening at the shore, one of the best ways to learn what works is to look at other gardens in the area.

Basically, garden styles fall into three broad categories: informal, formal, and naturalistic. Each style tends to work best with particular kinds of houses and lifestyles.

A garden's formality or informality is determined by the way it is laid out, the plants that grow in it, the colors used, and how the plants are maintained.

Informal. Many seashore homes are informal cottages and bungalows that are well served by casual, relaxed gardens. Informal gardens typically employ curves and diagonals, which make them feel lively and dynamic. Beds and borders are laid out in sweeping curves and softly undulating shapes, with plants spilling over the edges and onto pathways. Informal gardens generally have curved edges, and the beds are ovals or soft-edged free-form shapes. Within the garden, plants are allowed to assume their natural forms, growing together in flowing drifts and intermin-

These plants have a loose, open, or rambling habit, and work well in informal gardens.

Achillea, yarrow

Arctotis × hybrida, African daisy

Artemisia spp., artemisia

Aster spp., aster

Astilbe spp., false spirea

Buddleia spp., butterfly bush

Campsis radicans, trumpet creeper

Clethra alnifolia, sweet pepperbush

Coreopsis spp., tickseed

Cosmos spp., cosmos

Cytisus scoparius, Scotch broom

Gaillardia × grandiflora, blanketflower

Hemerocallis spp., daylily

Hibiscus spp., rose mallow, rose of Sharon

Ilex glabra, inkberry

Ilex verticillata, winterberry

Ilex vomitoria, yaupon holly

Juniperus spp., juniper

Lantana camara, lantana

Lonicera spp., honeysuckle

Monarda didyma, bee balm

Nepeta × faassenii, catmint

Oenothera spp., evening primrose

Ornamental grasses

Perovskia atriplicifolia, Russian sage

Petunia × hybrida, petunia

Philadelphus spp., mock orange (pictured)

Pittosporum tobira, Japanese pittosporum

Rudbeckia spp., black-eyed Susan

Rosa spp., rambler rose, rugosa rose, shrub rose

Salvia spp., sage

Sedum spp., stonecrop

Solidago spp., goldenrod

Spiraea spp., spirea

Thalictrum spp., meadow rue

Tropaeolum majus, nasturtium

Viburnum spp., viburnum

Vitex agnus-castus, chastetree

Wisteria spp., wisteria

Zinnia angustifolia, narrow-leaved zinnia

Mock orange is a classic choice for cottage gardens.

gling their colors where two drifts meet. Paths and walkways wind and curve, and they are surfaced with loose materials such as gravel, crushed bluestone, pebbles, and wood chips. Stepping-stones might be made with irregular fieldstone or wood rounds sawn from logs and sunk into the soil with their top surface at ground level.

In an informal garden you can mix and match colors in any combination you like, although there are traditional ways to create pleasing color schemes. See "Working with Color" on page 36 for information on mixing colors.

Saltboxes, cottages and bungalows, capes and ranch houses are all examples of house styles that usually work well with informal gardens. If you are unsure whether or not you have an informally styled house, consider its architectural features. Is the front door off to one side of the façade, with unequal numbers of windows on either side? That's one clue that you have an informal house. What is the house built of? If the construction is wood shingles, siding, or logs, for example, the house is probably informal.

There are many kinds of informal gardens. Cottage gardens of old-fashioned plants and plants chosen for their particular qualities and personal associations represent one style. The garden described in "A Secret Garden by the Sea," in chapter 4, is a charming example of a cottage-style

Neatly sheared shrubs and topiaries make an elegant formal statement in this seashore garden.

garden. Although many plants can be at home in both formal and informal gardens, some plants are just inherently less formal than others. Ornamental grasses, for instance, are by nature informal, with their fountainy, billowy forms and their constant swaying and dancing as their leaves are ruffled by passing breezes. See "Informal Plants" (page 32) for more examples.

Formal. Some seashore houses, particularly in traditionally upper-class enclaves like Newport and the Hamptons, are grandly formal and often complemented by formally designed gardens. Formal homes are built of solid, traditional materials such as stone and brick, often with classic columns and broad staircases. The façade of a formal house is typically symmetrical, with the front door in the center and equal numbers of windows on either side of it.

The formal gardens that suit such homes are laid out in precise geometric shapes — squares, rectangles, and circles — with beds and borders arranged around straight axes (lines of sight) that lead directly to prominent features of the property, such as the house itself, or important ornaments, such as fountains and works of art. The axes are often paths, with the main axis path being widest and bisected at a 90-degree angle by a narrower, secondary axis. Formal gardens have neat,

sharp edges, and the plants are meticulously groomed and shaped. Topiaries are classic components of formal gardens, as are neatly clipped hedges. The overall feeling in a formal garden is one of serenity and calm. Colors are restrained, and the color scheme is usually simple — cool blues and crisp whites, for example.

Many seaside communities are populated by contemporary homes constructed of simple geometric forms. These kinds of houses can be well served by updated formal gardens of bold, sculptural plants. Spare, weeping junipers and large, spiky yuccas are at home in these modernistic settings. Another way to landscape a contemporary home, depending on its setting and design, is with the third kind of garden: the naturalistic garden.

Naturalistic. Naturalistic gardens aim to evoke the look of particular natural environments — woodlands, deserts, prairies, beaches, and marshes — and they can beautifully integrate a home with its site. Naturalistic gardens also call for plants that are naturally adapted to the growing conditions present in the garden environment. The best of them are native plants,

FORMAL PLANTS

These plants have a neat growing habit and work well in formal gardens.

Catharanthus roseus, Madagascar periwinkle
Clematis spp., large-flowered clematis
Cryptomeria japonica, Japanese cedar
Dahlia spp., dahlia
Euonymus japonicus, evergreen euonymus
Hosta spp., plantain lily
Hydrangea macrophylla, bigleaf hydrangea
Ilex crenata, Japanese holly
Ilex opaca, American holly
Ilex pedunculosa, longstalk holly
Ligustrum spp., privet
Liriope muscari, lilyturf
Nerium oleander, oleander
Pelargonium × hortorum, geranium
Phormium tenax, New Zealand flax
Picea spp., spruce
Prunus caroliniana, Carolina cherry laurel
Rosa cvs., hybrid tea roses
Santolina chamaecyparissus, lavender cotton
Stachys byzantina, lamb's ears
Tagetes spp., marigold
Taxus cuspidata, Japanese yew
Teucrium chamaedrys, germander
Yucca filamentosa, Adam's needle

NATURALISTIC GARDEN PLANTS

These plants are well suited to naturalistic gardens — beach gardens, meadow gardens, and native plant gardens. The letter following each plant, B, M, or N, indicates whether it is best suited to a beach, meadow, or other native plant garden.

Ammophila breviligulata, American beach grass, B

Arctostaphylos uva-ursi, bearberry, N

Aronia spp., chokeberry, N

Artemisia stelleriana, beach wormwood, B

Asclepias tuberosa, butterfly weed, M, N

Aster spp., aster

Baccharis halimifolia, groundsel bush, B, N

Campsis radicans, trumpet creeper, B

Caragana arborescens, Siberian pea tree, B

Elymus arenarius 'Glauca', blue lyme grass, B

Eryngium maritimum, sea holly, B

Gaillardia pulchella, Indian blanket, N

Gelsemium sempervirens, Carolina jessamine, N

Hippophäe rhamnoides, sea buckthorn, B

Ilex glabra, inkberry, N

Ilex opaca, American holly, N

Ilex verticillata, winterberry, N

Ilex vomitoria, yaupon holly, B, N

Juniperus chinensis 'Torulosa', Hollywood juniper, B

Juniperus conferta, shore juniper, B

Juniperus virginiana, eastern red cedar, B, N

Monarda didyma, bee balm, N, M

Myrica spp., bayberry, wax myrtle, B, N

Pinus mugo, mugo pine, B

Pinus rigida, pitch pine, B, N

Pinus taeda, loblolly pine, B, N

Pittosporum tobira, Japanese pittosporum, B

Prunus maritima, beach plum, B, N

Rhus spp., sumac, N

Rosa rugosa, saltspray rose, B

Sabal palmetto, cabbage palmetto, B, N

Solidago spp., goldenrod, N, M

Spartina pectinata, cordgrass, B, N

Tamarix ramosissima, tamarisk, B

Thuja occidentalis, American arborvitae, N, B

Trachelospermum jasminoides, Confederate jasmine, N

Uniola paniculata, sea oats, B

Vaccinium spp., blueberry, N

Viburnum dentatum, arrowwood viburnum, N

Zinnia angustifolia, narrow-leaved zinnia, B

Knautia macedonica seems to float on tall, slender stems in this meadow garden, like balloons tethered to the ground.

or plants from other parts of the world where growing conditions are similar. For instance, a house situated on the beach, just behind the dunes, looks great with plantings of bayberry, seaside goldenrod, and beach grass in garden areas closest to the dunes. If the house is set near a marsh or estuary, and parts of the property are wet, a pond edged with wetland plants can provide an ideal landscape solution. Along a rocky coast, a rock garden might be the best option. For a house in a wooded area, a woodland garden of shade-tolerant plants would nicely fill the bill.

A Sense of Place

IN ADDITION TO CREATING A GARDEN that works with your house, you might give some thought to making a garden that "fits" the seashore environment. The seaside is a beautiful place to be, and having a landscape around your house that captures the essence of the surroundings can enhance your experience of and appreciation for it.

IN PRAISE OF NATIVE PLANTS

One good way to create a garden with a sense of place is to feature native plants. Whether you simply build garden beds and borders with native species or opt for a truly naturalistic garden that evokes the look of dune and swale, woodland, marsh and wetland, or coastal plain, your garden will look like it belongs at the shore. Take a look at James van Sweden's garden on page 120 to see how beautifully a garden of primarily native plants integrates into its setting.

There are many good reasons to grow native plants. For one thing, they are adapted to the climate and conditions, and will thrive with less fussing than a lot of imports. Natives will be less likely than exotic species and flashy hybrids to suffer pest and disease problems. You won't need as much fertilizer or supplemental water — native plants are far less demanding of our dwindling natural resources.

Native plants tend to be less dramatic and showy than traditional commercial plant varieties, and for that reason many people turn up their noses at them, considering them little better than weeds. But don't sell native plants short. Natives have a quieter, subtler beauty that can be just as appealing as those grand English perennials, precisely because they are better suited to the environment. It's a different sensibility, a matter of seeing the garden in a new way. And natives can be richly colorful, too. Consider, for example, New England aster (*Aster novae-angliae*), which bears masses of yellow-centered daisy flowers in shades of rose, pink, purple, and white in late summer and fall. Or bee balm's (*Monarda didyma*) heads of brilliant scarlet, soft purple, or fresh pink flowers in summer.

As more and more homeowners are discovering the positive attributes of native plants, breeders are putting more energy into developing improved cultivars. New England aster is just one native that is available in many cultivar forms. There are new varieties of bee balm, butterfly weed (*Asclepias tuberosa*), sweet pepperbush (*Clethra alnifolia*), and many other plants as well. And more landscape designers are discovering the virtues of natives and using them in creative ways.

If you don't think you would be happy with an all-native garden, how about a compromise? Create a basic framework

Using native plants ties a garden to the natural landscape beyond its borders and enhances the sense of place. The windmill palm places this garden unmistakably in the Southeast.

with natives and add plants — such as ornamental grasses — with a similar spirit. Inject extra shots of color by adding some more-traditional perennials. Grow flowering annuals in containers to use around the house and outdoor living areas or as accents right in the garden. Create a separate garden "room" enclosed by hedges or fences for a flower garden bursting with color and texture.

Working with Color

In this perennial garden, shades of green blend with silvers, whites, and pale pastels for a peaceful, cooling effect near the sea, where the summer sun glows hot.

Displaying a single type of flower, such as this purple coneflower (*Echinacea purpurea*), against green foliage is a simple, effective way to work with color.

IF YOU ARE GOING TO HAVE A FLOWER garden, it goes without saying that color will be an important part of the design. Here are some guidelines to use, and some issues to ponder, in choosing colors for your garden.

First, think about the basic kinds of colors you like in other areas of your life — your home and its furnishings, your clothes and accessories. Do you generally prefer bright, warm colors (reds, oranges, and yellows) or cool, peaceful colors (blues, greens, and violets)? Are you drawn to subtle, harmonious blends of colors or to contrasting colors? Rich, deep tones, brights, or pale pastels? Do you like the serenity of white instead of other colors?

What are the colors on the exterior of your house? You might consider trying to echo a trim color from the home in the landscape to create a visual link between house and garden.

If you have a good sense of the colors you like, you can mix them in whatever combination you want in the garden. Your garden should please you above all. Don't feel you have to be a slave to the laws of garden design. Nothing is written in stone. But if you feel at a loss about where to start, you may find it helpful to learn a bit about how designers have traditionally used color. Very basically, there are four ways to work with color in the garden: you can combine harmonious or analogous colors; you can use contrasting or complementary colors; you can rely on a single flower color contrasted against green foliage; or you can plant in an assortment of mixed colors.

HARMONIOUS COLOR SCHEMES

Harmonious, or analogous, colors are related; they are located near one another on an artist's color wheel and blend smoothly with one another. Examples of harmonious colors are red, orange, and gold, or blue, purple, and cool pink. Analogous color schemes are often quiet and subtle, as in the case of a pot full of pastel shades of pink, rose, and lilac petunias. But they can also be surprisingly dramatic, as in the case of a bed of chrysanthemums in brilliant gold, rich orange, russet, and

crimson. These combinations of closely related colors are most appealing to the eyes of some people. For others, more contrast is needed to bring more life to the composition.

CONTRASTING COLOR SCHEMES

Contrasting colors are farther apart on a color wheel, and placing them next to each other emphasizes their different qualities. Complementary colors lie opposite one another on the color wheel and contrast more intensely than any other juxtaposition of colors. Examples of complementary colors are blue and orange, purple and yellow, and red and green. The nineteenth-century English landscape painter John Constable placed in his paintings small strokes of red amid expanses of foliage to make the greens look greener. If you look closely, you may perceive the same effect in a garden.

If you want to plant a garden of complementary colors, you will probably find the most pleasing results by planting the softer of the two colors over a larger portion of the garden and using the brighter color sparingly, as an accent. For example, if you want to combine blue salvia with orange marigolds, plant lots more salvia than marigolds. If you plant more marigolds and fewer salvia, the orange will overwhelm the blue.

Another way to tone down a contrasting scheme is to soften the shade of the brighter color. Instead of using orange marigolds with the salvia, you could plant salmon-colored geraniums.

A third way to soften intensely contrasting colors is to introduce some neutral tones — white flowers or silver foliage, for example — to blend the colors, or to surround the contrasting hues with lots of green foliage to absorb some of the color.

BELOW: A magenta cranesbill (*Geranium* sp.) and the chartreuse-gold sprays of lady's mantle (*Alchemilla vulgaris*) make an electric duo in early summer.

Monochromatic gardens need not be boring. This juxtaposition of clear pink roses with the raspberry-hued flower clusters of Japanese spirea is lovely and long blooming.

SINGLE-COLOR GARDENS

The simplest color scheme of all is built on a single color, perhaps expressed in several different shades and tints, and perhaps with just a small amount of a second color added as an accent. Monochromatic gardens can be quite soothing to the eye, and their simplicity can work extremely well in a formal setting. You might like a garden of all white flowers, or pink, or blue. Or you could combine soft pale yellows with rich deep golds. A single-color garden need not be boring; you can vary the types of flowers; plant heights, shapes, and textures; flower sizes; and tones of color (pale, bright, or dark). Or you can mix in some variegated foliage for added interest.

MULTICOLORED GARDENS

In a mixed-color, or polychromatic, garden, the variety of colors included depends entirely on the gardener's preference. Multicolored gardens can be blindingly brilliant, if all strong colors are used, or they can be cheerful and festive, if you mix pastels and soft shades. You can create a multicolored garden by planting a favorite flower, such as daylily or iris, in mixed colors or by planting a selection of plants, each in a different color, for a rainbow of blossoms.

A polychromatic garden generally works best if one color is dominant, to bring a sense of cohesiveness to the overall scheme. And don't spread the plants of each color throughout the garden like so many polka dots; you will lose the visual impact, and your garden will look like just a motley collection of plants. Instead, plant in color groups, in bands, or in drifts or clumps. Don't plant one yellow coreopsis; plant five or nine or fifteen.

To get the best effect from a polychromatic garden, surround it with lots of green to provide some visual relief and give the viewer's eye some rest. Set your flowers of many colors in front of evergreens, or a hedge, or in a bed in the middle of a lawn.

If you are not sure what sort of color scheme would most please you in your garden, start with a simple blend and add to it in subsequent years if you feel you need more color. It is easier and more satisfying to add color than to subtract it.

Outdoor Living

Part of a successful landscape design lies in tailoring the outdoor space, whether you do it yourself or work with a professional, to accommodate the ways in which you use it. As you get started on the design process, then, give some thought to what you like to do outdoors. Do you, for example, enjoy dining outdoors in nice weather? If so, you'll want to create a sheltered spot for a picnic table, or perhaps a more elaborate dining area, with enough seating to accommodate your family and whatever guests you are likely to be entertaining. Decks and patios are often good places for socializing. Or perhaps a vine-covered arbor would suit your needs.

Will the kids need a place to play? Then you will probably want to have a lawn, and perhaps a screened-off area for a jungle gym or other play equipment. Would you enjoy a bench or lounge chair in a quiet, private nook at the end of a path where you could curl up with a good book and get away from the world?

WHAT DO YOU WANT IN YOUR GARDEN?

As you set about creating your seashore garden, whether you are starting from scratch or renovating an existing garden, asking yourself these questions will help guide you toward the kind of garden that will work for you. This should be helpful whether you intend to do the work yourself or hire professionals to do it for you.

How Will You Use Your Outdoor Space?

- Secluded, quiet spot for reading and relaxing
- Dining outdoors
- Entertaining, outdoor parties
- Sunny area for sunbathing
- Play space for kids
- Other recreational space: tennis, croquet, badminton, etc.
- Swimming pool
- Pet exercise area

What Qualities Do You Want in the Garden?

- Lots of color
- Easy maintenance
- Privacy
- Peace and serenity
- Neat, well-groomed look
- Casual, informal but traditional look
- Natural, beachy look

Swimming pools are often included in seaside landscapes. Choose the best site for your pool and design plantings around it for privacy.

Structures and Hardscape

AN IMPORTANT CONSIDERATION IN planning and laying out a landscape is the nonplant areas. Before you create beds and borders, you need to figure out the overall spatial relationships on the property. Where will the driveway go? Where will you need paths and walkways, both for practical reasons — to get from one place to another — and for design purposes? What kinds of structures do you have or will you need? Will you want fences or walls to divide space, confine pets, demarcate the property line, or retain soil on a slope? Is there a swimming pool? Will you want to have a gazebo, arbors or arches, a storage shed? Even if some of these structures will be built in the future, it is best to plan for them now so you don't have to move beds and borders later on.

When considering the design of structures — decks, boardwalks, fences and walls, arbors and gazebos — plan for an open construction that will allow air to pass through. See "Creating Sheltered Places" on page 41 for an explanation of the importance of air permeability. An open construction, particularly for decks and boardwalks that sit on or near the ground, will also permit rainwater to drain away readily and find its way back to the water table.

For wooden structures, use rot-resistant woods such as redwood, teak, cypress, and cedar, or a composite material like Trex. These materials hold up best under salt spray and wind. Any metal you use should be galvanized, again to withstand the salt.

BELOW: Hardscaping, or pavement, forms part of the basic structure of the landscape. It leads you through the garden and ties the garden to the house.

RIGHT: A small fountain set on stone provides an elegant focal point in a quiet, sheltered garden room.

Creating Sheltered Places

S EASHORE WINDS AND SALTS ARE hard on gardens. Where plants — even tough trees and shrubs native to coastal areas — are continuously exposed to strong winds with a high concentration of salt, along ocean beaches, for instance, the plants will stop growing, or grow only very slowly, on their windward side. The back side of the plant continues to grow, though, and eventually the plant becomes asymmetrical and unbalanced looking — it takes on the windswept appearance so typical of seaside trees and shrubs.

Strong winds can snap stems and shoots and detach leaves. During storms, winds can be strong enough to break large branches and even uproot entire trees. Wind also speeds up the rate at which plants transpire moisture from their leaves, and the resulting lack of moisture in plant tissues can cause scorching. Salt exacerbates the drying effect and can result in discolored, windburned growth, especially in evergreens. Where I live on eastern Long Island, eastern red cedars (*Juniperus virginiana*) growing in exposed oceanfront locations often appear brownish in winter from the harsh, salty winds.

Wind can cause erosion of light, sandy soil, too, if there's nothing to anchor the soil. It simply blows away.

A final problem wind can produce near the sea is when it becomes concentrated and even stronger. Wind tunnels can be created on beachfront properties by, for example, a break in the dunes or a gap between two adjacent dunes. The wind is channeled through the narrow space and blows faster and harder. When assessing your property for prevailing wind directions, look also for potential wind tunnels that would be terribly destructive to plants.

FENCES AND SHELTERBELTS

Unless you plan to grow only the toughest native plants, you are going to need to create sheltered places on your property in which to garden. The best way to provide protection for plants is with a windbreak. Windbreaks can be made with trees and shrubs, or they can be structural — high fences or walls of open construction. A windbreak of plants is more correctly called a shelterbelt, but I've used the terms more or less interchangeably in this book. Traditionally a windbreak of plants is narrow, a single or double line of trees whose purpose is simply to slow the flow of wind. A shelterbelt consists of several rows of a variety of trees and shrubs intended to slow the wind and trap sand and salt.

A hedge can also serve as a windbreak, but a hedge by itself generally will not provide enough protection on an ocean beach. A hedge can, however, serve as a second line of defense at the beach, located some distance inside the primary shelterbelt, and hedges can also provide

Tall plants like rose of Sharon could snap in the wind in an exposed location, but they can thrive behind a sheltering wall, fence, or hedge.

good protection for gardens a bit inland, away from the beach. An evergreen hedge provides protection year-round, but even a deciduous hedge will afford a reasonable degree of shelter in winter when the leaves are off, if it is dense enough.

With the right plant choices or the right kind of construction, either a living or a constructed windbreak will slow the speed of the wind as well as block salt and sand from blowing into the garden. The overall

Wind striking a solid wall is forced up the front side and over the back, where it can slam down hard onto plants or eddy in unpredictable patterns. Windbreaks need to allow for air to pass through them.

aim is to create protected areas for gardening and also to make the outdoor space around the house more comfortable for people to be in. Ideally, you want to provide shelter without blocking the view. The windbreak can also shelter the house, allowing seashore dwellers to save money on winter heating bills. You'll also get the bonus of added privacy when you plant or erect your windbreak.

Whether you opt for a windbreak of plants or a fence, be sure that air can pass easily through it. An air-permeable windbreak will allow the wind to flow through it and will slow the wind's speed as it passes. The ideal windbreak allows about 50 percent air penetration. This means the plants in a shelterbelt or hedge will have plenty of small spaces between them, and a wooden fence will have some room between the boards. When you stand right next to the windbreak, you should be able to see through it. The spaces in the windbreak should be small, though. Larger gaps will create wind tunnels as described above, and will actually increase the wind speed rather than moderate it.

A solid wall or closed-board or solid-panel fence would create problems of its own if you tried to use it as a windbreak. The solid structure forces wind to shoot up and over its face, and the wind then slams down the back side of the wall in a downdraft, creating nasty currents and eddies that can do more damage to the plants behind the walls than would the unobstructed wind.

SITING A WINDBREAK

Whatever kind of windbreak you choose, you will need to plan its location carefully. In order to be effective, a windbreak or shelterbelt must be set where it will block the prevailing wind. The best way to do this is to position the windbreak so it lines up at a 90-degree angle to the direction of the prevailing winds. Depending on the location and exposure of your property, you may need to provide shelter in two different places — one to block summer winds and another to deflect winter winds.

The first step, then, is to determine your property's orientation and exposure, and to find out which way the prevailing winds blow in winter and in summer. When you know on which side or sides of the property the windbreak or windbreaks must go in order to protect the garden areas, the next step is to calculate how far away from the house and garden it should go. The obvious solution would be to put a windbreak along the property line, but that might not be the most effective location. A well-designed windbreak will cut wind speed in half over an area on its lee side (away from the wind) that is 5 to 10 times the windbreak's height. It will reduce wind speed to a lesser extent over a distance up to 20 times its height. Thus, a windbreak of 10-foot-high shrubs would slow the wind speed 50 percent for a distance of 50 to 100 feet, and to a lesser degree up to 200 feet behind it.

Interestingly, a windbreak will also slow down the wind in front of it, on the side facing into the wind, over a distance two to five times the windbreak's height. So our 10-foot shrubs will also moderate the wind 20 to 50 feet in front of them.

The third step in windbreak planning is to calculate the size of the area you need the windbreak to protect. If you know what kinds of trees and shrubs you want to use in your shelterbelt, you can use their height to calculate their positioning based on the size of the necessary protection zone. Thus, if you know that your windbreak will be 20 feet high and you need to protect a garden that is 100 feet deep, the inside edge of the windbreak should go within 5 to 10 feet of the garden to afford the maximum protection for the most sensitive plants. If you plan to grow plants with some tolerance for salt and wind, the windbreak could be 20 feet away. You will notice that I said "the inside edge" here. That's because a shelterbelt of several rows of trees and shrubs can be quite wide. You have to allow enough room for the depth of the windbreak. Hedges and fences, of course, are much narrower than shelterbelts.

Alternatively, you could design a wind break by determining the best height for the windbreak based on the size of the garden. The windbreak should be one-fifth to one-tenth as high as the depth of the area you need to protect.

Another factor to take into account is how long the windbreak will be. The rule of thumb for this is that it should extend 50 feet past the sides of the area to be protected. If the windbreak is too short — say, the same length as the garden's width — strong wind gusts can swirl around the windbreak's ends right into the garden and wreak havoc with the plants.

If your beachfront property is flat and quite large, you may need to have a series of windbreaks to adequately protect the plantings. In such a case, you might make the outermost windbreak a good shelterbelt, and for the inner windbreaks use a series of hedges incorporated into the landscape design to serve as the walls of garden rooms or otherwise act as space dividers. Place the windbreaks a distance apart that is equal to 10 times their height. For example, 10-foot hedges would go 100 feet apart from one another.

Properties that are near the ocean but are not flat are a lot harder to protect with windbreaks. Wind does not flow straight across hilly land, and the wind patterns are complicated to figure out. In this case it would be wise to consult an experienced professional landscape architect or engineer to plan the necessary windbreaks.

A windbreak of 10-foot-tall shrubs will slow wind speed over an area up to 100 feet behind it and 20 to 30 feet in front of it.

SHAPING A WINDBREAK

Near the sea, a windbreak or shelterbelt must do more than simply slow the force of the wind in order to be effective. You need the windbreak to deflect the wind up and over the garden to carry its cargo of salt past your garden plants. The best way to direct the wind is to design the windbreak of plants in a gradation of heights. Viewed from the side, the windbreak is shaped like a wedge. Each row of plants protects the plants behind it. The lowest and most salt-resistant plants — such as beach grass (*Ammophila breviligulata*), sea oats (*Uniola paniculata*), and Adam's needle (*Yucca filamentosa*) — go closest to the beach. Behind them go shrubs of increasing height, and behind them, on the inner side of the windbreak, go taller evergreen trees.

This layered construction will draw the wind up and over the tallest trees in the barrier and allow it to flow above the garden. If the windbreak is made of only shorter plants, the wind will pass lower over the garden and will likely be slowed enough to drop its load of salt right on the plants in the garden, just where you don't want it to go.

PLANTING WINDBREAKS

When planning a shelterbelt of plants, start with the toughest ones on the ocean side, or on the outside facing into the prevailing winds. It is best to put in young plants, even if it means delaying the rest of your garden for several years — younger plants will adapt better to the harsh conditions than larger, more mature specimens. It's worth the wait. While you wait for the windbreak to grow tall enough to be effective, you can grow some plants in containers in protected spots, such as behind the house. You could also put up a fence and grow behind it plants with some degree of salt tolerance.

Be aware that trees and shrubs in seaside windbreaks and other very exposed locations will probably not grow as large as

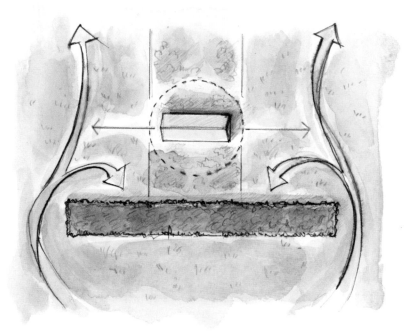

A windbreak meant to protect a house needs to extend 50 feet beyond the sides of the house so that wind currents sweeping around the edges will not blast the building.

they would farther inland. Seaside trees and shrubs are also likely to take on a gnarled, windswept look over time as the fierce salt winds stunt their growth on the seaward side.

Another point to keep in mind is that trees and shrubs growing in exposed seashore locations often appear to grow very slowly, if at all, during their first few years. That's because in dry, sandy conditions, they first put their energy into sending roots deep into the sand to find a source of water and to provide a secure anchor. When the roots reach the water table, the aboveground parts of the plant will start to grow faster.

When the windbreak is established and you begin to plant inside it, you may want to choose shade-tolerant ground covers for the area immediately to the lee of the windbreak. This space will tend to be shady and dry, especially if the windbreak is to the south, because the trees and shrubs will block much of the sunlight and rain from reaching the ground there. This area will also be cooler than sunnier locations.

One final caveat: If your windbreak will be located close to your property line, be sure to set the plants far enough back from the boundary that they will have room to fully mature without encroaching on your neighbor's property. Remember to consider the spread, as well as the height, of each tree or shrub.

To deflect salty winds up and over your house or garden, plant a windbreak with several layers of plants of increasing height. From the side, the windbreak appears wedge-shaped.

PLANTS FOR WINDBREAKS

Acer pseudoplatanus, sycamore maple

Agave spp., century plant

Baccharis halimifolia, groundsel bush

Caragana arborescens, Siberian peashrub

Chamaecyparis obtusa, Hinoki falsecypress

Crateagus spp. (deciduous, but will filter the worst of the wind in summer; fairly small but very tough)

×*Cupressocyparis leylandii*, Leyland cypress

Cytisus scoparius, Scotch broom

Elaeagnus commutata, silverberry

Euonymus japonicus, evergreen euonymus

Hippophäe rhamnoides, sea buckthorn

Ilex vomitoria, yaupon holly

Iva imbricata, marsh elder

Juniperus conferta, shore juniper

Juniperus horizontalis, creeping juniper

Juniperus virginiana, eastern red cedar

Magnolia grandiflora, southern magnolia

Myrica cerifera, southern wax myrtle

Myrica pensylvanica, bayberry

Nerium oleander, oleander

Ornamental grasses (*Schizachyrium scoparium*, *Panicum amarulum*)

Pinus mugo, mugo pine

Pinus nigra, Austrian pine

Pinus rigida, pitch pine

Pittosporum tobira, Japanese pittosporum

Prunus maritima, beach plum

Quercus virginiana, live oak

Rosa rugosa, saltspray rose

Sabal palmetto, palmetto

Tamarix gallica, French tamarisk, saltcedar

Tamarix ramosissima, tamarisk

Uniola paniculata, sea oats

Vitis rotundifolia, muscadine grape (use on lee side of dunes to help stabilize)

Yucca filamentosa, Adam's needle

A board-on-board fence like this one allows air and light to flow between the boards but still provides privacy.

OTHER WINDBREAK OPTIONS

While a shelterbelt of mixed trees and shrubs is probably the best kind of windbreak for properties along ocean beaches, homeowners a bit farther inland have other options to consider.

For a property away from the beach, or as a second line of defense for beachfront locations, a tall clipped hedge or an informal screen of unsheared evergreens can be a good option. Hedges and screens afford welcome privacy and are also useful for delineating space in the landscape. Hedges can mark property boundaries, enclose swimming pools and tennis courts, and separate the driveway from the garden. Privet (*Ligustrum* spp.) is by far the most popular hedge plant, and most types have some degree of salt tolerance. But you can also make hedges or screens of arborvitae or juniper, and southern gardeners can use pittosporum or oleander.

Fences also make good windbreaks if they are of permeable construction. Picket styles, board-on-board, stockade fences, woven panel and louver designs, even snow fencing, all can work. In fact, snow fencing, though not much to look at in terms of aesthetics, will slow the wind speed by as much as 80 percent. Do not use a solid-panel or closed-board fence as a windbreak. Stucco and cinderblock walls are also poor choices. A brick wall could serve, however, if it is made with screening brick, or if holes are left between bricks at regular intervals to permit airflow. In the Delaware garden described in chapter 4 ("A Secret Garden by the Sea"), the brick wall surrounding the courtyard is a fine example of this kind of permeable yet solid wall.

This brick wall at an oceanfront home in Delaware includes spaces for air to pass through, making it a most effective — and sturdy — windbreak.

It's not a good idea to clear all the vegetation from an oceanfront lot when building a house, but some developers still do it. If you have purchased a beachfront home on an empty, bulldozed lot, here is a basic plan of attack that might work for you.

First, take photos of the property from various angles. Make sure you photograph the view of the water, and also the street and neighboring properties. You can use these photos later in planning for your landscaping.

The next order of business is to create some protection for the house and grounds. First, you need to create sand dunes if none currently exist. Probably the best way to encourage dune formation is to erect a line of snow fencing at the front edge of your property, well back from the high-water mark and running parallel to the beach. Put up a second line of fencing 30 to 40 feet behind the first one. (If you want to stabilize existing dunes on your property, run the first line of fencing at the base of the dunes.) The fencing should run at a right angle to the prevailing winds. If the prevailing winds do not come off the water, run a fence that is at the proper angle in relation to the wind and 30 feet away from the first fence.

The snow fencing will trap and hold sand. When the dune is high enough to provide reasonable protection, plant American beach grass (*Ammophila breviligulata*) to stabilize it. Southern gardeners can use beach grass or sea oats (*Uniola paniculata*) to help stabilize dunes. Beach grass spreads readily by means of underground stems. Local nurseries sell small clumps of beach grass ready for planting. The best planting time ranges from October 1 to April 30; ask the nursery about the best time for your area. Set the clumps 8 inches deep and about 18 inches apart, in a staggered pattern like you'd use for planting other ground covers.

Water thoroughly after planting, so the water soaks down to the roots of the grass. Keep the grass watered so it stays as evenly moist as you can manage until it becomes established and sends out new roots. Fertilize heavily in spring with a balanced fertilizer such as 10-10-10, applied at a rate of 100 pounds per quarter acre. Fertilize again at the same rate in midsummer.

After a couple of years when the beach grass has stabilized the dune, it will start to lose its vigor. At that time you can begin putting in more permanent plants, such as seaside goldenrod (*Solidago sempervirens*), beach plum (*Prunus maritima*), sea oats (*Uniola paniculata*), beach wormwood (*Artemisia stelleriana*), and groundsel bush (*Baccharis halimifolia*), to hold the dune in place.

When more permanent dune plantings are in place, you can start working to improve the soil so you can plant shelterbelts and, eventually, gardens. See "Improving the Soil," on page 48, for information. The next step is to form windbreaks to create sheltered locations for gardening and to help protect the house. You might also decide to build a berm, with shrubs along the top, to help deflect wind.

With windbreaks in place, get out the photos you took of the property. If you can have a local copy shop make blowups for you, you can use tissue paper overlays or paper cutouts of tree, shrub, and hedge shapes to play around with different locations for ornamental plantings. Lay the cutouts on the photo enlargements to try out different arrangements of plants. Think about using groups of trees and shrubs to frame views; provide shade; and screen decks, patios, and other outdoor living areas from view. When planning windbreaks, be sure to place them between the prevailing winds (in winter or summer or both, if necessary) and the future garden.

Improving the Soil

Pure sand is a difficult growing medium for plants. If you want a garden, you will need to add lots of organic matter.

As explained in Chapter 1, pure sand is not a good growing medium for most plants. Even if you don't live right on the beach, if you live at the seashore, your soil is probably very sandy. There are exceptions to the rule, of course. In my area, rich, beautiful, loamy soil can be found in the village of Bridgehampton within sight of the dunes.

Bridgehampton loam is some of the best farmland in the country (although now, alas, it is sprouting more and more houses instead of vegetables). On the other hand, my garden 15 miles away is a few thousand feet from a bay, and my soil is sandy but poorly drained in spots, low in fertility, and highly acidic. My neighborhood was once a pine-oak coastal forest, a tiny remnant of which remains in my backyard. But often, sandy seashore soil is alkaline because of the salt it contains. The pH of beach sand can range from a mildly acid 6.5 to a decidedly alkaline 8.0. If you don't manage to have the soil tested, a general improvement strategy is to work in 50 pounds of ground limestone per thousand square feet.

But it's always a good idea to have your soil tested before beginning a new garden. Most USDA county Cooperative Extension offices do soil testing, and along with your test results they provide recommendations on how to amend your soil to create a better growing environment for plants. There are also private soil-testing labs, and various sorts of do-it-yourself test kits. If you choose this last option, purchase a good kit — one that tests more than just the soil's pH.

ADDING ORGANIC MATTER

Whether or not you garden organically, the best thing you can do for your seashore soil is to add copious amounts of organic matter to it. Organic matter — compost, leaf mold, livestock manure, and other natural materials — improves the soil's texture and the ability of sandy soil to retain moisture. It aerates and improves drainage in compacted soils, and improves nutrient content as well. Seashore gardeners can take advantage of local materials, particularly seaweed. Some gardeners prefer to rinse or soak seaweed gathered from the beach in freshwater before digging it into the garden or tossing it onto the compost pile. Other gardeners do not rinse and do not find the salt problematic. It is a good idea, though, to add a nitrogen source such as dried blood or cottonseed meal at the same time to help the seaweed decompose more quickly. In very poor sandy soil, you could add as much as three parts by volume of compost to one part of the existing soil. Or use two parts compost and one part good topsoil to one part existing soil.

A more useful guideline is to spread the compost and/or topsoil over the entire garden area before making beds and borders

BELOW: Seaweed that washes up on the beach can be an excellent soil amendment. Add a nitrogen-rich material to the soil along with seaweed to speed its decomposition.

or other planting areas. This is easiest to do if nothing is currently growing on the site. If there are any existing indigenous trees you want to keep, you will need to build individual retaining walls around them to keep the soil around the trunk at the same level it is now. If these measures aren't taken, the tree could die.

You will need lots of compost and/or topsoil to make an appreciable improvement in the soil. Plan on at least a three- to four-inch layer for an area where you will have a lawn; six to eight inches would be even better. For beds and borders, foundation plants, and trees and shrubs, 8 to 12 inches of compost and/or topsoil is the goal.

After spreading the compost/topsoil, work it into the top few inches of the existing sand. You could also spread 15 pounds per 1,000 square feet of a fertilizer high in phosphorus and potassium, such as a 5-10-10 or a 6-12-12 formula, and work it in.

An alternative to spreading compost and topsoil over the entire garden area is to create a series of raised beds in which to garden and simply amend the soil in the beds. The spaces between the beds become paths. Working in raised beds reduces the amount of compost and topsoil you will need, and the design and layout of the beds can become the basis of an elegant formal flower garden or a charming herb garden.

To hold the compost, buy some bins (available at most garden centers) or make simple enclosures of hardware cloth or turkey wire. Or you can dig a pit in the ground six to eight inches deep and line the bottom with hardware cloth or heavy-duty plastic into which you will punch lots of holes, which will keep roots from growing into the compost pile from nearby trees while still allowing for drainage.

In the bottom of the enclosure, spread a six-inch layer of shredded leaves, weeds pulled from the garden that have *not* gone to seed, or upside-down chunks of sod. Next, add a four-inch layer of kitchen waste (excluding fats, oils, and meat remains) and/or manure. If you have fresh grass clippings, spread a *thin* (no more than ½ inch deep) layer on top. Then sprinkle with ground limestone, dried blood, or other organic fertilizer.

Repeat the layers as you acquire more materials. Turn the pile with a pitchfork or garden fork once a week, moving the ingredients from the outside to the inside of the pile. Water the compost thoroughly once a week in dry weather. The compost is ready to use when it has become dark and crumbly and you can't distinguish the different materials that went into it.

For a homemade fertilizer that's especially useful for container plants, you might try your hand at making compost tea. Put a couple of shovelfuls of finished compost into a burlap sack or other similarly porous container and place the bag in a tub of water (outdoors). Let it steep like a tea bag until the water turns dark brown. Then toss the compost into the garden and use the "tea" to water plants. If the tea is very dark colored, dilute it with water until it is the color of weak coffee. You can also fill the bag with manure instead of compost and make manure tea.

Deciding What to Grow

Petunias, ageratum, and marguerites thrive in full sun in northern gardens but prefer some shade in the afternoon farther south.

EVEN IN THE SHELTERED PLACES behind windbreaks and in gardens not right at the beach, some plants just do better at the seashore than others. In chapter 5 you'll find profiles of 100 of the best plants for Atlantic coastal gardens. But you still need to consider the usual particulars of the growing environment when you set out to select plants for your garden. Before you go shopping at local nurseries, assess the planting sites you will be using so you will be able to make wise choices.

GROWING CONDITIONS

To choose the best plants for any garden, you need to have a good understanding of the growing conditions present in the garden site. Seashore climates vary, and different locations come with different sets of challenges. On eastern Long Island, where I live, spring weather is cool and rainy, and late cold snaps and even frosts are not uncommon. Hydrangeas and other sensitive plants that begin to emerge from dormancy when the weather warms in spring can have their flower buds blasted by a late frost, and the hoped-for display of summer color will be cut off for the year. Planting of potatoes and other commercial crops may have to be delayed, pushing back the harvest at the end of the season.

For southern gardeners, winter can be difficult when a spell of warm weather is followed by a sudden, steep drop in temperature that chills plants before they have had time to harden their growth.

A problem in both northern and southern regions is that so many seashore plants that are drought tolerant in summer need good drainage year-round. Prolonged rainy weather in the South and snowpack in the North can lead to soggy soil in winter that is deadly to these plants.

Temperature. The average temperature range is an important factor in where plants will thrive. Most gardeners are aware that it's important to know the cold hardiness of a plant — the lowest winter temperatures at which it is likely to survive — to determine whether or not they can grow it. But for southern gardeners, especially, a plant's heat tolerance is just as important. See the appendix for the USDA Hardiness Zone Map and visit www.ahs.org to see the the AHS Heat Zone Map.

Sunlight. The amount of light your garden receives is another critical component of the growing environment. Full, unobstructed sunlight can be very intense at the seashore, and it can be amplified near the beach, where it bounces off white sand and reflects off the water. In understanding how much sun your garden gets, the duration of the sunlight is as important as the quality. Full sun is defined as unobstructed sunlight directly striking the

garden for at least six hours a day. Partial shade is a location that receives two to six hours of sunlight a day, in either the morning or the afternoon, or dappled sunlight all day long. Light or thin shade, sometimes called medium shade, can be found under trees with a high, lacy canopy; such a location may receive a couple of hours of sun a day but is brightly, though indirectly, lit the rest of the day. Full shade is found under mature trees with dense canopies, and deep shade is cast by large evergreens and nearby buildings. Deep shade is dim and cool all day, and very difficult for gardening.

How much sun or shade a plant can take depends in part on where it is growing. Many plants that need full sun in northern gardens do better with some shade, especially in the afternoon, in the South. The quality of light affects colors in the garden, too. Bright colors stand up better under the strong southern sun, where lighter, softer tones would wash out in the glare. Pastels often work better in the cool, misty air of New England, where bright, hot colors can sometimes seem too strident.

Precipitation. Rainfall and humidity are also important factors. The East Coast generally receives adequate rainfall to support a wide variety of plants. But sandy seashore soils drain quickly, and the wind and salt are also drying, so many plants need to be drought tolerant in order to survive. Supplemental watering is helpful, indeed a must for many gardens, but a watering system should be installed before the garden is planted. High humidity levels can also be problematic, especially in southern gardens. Not all plants that thrive in high temperatures can also withstand very humid conditions. In addition, when temperatures soar above 90°F and the atmosphere is very humid, garden soil that heats up during the day cannot cool down during torrid southern nights, stressing plants and encouraging the growth of pathogens.

Finally, the soil itself is all-important. Seashore soils are usually — but not always — sandy, and it is important to understand your soil type, how well it drains, its pH level, and its fertility. See "Improving the Soil," on page 48, for information on building good soil for your plants.

For a flourishing garden like this one, the first step is to understand the growing conditions present on your site. Fences or other windbreaks provide shelter, but can also shade the garden.

Along a sunny driveway, naturalistic drifts of purple Russian sage (*Perovskia atriplicifolia*), golden rudbeckia, grasses, and other perennials flourish in the coastal conditions.

CHOOSING PLANTS

The universe of plants is vast indeed, but some plants are undeniably better suited than others to life near the sea. Plants native to seashore environments, such as bayberry (*Myrica pensylvanica*), sea oats (*Uniola paniculata*), and seaside goldenrod (*Solidago sempervirens*), are some obvious choices. So are halophytes like sea pink (*Armeria maritima*) and sea lavender (*Limonium*). Plant names can offer clues to species that might be well suited to seashore gardens. If you see a word like *beach, coast, sea,* or *seaside* in a plant's common name, it is probably worth checking out. Botanical names containing such words as *maritima* and *littoralis* (of the seacoast) also tip off likely candidates.

Traits to Look For. When you begin to seek out other likely candidates, you can look for some particular characteristics. Low-growing, mat-forming plants such as thymes (*Thymus* spp.) and ceratostigma (*Ceratostigma plumbaginoides*) allow the wind to pass easily over them. Plants with small or narrow leaves, like tamarisk (*Tamarix ramosissima*), are also resistant to wind. Silver-leaved plants like artemisias and curry plant (*Helichrysum italicum*) are able to withstand intense sun, dry soil, and salt. Blue-toned conifers have a waxy coating on their needles that protects them from the effects of salt winds and spray.

Trees are essential for providing shade from the strong summer sun. Removing lower limbs allows sunlight to reach the ground and light up the space beneath.

Plants native to the Mediterranean region and other hot, dry places, such as lavender, rosemary, and santolina, stand up well to hot sun and drought. Deep-rooted plants like sea buckthorn are also very resistant to drought.

Attributes to Avoid. At the other end of the plant spectrum, there are those that are generally *not* good choices for seaside gardens. Tall, top-heavy perennials, such as delphiniums, whose stems need staking even in calmer conditions, may snap and topple under seashore gusts. Plants with large leaves can look ragged in exposed, windy sites. Trees with brittle wood or narrow crotch angles, such as are common in Bradford pear, would be at risk of damage from the wind.

It is also the wise and responsible course to refrain from planting invasive species. This is a difficult issue, since many of these tough plants are favorites along the coast because they can tolerate the harsh environment and grow where little else will. But even at the seashore these plants can get out of bounds and spread into natural environments and habitats, where they crowd out native plants and, in so doing, eliminate some of the food sources relied upon by local wildlife. Other popular and widely planted imported species are at risk from pests and diseases. Where I live, for example, Japanese black pines that were planted for their tolerance to salt, wind, and drought are now being killed off by beetles and bacterial disease. See "Plants to Avoid" (page 54) for a list of undesirables.

TREES AND SHRUBS

Trees and shrubs are invaluable in seaside gardens. Although a rarity down on the beach, trees and shrubs are important in windbreaks, for hedges and screening, to provide cooling shade, to bring order to the landscape, to help support wildlife, and for ornamental purposes. Evergreens offer year-round color, protection, and structure. Some of the best conifers for seaside gardens are those with a bluish coloration. The blue color comes from a waxy coating on the needles, which protects them from salt damage near the beach. The best broad-leaved evergreens are those with thick, leathery leaves; some also carry a glossy, waxy surface on the leaves that has a protective effect. Many broad-leaved evergreens have ornamental flowers, too.

Deciduous trees may offer ornamental flowers, welcome shade, colorful autumn foliage, attractive bark, or fruit that is edible to people or wildlife or simply decorative.

Deciduous trees and shrubs for seascape gardens need a sturdy framework with wide crotch angles and well-spaced scaffold branches. Both evergreen and deciduous trees need enough flexibility to bend before the wind without snapping.

TRIAL AND ERROR

As in gardening anyplace else, learning what will grow best in your seashore garden is a process of experimentation, trial, and error. It takes time. You can obtain guidance on what generally grows well in your area by talking to your neighbors, joining a local garden club, and taking tours of public and private gardens when they are offered. You can visit good local nurseries and ask questions of knowledgeable staff. But experience is still the best teacher. Take time to get to know your particular property and its growing condi-

tions. If there's already a garden in place from previous owners, wait a season to see what does well before making changes. Spend time in the garden and on the grounds. Watch and learn.

When you do start gardening on your own, keeping a garden journal is an invaluable aid. Jot down when trees leaf out, when roses and perennials bloom, what thrives and what languishes, which plants suffer from pests or disease. Note weather conditions: dates of major storms, periods of drought, floods, first and last frosts. As the years pass, your journal will become an ever-more-detailed portrait of the climate and your landscape, a better guide than even the best reference book.

An ancient copper beech (*Fagus sylvatica* var. *purpurea*) lends a sense of history to this Massachusetts harbor.

Gardening in Containers

CONTAINERS OFFER GREAT FLEXIbility for seashore gardeners. Where the soil is poor, or during the time you are building better soil for gardening or waiting for a protective windbreak to grow in, containers can be the focus of your gardening efforts. You might set large tubs holding small shrubs, perennials, trellised vines, or topiaries in sheltered locations behind the house, on a patio protected by a fence or hedge, or in low spots in the lee of the dunes.

In more established gardens, containers of plants can accent beds and borders, porches, decks, patios, and swimming pools. Colorful combinations of well-chosen annuals will bloom all summer, many until frost shuts them down. Neatly clipped evergreens in containers can add elegant touches to formal gardens. Tubs of bold tropicals inject a dramatic note to foliage beds and outdoor living spaces.

When choosing places for pots and plants to put in them, it is important to carefully assess sun and shade conditions and wind exposure. And be honest: a spot that gets a few hours of morning sun and is shaded by the house the rest of the day is not a "sunny" spot. For pots in a shady location, use shade-tolerant plants.

In a windy location it is a good idea to rely mostly on plants that stay reasonably compact. Tall plants in narrow pots will be blown over. Large leaves can become tattered. Brittle stems can snap. Smaller-leaved plants with flexible stems are better able to bend with the wind.

Try to use heavy, sturdy pots rather than small, lightweight plastic ones. Fewer, larger pots will be more stable than lots of smaller ones. Water the pots well to keep them heavy. If the pots are in garden areas, you can sink them partway into the ground to hold them in place.

Hanging baskets overflowing with cascading and trailing plants are delightful additions to summer landscapes. But be sure they are well anchored, with sturdy hangers. Keep them out of the most exposed locations and place them instead in more protected places — on the lee side of the house rather than on the windward side, or under an arbor, perhaps. Take down hanging baskets (and wind chimes and other dangling ornaments) when you expect a storm or higher-than-usual winds.

Remember that plants in containers need plenty of water, especially in sunny, windy seashore locations. See chapter 3 for information on watering.

Finally, if you are a weekend resident, you may want to have a local nursery or gardener plant and maintain your pots for you.

Container plantings can enhance the garden and outdoor living space in myriad ways, offering an easy way to add color to porches and decks.

Planting and Maintenance

ABOVE: Drought-tolerant yucca provides an architectural presence in the seaside garden.

RIGHT: This well-maintained garden benefits from the protection of a stone wall. A greenhouse can expand your plant palette by offering a warm site to overwinter tender species.

WHEN THE DESIGN IS IN PLACE AND THE SITE PREPARED, it's time to get growing. This chapter provides a summary of the best gardening techniques for seaside gardens. You'll find guidelines for planting, watering, fertilizing and maintaining good soil quality, mulching, deadheading and pruning, preventing and controlling pests and diseases, and getting ready for winter. There's also information on what to do after a storm.

Bear in mind that you will need to adapt these techniques to fit the particular microclimates in your garden. Weather conditions also will vary from year to year and may necessitate adjustments in planting dates, amount of watering, and other aspects of plant care. Watch your garden and be sensitive to its needs.

Planting Guidelines

Before you plant a tree or shrub, find out what its mature size is likely to be, and be sure to allow enough space for it to reach its full height and spread.

PLANTING TECHNIQUES FOR SEA-shore gardens are basically the same as those used in other gardens, although, as I will explain in a minute, you do need to be aware of the effects of wind and intense sun. Before you plant anything, make sure the plant you are putting in will have enough space to reach its full mature size without crowding. Space considerations are especially important along property lines, the street, driveways and paths, and alongside the house. Large shrubs such as hollies and false cypress can easily grow to six or more feet wide, and evergreen trees can be even wider.

Investigate the best planting times in your area. Trees and shrubs can be planted in either spring or fall in many seashore areas. In the South, woody plants can go into the ground in February, while they are still dormant. Farther north, you have to wait until the soil thaws and becomes workable.

It's best to plant on a cloudy day, or in the morning if the weather is hot and sunny. First, water the soil deeply before planting. If you are planting bare-root nursery stock, it's important to prevent the roots from drying out before you get the plants in the ground. Many mail-order plants are shipped in bare-root form in a loose, light packing material; roses are also sold this way. If you cannot plant as soon as the stock arrives, unwrap the plants to inspect them and moisten the roots if they are very shriveled and dry. Pull a plastic bag over the roots to hold in moisture until you can plant (which will be, hopefully, in 24 hours or so). A few hours before planting, set the roots in a bucket of water and let them soak to rehydrate them. When you are ready to plant, carry the bucket to the planting site, or put each plant's roots into a plastic bag to hold in the moisture. If you're working in the sun, cover the bag with a cloth to keep it from heating up and damaging the plants.

PLANTING TREES AND SHRUBS

For trees and shrubs, dig a planting hole as deep as the root-ball is high and twice as wide. There is one exception to the rule: If you are planting in sand rather than soil, set plants an inch or two deeper than they were growing at the nursery. Also, if you are planting on or very near the beach, it's not a bad idea to scrape away the top few inches of dry sand before you dig the hole. Fine, dry sand is hard to moisten—it sheds water like dry peat moss does. Removing the top layer of it decreases the chance that some of the sand will fall into the planting hole and create a dry spot around plant roots.

Excavate two bucketfuls of sand or existing soil from the bottom of the hole and mix it with two bucketfuls of compost or good-quality topsoil. Mix some of the amended soil with the soil in the hole, and

set the plant in the hole to check the depth. Remove more soil as needed to correct the depth. An alternative method is to dig the hole a little deeper and work some compost or leaf mold into the bottom before planting. In any case, the plant should sit at the same level it was growing in the nursery, which you can see by a difference in color at the bottom of the trunk. The part that grew below the soil line should appear darker than the rest of the trunk. If you aren't sure about the planting depth, it is better to err by planting too high than too deep, because the plant will settle after it is in the ground. Make sure all the roots are covered, but don't cover the trunk. If the plant has a long taproot, make sure the hole is deep enough to accommodate it.

When the planting hole is ready, if the soil is mostly sand or otherwise of very poor quality, make two slits in the bottom of the hole with a trowel and put about a tablespoon of all-purpose fertilizer into each one. Or you can pour a liquid fertilizer solution, such as compost tea, a fish/seaweed product, or a synthetic all-purpose liquid fertilizer diluted to half strength, into the hole. Or add an organic fertilizer to the amended soil that will go into the hole around the plant.

If the tree or shrub is in a container, remove it (cut off the container if you need to). Lay the plant on its side and gently

PLANTING A TREE OR SHRUB

When planting in sand, set a tree or shrub one to two inches deeper than usual (1). Remove some sand from the planting hole, mix with compost, and return some to the hole (2). Set the plant in the hole and partially fill with soil (3). Check to make sure the plant is at the proper depth (4). Make a saucerlike depression around the stem to catch and hold water for the roots (5).

untangle the roots as best you can. If the root-ball is very tight, try to tease out a few of the bigger roots without breaking them. If the plant has a taproot, handle it carefully to avoid breaking it. Fill the hole halfway with amended soil, working it

PLANTING A PERENNIAL

To remove a perennial from its nursery pot, support the top growth with one hand as you turn over the pot with your other hand, and slide out the root-ball.

around the roots with your fingers. Water well to settle the soil and get rid of air pockets. Fill the hole the rest of the way, gently rock the plant a bit, water again, and firm the soil around the base of the plant with your hand or, for a larger specimen, with your foot. Make a depression in the soil around the trunk to catch water and channel it down to the root system.

Staking is not generally recommended for trees and large shrubs anymore, but you may need to stake them in exposed seaside locations. If you do need to stake, thread the wires through pieces of garden hose where they touch the trunk. Leave just enough slack in the wires for the trunk to be able to flex a bit in the wind — it makes for a stronger trunk and better anchorage in the roots.

PLANTING PERENNIALS AND ANNUALS

When planting a perennial or annual, you will probably be planting in soil that already has been improved (such as in a prepared bed). Dig a hole just deep enough for the plant and fill it partway with water. While the water drains away, remove the plant from its pot. To do this, tap the bottom of the pot with the handle of a trowel to loosen the plant. Turn the pot over and support the top of the soil ball with one hand, placing a finger on either side of the stem for support. With your other hand,

slide the pot off the root-ball. If the root-ball does not slide out easily, lay the pot on its side and roll it back and forth while pressing on it to loosen the soil ball. If it still doesn't come out easily, cut away the pot with shears.

If the plant is severely root-bound, make two or three vertical cuts a few inches up into the root-ball from the bottom and gently spread apart the root-ball.

Set the plant gently into the planting hole. Make sure the plant sits at the correct depth in the hole, and proceed as directed above for trees and shrubs. If the plant grows as a rosette of leaves close to the ground, be sure you do not cover the crown of the plant (where roots meet the stem) or the plant could rot. Bushy, branched plants generally can be set a bit deeper in the soil without harm.

Water to settle the soil around the plant and ensure good root contact, then fill in any holes that remain.

To remove a plant from a market pack or cell pack, tap or lightly press on the bottom of a cell to loosen the plant. If the plant does not slide easily out of the cell, cut the plastic with scissors and tear it away from the soil ball. Grasp the plant *very gently* by two upper leaves (but not the growing tip, or you could damage the plant) and slip it out of the cell. When the plant is out, support it underneath and plant as described above.

Watering

SOAKER HOSES

Soaker hoses are a very efficient way to water, trickling moisture slowly onto the soil where it is readily absorbed. Lay the hoses on top of the soil, snaking them among plants in a pattern that allows all the plants to get water.

Unless you are growing only tough native plants that are highly drought resistant, your garden is going to need supplemental watering. Many seashore residents install automatic watering systems; if you're not a full-time resident, that's probably the best course of action. There are several different kinds of watering systems, and each has its own benefits and disadvantages.

OVERHEAD SPRINKLERS

Overhead sprinklers are the least efficient means of watering; some of the water evaporates into the air before it gets to plants, and some runs off before it can soak into the ground. Overhead watering can cause soil to splash up onto plant leaves, which can lead to the transfer of disease organisms from soil onto susceptible plants. And drought-tolerant plants do not always fare well under overhead watering — the crowns may rot if they get wet on a regular basis, and the plants will eventually die.

On the other hand, overhead sprinkling can be beneficial because it rinses salt off plant foliage and dilutes salts that have settled on lawns and ground covers. This is especially important for gardeners who aren't at their seaside homes every day to keep an eye on plantings and rinse them as needed. Despite its detractions, therefore, you may decide that an overhead sprinkler system is right for you.

SOAKER HOSES

Soaker hoses are a very efficient means of watering. They deliver water directly to the soil, where it can reach the roots, and little water is lost to evaporation. Soaker hoses emit water in a slow trickle, so it doesn't run off before soaking in, and they don't cause soil to splash onto plants. They are easy to install — you simply lay out the hoses on top of the soil near plants, and you can cover them with mulch to hide them. And many soaker hoses are made from recycled tires, making them environmentally helpful.

The downside is that soaker hoses have to run for a pretty long time in order to deliver enough water. Depending on the quality of your soil and the plants you are growing, you may need to run soaker hoses for several hours at a time.

HOW LONG TO WATER

Timing is important where sprinklers are concerned. You need the system to run long enough that the water it puts out can soak deep enough to reach the root zone. It is generally better to water longer and less often than to let the system run 10 or 15 minutes every day. Many municipalities have regulations that forbid overhead watering during daylight hours. In such a case (or even when no watering restrictions are in place, for that matter), it is better to have the system run early in the

USING DRIP IRRIGATION IN SANDY SOIL

Drip irrigation is the most efficient way to water; its slender plastic tubes deliver water directly to the root zone, where plants can best use it. However, drip systems don't always work well in very sandy soils, because the water lines can clog. Robert Kourik, author of *Drip Irrigation for Every Landscape and All Climates* (Metamorphic Press, 1992), offers the following tips for using a drip system in sandy soil:

- Don't install the system underground. Instead, keep the emitters on top of the soil and cover them with mulch.
- Use tubing that does not have built-in pressure compensation (as some do); the higher water pressure will help to flush the lines.
- Use tubing with one-foot intervals, and place the lines a foot apart in the garden.

To revive a wilted plant in a pot, submerge the pot in a bucket of water. When the bubbling stops, remove the pot and let the excess water drain away.

SOIL PREPARATION FOR MOISTURE LOVERS

If you yearn to grow moisture-loving plants in sandy, fast-draining soil, try preparing a special area for them. Excavate the soil from the bed to a depth of two feet. Line the bed with heavy-duty plastic, and poke holes in the plastic to allow water to drain away. The idea is to slow the rate of drainage, not prevent drainage altogether. Mix the excavated soil with equal parts (or more) of compost or good-quality topsoil and replace it in the planting area. (Using all the amended soil will create a raised bed.) Plant the moisture lovers in the bed and water well whenever the soil gets dry.

day so foliage will dry in the morning sun, rather than in the evening, when moisture sitting on leaves overnight could promote the growth of disease organisms. It is also important to adjust the watering schedule according to the weather so you are not watering when it rains.

The other way to water is with a hand-held hose. It's a time-consuming chore if you've got more than a few plants, and there's a tendency not to water long enough to allow the water to soak deep into the ground.

Many localities have ordinances governing watering. Become familiar with regulations where you live and abide by them: they are for everyone's good.

WHEN TO WATER

Be sure to water new plants thoroughly after planting. Thereafter, water as needed to keep the soil moist until the plants can send out new roots and establish themselves in the soil. How long this process takes depends upon the plant. Annuals and perennials will settle in in a couple of weeks, but trees and shrubs will take longer. Trees in exposed locations should be watered during dry weather for the first year after planting.

The old gardener's rule of thumb for watering — that plants need one inch of water per week — does not necessarily apply to seashore gardens. Sandy soil drains so quickly that an inch of water a week might not be enough. On the other hand, it might be too much moisture for drought-tolerant plants like arctotis and prickly pear. A better general guideline for seashore gardens is to make sure gardens of nonnative plants that are not highly drought tolerant receive one deep watering, thorough enough to send water 1 to 1½ feet down into the soil, once a week if no rain falls.

More sensitive perennials and other plants that thrive in soil that is "moist but well drained" would probably fare best in soil amended with lots of organic matter where they receive water two or three times a week. Drought-tolerant plants should need water only during prolonged periods of dry weather. If you want to grow plants with different needs, try to group like-minded ones together in separate beds or even in different parts of the garden. Water each group according to its needs.

WATERING CONTAINERS

Containers need watering much more frequently than gardens in the ground. In hot, windy seashore conditions, plants in containers may need watering every day or even more than once a day. How often your containers will require watering depends in part on the moisture needs of the plants growing in them. But a number of other factors also come into play.

Ask yourself these questions:

- Is it hot? The higher the temperature, the more water plants need.
- Is the humidity high or low? On dry days, pots need water more frequently.
- Is the container in sun or shade? Plants in the shade need less water than plants in full, blazing sun.
- Is it windy? Pots dry out faster on windy days.
- What kind of soil mix is in the pot? Lightweight, soilless, peat-based planting mixes dry out faster than potting mixes containing a larger amount of soil and/or compost.
- How big is the pot? The smaller the pot, the smaller the volume of soil it holds and the faster it dries out.

To help reduce watering frequency, mix a polymer gel into the potting mix before planting. These polymers come in the form of crystals that can absorb many times their volume in water, turning into blobs of gel. They release their moisture gradually, so the potting mix dries out more slowly. Follow package directions; if you use too much polymer, the expanding gel will cause the potting mix to overflow the container.

Don't wait until your plants look wilted before watering — wilted plants are stressed, and their growth can be adversely affected. The best way to tell when plants need water is to poke a finger into the soil. When it feels dry an inch below the surface, it's time to water. To judge if a hanging basket needs water, place your hand under the basket and let the basket rest on your palm until you can feel its weight. If the pot feels heavy, it is probably still moist; if it feels very light, it's in need of water.

When you do water, do it thoroughly. Water enough for some excess to drain from the holes in the bottom of the pot. The goal is to moisten the potting mix all the way to the bottom. Use a watering can or a hose. A long-handled watering wand makes it easy to reach hanging baskets. If you have an automatic drip system in your pots, make sure it runs long enough to provide a thorough watering. A drip system will emit water far more slowly than a hose and will need to run for a much longer time. Experiment by connecting the drip line to just one pot and water until the potting mix is moist throughout. Keep track of the time so you know how long to run the system in the future.

TOP: Drought-tolerant plants like these sedums, echeverias, and aeoniums are a good choice for weekend gardeners.

BOTTOM: Pots may need watering daily — or more than once a day — in hot, windy summer weather.

Fertilizing and Soil Care

Soil building is an important, continuous process for seashore gardens, especially if you want to grow heavy-feeding flowers like these lilies.

BUILDING GOOD SOIL IS NOT A ONE-time proposition. When you've spent time and money to improve your soil, you will want to keep it in good condition so your garden will continue to thrive. Organic matter, as we saw in chapter 3, is tremendously valuable for improving the quality of sandy soil. But it doesn't last forever. Organic matter breaks down and disappears quickly at the seashore; the sandier the soil and the hotter the weather, the faster organic materials get used up in the soil. It's important to replenish the supply every year.

Try to add an inch or two of compost to your garden each year. That's easy to do if you're growing annual flowers or vegetables — you simply spread the compost over the empty garden in spring and till it in before you plant. In a perennial garden, drop the compost in between plants and spread it around and among them with your hands or a hoe. But be careful not to cover the plant crowns. For shrubs, a more feasible method of application is to spread the compost around the base of each plant, keeping it a few inches away from the main stems. For trees, the layer of compost should, ideally, cover an area from a foot or so away from the trunk outward to the drip line (an imaginary line on the ground beneath the limit of the tree's canopy). That's because a tree's roots don't just go straight down into the ground; they spread out and cover an area equal to or greater than the spread of the tree's branches. If you apply compost just around the base of the tree, it won't benefit much of the root system.

Plants native to beach and dune areas are adapted to dry, infertile sand and may not thrive in fertile soil rich in organic matter, so salt windbreaks and dune-stabilizing plantings may not require these yearly infusions of organic matter. But garden beds and borders will definitely benefit.

When applying compost or other soil amendments under a tree, spread the material over an area from a foot away from the trunk to the drip line, to ensure that the entire root system receives the benefit.

Roses and other flowering plants appreciate a fertilizer rich in phosphorus. Apply fertilizer around the base of each plant and work it gently into the soil.

HOW TO FERTILIZE

Fertilizing at the beach can be a tricky proposition. Garden beds and borders in very sandy soil will need fertilizing in order to thrive, especially if the soil is not being regularly amended with organic material. But well-adapted native plants will need less fertilizer than more conventional garden plants.

How and when you fertilize also depends upon the kind of fertilizer you are using. Synthetic fertilizers such as granular 5-10-5 and 8-8-8 products work quickly and can be very effective. But they are more concentrated than organic products, and they can cause problems in sandy soils if not handled correctly. For one thing, granular fertilizers mixed into soil that is mostly sand can become more concentrated if the sand dries out during spells of hot, dry summer weather. The concentrated salts can burn plant roots with which they come into direct contact. To avoid damaging plants, sprinkle granular fertilizers on top of the ground, in a circle around the base of each plant, and water them in, instead of placing them into planting holes.

Synthetic fertilizers also leach quickly through very porous, sandy soil. You need to be careful not to overfertilize your garden. Fertilizers that are not absorbed by plant roots travel through soil in rainwater and can eventually reach the water table.

From there the runoff can get into rivers, estuaries, and bays. Fertilizer runoff wreaks havoc with coastal waterways. (On eastern Long Island, for example, fertilizer runoff is believed by many environmentalists and other experts to be a possible contributor to the demise of the once abundant population of bay scallops and the subsequent ruin of the shellfishing industry.)

A better fertilizer option is to use a timed-release product or an organic formula, which will naturally release its nutrients gradually. Timed-release fertilizers are especially helpful for heavy feeders like annuals (either in the ground or in containers) and roses that repeat bloom. Read labels carefully: a timed-release fertilizer may not be effective until the soil temperature reaches 50°F. And fertilizers are used up more quickly in hot weather. Soaring temperatures may mean you will have to apply the fertilizer more frequently than the advertisements or the large print on the front of the package promises.

Use fertilizers rich in phosphorus, such as 5-10-10 and 5-10-5, for flowering and fruiting plants. Powdered rock phosphate is an organic source of phosphorus. For grasses, lawns, and other foliage plants, use a high-nitrogen fertilizer such as 20-10-10. Some plants need less fertilizer than others. Achillea and artemisia, for instance, need less fertilizing than lilies and roses.

Natives also will need little in the way of fertilization once they become established. See the plant profiles in chapter 5 for information on the nutritional needs of individual plants.

Liquid fertilizers are great for plants in pots, and you can also use them diluted to half or one-quarter strength as a foliar feed sprayed onto leaves to give plants a quick boost. Foliar feeding is a good way to provide plants with trace elements; use an organic liquid such as kelp or fish products or compost tea to supply them. There are numerous all-purpose liquid fertilizers available at garden centers and home improvement stores.

Intensively planted container combinations will need frequent water and fertilizer to keep them flowering through the summer.

WHEN TO FERTILIZE

You may or may not want to fertilize at planting time, depending on what you are planting and where you are planting it. As described below, many plants in beds and borders benefit from fertilization at planting time. But do not fertilize dune-stabilization plantings when you put them in unless you are using an organic product.

Trees and Shrubs. Fertilize new trees and shrubs with an organic fertilizer at planting time, working the material into the soil at the bottom of the planting hole. Fertilize young trees again in early summer with an organic or timed-release product, or monthly with a granular synthetic until six to eight weeks before the average date of the first fall frost in your area.

Fertilize established trees and shrubs once a year, when growth begins in spring, with an all-purpose organic or synthetic fertilizer. Follow package directions for rate of application. For shrubs and young trees, spread the fertilizer on top of the soil in a ring around the base of the plant and a couple of feet out from the trunk or main stems. Work it into the top inch of soil. For older trees, drill holes two feet apart and 12 to 18 inches deep over an area from two to three feet out from the trunk to the drip line (where most of the roots are concentrated). Put the fertilizer into the holes.

Tough plants like these hens-and-chicks (*Sempervivum* spp.) need so little water and nutrients that they can even grow from a pocket of soil in a stone wall.

Perennials. Feed perennials at planting time with an all-purpose or high-phosphorus fertilizer. Thereafter fertilize every two or three weeks in sandy soil, once a month if you are using an organic fertilizer, or once in early summer if the soil is rich in organic matter. Stop feeding six weeks before the first expected fall frost — late July in the North, around the middle of August in the mid-Atlantic region, or September in the South. Cessation of fertilizing allows plants to slow their growth so they will not be producing a lot of tender new leaves right before the onset of cold weather (new growth can be seriously damaged by cold). Instead, plant tissues, especially in the crown, will be able to harden off in preparation for the winter dormant period.

Roses. Amend the soil for roses before planting with plenty of organic matter (this is less important for rugosas, which are very tough). Also work in an all-purpose or high-phosphorus organic or timed-release fertilizer, according to package directions. After planting, wait three to four weeks for plants to establish themselves in the soil, then begin to fertilize every two or three weeks in sandy soil, or once a month if you are using an organic fertilizer. In subsequent years, fertilize bush roses when plants begin to grow in spring, again after the first flush of bloom, and once a month until midsummer. Feed shrub roses and climbers in spring when growth begins and just once or twice more, in late spring and early summer. Stop fertilizing six to eight weeks before the first expected fall frost to allow plants enough time to harden their canes and buds before winter.

Annuals. Fertilize annuals at planting time with all-purpose or high-phosphorus products. As soon as the plants show new growth, begin to fertilize weekly in sandy soil, or monthly with organics throughout the growing season. If your soil is heavier, feed every two or three weeks. Follow package directions for rates of application. It's a good idea to water before fertilizing if the soil is dry.

Container Plants. Mix an organic or timed-release fertilizer into the potting mix when planting. Then feed every week or two with an all-purpose liquid fertilizer diluted according to package directions. Or fertilize at every watering with an all-purpose liquid fertilizer diluted to half or one-quarter strength.

If you want to use an organic liquid fertilizer, look for fish emulsion or a product that combines seaweed and fish. Use according to package directions. Liquid fertilizers may be applied to the soil or sprayed onto plant leaves as a foliar feed.

Mulching

Buckwheat hulls dress up the King garden in Cohasset, Massachusetts. Mulch helps slow evaporation of moisture from the soil and adds organic matter as it decomposes.

Mulching — covering the soil under plants — is a great help to seashore gardens. Mulches laid on the garden in summer slow the evaporation of moisture from the soil and reduce weed growth. Mulch will also help moderate soil temperatures, preventing them from rising to levels harmful to plants — the sun won't heat up the soil under a layer of mulch as much as it will bare soil that just bakes under the beating summer rays. Mulches of natural materials offer the additional benefit of contributing organic matter to the soil as they decompose, improving soil texture and overall quality. They'll add some nutrients, too.

Be aware that mulches of wood products, such as wood chips, bark nuggets, and uncomposted sawdust, use nitrogen from the soil as they decompose, so it's a good idea to apply a nitrogen-rich fertilizer before laying a wood mulch.

Covering the soil with mulch keeps soil from splashing up during rain or waterings onto plant leaves, where it could possibly encourage soilborne diseases in susceptible plants. At the seashore, mulch can also help protect the soil from salt deposits. In addition, a layer of mulch gives the garden a neat, finished look.

SEASONAL MULCHES

The best time to put down a summer mulch is in spring, after the soil warms but before temperatures really start to climb. Most mulches are best laid two to three inches deep; see below for more information on particular mulch materials.

Mulches can be extremely useful in winter, too, but at that time of year their purpose is different. Where the ground freezes in winter, mulch helps to keep the soil frozen during spells of warm winter weather. It prevents or at least minimizes the kind of freeze/thaw/refreeze cycle that can cause the ground to heave and push the roots of perennials out onto the surface. Exposed roots in winter are likely to die as they dry out and freeze. If you want to give your garden a protective winter mulch, apply a six-inch layer in late fall or early winter after the soil freezes. Note that mulches will be washed away or at least moved around by floodwaters. If your property is prone to flooding, you may want to forgo mulching.

APPLYING MULCH

When you spread mulch in your garden, don't just dump it on top of the plants. Tuck it in around the base of each plant, taking care to keep it away from direct contact with stems. Don't bury the crowns of plants that sit close to the ground — the mulch will hold moisture that can cause crowns to rot. If laid too deeply, the mulch could suffocate the plants.

There are some times when mulching

Mulching with natural materials gives the garden a neat, finished look. Pine needles and pine straw make good mulches for many seaside gardens.

may not be a good idea. Earwigs, slugs, and mice love to hide out in mulch. If they're a problem in your garden, it may be better not to mulch. Also, if you have some plants that you want to encourage to self-sow and spread, leave the soil under them bare so the seeds can reach the ground.

When applying mulch, tuck it around the base of each plant, but do not cover the crown; the plant could rot.

The most widely used mulches are shredded bark, wood chips, bark nuggets, cocoa bean hulls, and shredded leaves. Seashore gardeners can also look for saltmarsh hay, which works well, and in the South, pine straw, which is an attractive dark brown. You can also mulch with compost or pine needles. Be aware that organic mulches will lighten in color over the course of a season. To retain a good dark color, spread fresh mulch each year.

Some gardeners like to use plastic mulches, or a layer of gravel or pebbles, to cover the soil around plants. Both can work, but they do hold heat in the soil and are probably best for northern gardens.

Here are some of the characteristics of various mulches:

• **Bark chips or nuggets.** Long lasting. The larger the pieces, the longer they last, but smaller chips are finer textured and more attractive under perennials and smaller plants. Add nitrogen fertilizer to soil, and apply a two-inch layer.

• **Shredded bark.** Long lasting. Partially composted mulch is an attractive dark color. Add nitrogen fertilizer to soil, and apply a three-inch layer.

• **Cedar mulches.** Fine textured and available in natural and dyed colors. The orange-red type is popular but can clash with flower colors and call too much attention to itself; use with care. Apply a two- to three-inch layer.

• **Cocoa bean hulls.** Nice brown color, and they smell like chocolate when first applied. Expensive, but fine textured and nice in perennial beds and formal gardens. Lightweight and may blow around on windy sites. Apply a two-inch layer.

• **Compost.** Dark brown and crumbly, excellent soil conditioner, and invaluable for sandy soils. But it won't keep down weeds — they'll grow right up through it. Apply a one- to two-inch layer.

• **Shredded leaves.** Free or inexpensive if you shred your own or obtain them from municipal recycling operations. Excellent soil builder, but best in informal or naturalistic gardens. Apply a two- to three-inch layer in summer; six inches as a winter mulch. Leaf mold (composted leaves) is also good. Don't use unshredded leaves — they tend to mat down and look messy.

• **Pine needles, pine straw.** Attractive brown color, especially nice in naturalistic and native plant gardens. Will tend to make soil pH more acidic; add some lime if using around plants needing neutral to mildly alkaline soil. Apply a two- to three-inch layer.

• **Saltmarsh hay.** Effective where available, though expensive. It is finer textured than agricultural hay, and contains no weed seeds, the way agricultural hay can. Decomposes well and adds trace minerals to soil. Apply a two- to three-inch layer.

• **Seashells.** Crushed seashells, where they are available, can be used for mulching or for surfacing paths. They will tend to raise soil pH. Apply a two- to three-inch layer.

• **Seaweed.** Free when collected from beaches. Adds minerals and organic matter to soil, but can be smelly when it decomposes. Best used in compost.

• **Stone (pebbles, gravel, marble chips).** Won't suppress weeds unless you first lay down a weed-barrier fabric. Looks best in a rock garden or under trees and shrubs. Apply a two- to three-inch layer, depending on size of stones.

• **Wood chips.** Often available free from tree-care crews. Long lasting, but not terribly attractive when chips are large. Usually light colored. Add nitrogen fertilizer to soil and apply a two- to three-inch layer, depending on size of chips.

Shredded bark mulch suppresses weeds beneath a newly planted tree.

Deadheading and Pruning

Even in the most naturalistic gardens, plants will need some grooming, however occasional. The more formal the garden, the more upkeep plants will require in order to retain their neat, carefully shaped forms. Annuals and perennials in general need more attention than shrubs and trees.

ANNUALS AND PERENNIALS

Two important techniques for flower gardeners are pinching and deadheading. Many plants with a branching growth habit can be encouraged to grow bushier when the growing tip is pinched off one or more times as the plants grow. Pinching out the tip stimulates dormant buds in leaf axils or farther down the stem to grow into side branches. The result is a fuller, bushier plant. Plants that benefit from pinching include chrysanthemums, asters, marigolds, nicotiana, summer phlox, and snapdragons.

Pinching off the flowers of basil, coleus, and other plants whose leaves are their most important feature will help hold the leaves in good condition for the longest possible time. Eventually these plants will bloom anyway, but pinching off buds as soon as you see them does delay flowering for a while.

Deadheading is picking off faded flowers. It can prolong the blooming period of many plants. Deadheading is particularly effective for annuals, whose mission is to flower and produce seeds in a single growing season. If old flowers are picked off before seeds can form, the plants will keep on producing more flowers. Many annuals will bloom all summer and right up until frost if you deadhead them regularly.

Pinch off the dead flowers between your thumb and forefinger; use pruning shears for stems that are thick, woody, or wiry, or use flower shears for slender stems. In many cases it is best to pinch or cut right above the nearest set of leaves so you don't leave a lot of headless flower stems sticking up from the plants. Not all plants follow this rule, though, at least not right away. Cosmos, for example, blooms in clusters of three successive flowers. After the first flower blooms, two new buds will form on either side of it, immediately below the old flower. The best way to deadhead is to cut the first blossom right below the head, then cut back to the next set of leaves after the second and third flowers in the group have bloomed. For some plants, it is best to carefully pick or clip off individual blossoms when they fade. For others, such as kniphofia, you can remove the entire flowering stem to the ground when the single flower on the stem or all the flowers on it are finished. See the plant profiles in chapter 5 for information on the deadheading needs of particular plants.

For plants with a basal rosette of leaves, such as kniphofia, cut off the stem at the base.

To deadhead many-branching plants, cut off the flower stem at the next lower set of leaves.

When pruning roses, cut above a bud eye (a crescent-shaped scar on the stem) to encourage a new shoot to grow.

In the case of plants that have a lot of small flowers that are too time-consuming to pick off by hand, such as sweet alyssum and threadleaf coreopsis, you can cut back the plants with a pair of flower shears when the first flush of bloom subsides, and they will rebloom.

Deadheading *is* time-consuming. But it is also a most rewarding activity. Regular deadheading keeps plants looking neat, and coaxes the maximum amount of bloom from them. It gives you a chance to spend quiet, relaxing time in your garden, too. It is well worth the time it takes.

ROSES

It's a good idea to deadhead roses unless you want them to form the seed cases called "hips." (Rugosa roses develop large, colorful hips that provide food for birds.) Deadheading encourages some roses to send out a second flush of flowers, called repeat blooming. The traditional advice for deadheading roses was to cut the spent flowering stem back to the nearest five-part leaf. But now experts recommend cutting right behind the flower head, to leave the maximum amount of foliage intact, thus making for a stronger plant.

If you need to prune roses to control their size or to shape the plants, look for a crescent-shaped scar on the cane (stem) with a slight swelling above it. A new shoot will be able to grow from this "bud eye."

Cut back the stem on an angle to ¼ inch above a bud eye on the outside (not the inner side) of the stem to produce a new shoot that grows outward. Roses are susceptible to black spot and other diseases, and a plant with an open form will permit good air circulation that helps minimize disease problems.

If you do need to prune out diseased growth, cut back to healthy green wood with a firm, white central pith. Prune away any winter-killed growth at the end of winter before the new season's growth begins.

GRASSES

Like perennials, ornamental grasses need to be cut back close to the ground once a year. When you cut them back depends, to some degree, on your personal preference and what kind of winter conditions your region experiences. Ornamental grasses really come into their own in autumn, when their silky, fluffy, or bristly seed heads wave at the ends of long stems, glistening in the sunlight, sparkling with droplets of rain, and dancing in the breeze. You can leave grasses in place over the winter to add interest to the garden and cut them back in early spring before new growth begins. The plants will slowly fade to varying shades of tan and beige. But if winter snows are likely to knock over the stems and leave plants looking broken and messy, it is better to cut them back in late fall.

WOODY PLANTS

The most important reason for pruning trees and shrubs is to remove dead or damaged growth. At the seashore, strong winds and storms cause plenty of broken branches. Salt exposure and tough winter conditions can result in dieback of stem tips and branches. Pests and diseases also can cause damage.

Dead or damaged growth should be removed whenever you notice it, whatever its cause. You will want to survey the plants on your property after a storm, of course, but it is a good idea to walk the grounds on a regular basis to inspect the condition of the landscape.

Structural pruning is also sometimes needed, to create a sturdy branch framework for a young tree or to thin the dense canopy of a mature tree to allow more light to reach the ground underneath. You may need to prune to thin out or rejuvenate old or overgrown shrubs.

Structural tree pruning is usually done while the tree is dormant, in late winter to early spring, or midwinter in mild-winter climates. Pruning of flowering shrubs depends on when they bloom. Shrubs that bloom in spring, such as lilacs, generally bloom on old wood. This means that after they finish blooming, they set buds for next year's flowers. These shrubs are best pruned right after they bloom, before new buds form, to avoid removing some of next year's flowers. Shrubs that bloom later, such as butterfly bush, tend to bloom on new wood, setting their buds during the current growing season. Prune these shrubs in spring.

Trees and shrubs in formal gardens will need pruning to maintain their idealized shapes. Hedges need to be sheared and topiaries precisely clipped. Pruning of large trees is best handled by a certified arborist, and you will probably also want a professional gardener to maintain high hedges and topiaries in a formal garden. But you may want to do minor pruning yourself. Either way, it's useful to understand the basic techniques involved.

Thinning. Thinning means cutting off crowded or weak stems or branches back to their base. You might thin to lighten a heavy tree canopy or to keep an older flowering shrub vigorous. Use lopping shears to remove thinner stems and branches, or a pruning saw for thicker growth.

To thin an overgrown shrub, cut off crowded or weak stems at the base with loppers or a pruning saw.

Heading Back. Heading back involves removing the end of a branch or stem in order to improve a plant's shape or promote new or bushier growth. You might, for instance, decide to head back a flowering shrub that blooms on new wood to give it a more pleasing shape. Cut back stems to ¼ to ½ inch above a bud; cut on an angle, with the bottom of the cut being about even with the top of the bud. The cut will stimulate the bud to grow and produce new shoots. Step back from time to time as you work to look at the overall shape of the plant. Unless your garden is very formal, try to work with the plant's natural form; don't try to force it into a whole new shape.

Rejuvenation Pruning. Hard pruning can reinvigorate multistemmed flowering shrubs that have become overgrown and neglected. The most severe way to rejuvenate a shrub is to cut back all the stems at once to a few inches above the ground. A better approach is to do the rejuvenation over a period of three years, cutting back one third of the old stems each year. Not all shrubs respond well to rejuvenation. Those that form clumps that expand over time — spirea, lilac, and forsythia, for instance — usually do.

Removing Tree Branches. Removing dead or damaged branches not only improves a tree's looks, but it also can prevent the spread of diseases and insects like carpenter ants. You might want to prune a young tree to remove crossed branches, or to eliminate weak crotches where branches meet the trunk at a sharp angle that leaves them more liable to breakage and storm damage. Old, dense trees can tolerate having some lower branches removed (a procedure called "limbing up") to raise the canopy and let more light into the landscape.

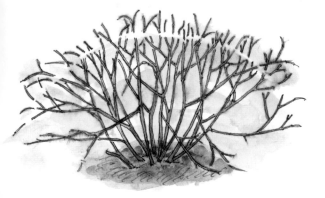

To head back a shrub, remove the ends of the stems, cutting back to ¼ to ½ inch above a bud so you don't end up with bare stem tips.

To rejuvenate a neglected old shrub, cut back one third of the oldest stems to the ground each year over three years to promote vigorous new growth.

To remove a large branch safely, make the first cut up into the underside of the branch, then a second cut down from the top of the branch. Then remove the stub by cutting through the branch next to the collar.

There is a standard procedure to follow in removing large branches without tearing the bark of the trunk. First, make a cut up into the underside of the branch one to two feet out from the branch collar (the raised ridge of bark where branch meets trunk), cutting about halfway through the branch. Second, a couple of inches out beyond the first cut, saw downward from the top of the branch all the way through it. Third, saw off the remaining stub by cutting right next to the collar (the cut will be slightly angled to follow the line of the collar). Do not cut into the collar or leave a stub beyond it — either could increase the possibility of disease.

Remove smaller branches with loppers, a pole pruner, or a pruning saw, cutting right alongside the collar.

If you need to prune a diseased branch, cut back to healthy wood, several inches away from the damaged site. Dip your tools into a solution of liquid chlorine bleach and water after each cut to sterilize them and avoid spreading the disease.

After pruning, make sure to water and fertilize according to the guidelines given earlier in this chapter, to keep the tree or shrub healthy and help it recover.

Shearing. Shearing is simply cutting off a certain amount from the ends of stems all over a plant to create a uniform surface or a precise, particular shape. The technique is

used to trim hedges and clip topiaries. In order to tolerate shearing, a plant must be able to sprout new growth from farther back on the stem than the tip. Many plants cannot tolerate shearing, so it's important to choose hedge and topiary plants carefully.

Shear hedges and evergreen topiaries in late spring or early summer every year, at least once. Do not shear late in summer in the North, or you will promote new growth late in the season that may not have time to harden properly by winter. Insufficiently hardened growth is susceptible to winterkill. Clip stray shoots from topiaries as needed throughout the growing season.

Keep hedges neat by shearing them at least once a year, in late spring or early summer. Where the growing season is long enough, you may shear again in mid- to late summer.

Controlling Pests and Diseases

This sea holly (*Eryngium* sp.) is one of the most deer-resistant plants you'll find.

Pᴿᴼᴮᴸᴱᴹˢ ᴄᴀɴ ᴄʀᴏᴘ ᴜᴘ ɪɴ ᴇᴠᴇɴ the most carefully tended gardens. Lots of seashore gardeners have to contend with deer, and diseases like mildew and black spot can be troublesome, too. In general, when dealing with pest and disease problems, the best approach is to try to prevent problems in the first place. As they say in the sports world, the best offense is a good defense. If you grow a lot of native plants in your garden, you're already a step ahead of the game. Natives are far less bothered by pests and diseases than are exotic plants, especially varieties bred to be bigger, brighter, and earlier than their less flamboyant ancestors.

But no matter what grows in your garden, keeping the garden clean will go a long way toward preventing disease and insect infestation. Practice good sanitation. Pick up and remove dead and fallen leaves and other debris. Deadhead to get rid of old flowers. Keep the weeds pulled — they offer good hiding places for bugs, and they compete with garden plants for water and nutrients. When you plant, allow enough space between plants for air to circulate freely. Mulch the garden to prevent mud that could contain pathogens from splashing up onto plant leaves. Clean up the garden promptly after a storm.

To prevent disease, don't use overhead sprinklers. Instead, install a drip-irrigation system or lay soaker hoses. If you do water from above, do it in the morning or late afternoon (early enough so foliage will dry before dark). Try not to work among the plants when they are wet, so you don't inadvertently transfer any lurking pathogens from one plant to another.

Be vigilant. Keep an eye on your garden. If you spend time among your plants, you will notice when things go wrong before little problems turn into big ones. And after all, isn't a big reason you have a garden to enjoy the plants in it? When you do spot a problem, take action right away. Don't wait until a few bugs turn into a full-scale infestation or a disease spreads from one plant to many.

With experience, you will learn which pests and diseases are likely to invade your garden and which plants they are most likely to attack. But you can be proactive and investigate for yourself. Learn to identify the insects in your landscape. Some will actually help combat pests by preying on them. You don't want to get rid of the beneficial wasps, flies, and other insects that prey on pests. Indeed, you should encourage them. Growing native plants is one good way to support beneficial insects. Also, if you have an herb garden, include dill, caraway, angelica, and other plants in the Umbelliferae family — they attract a variety of beneficial insects. Include some blue lace flower (*Trachymene coerulea*) in a flower garden; it's in the same family.

PEST CONTROL

Deer take a toll on many a seaside garden. As the march of development eats up natural habitat areas, deer find their way into more and more gardens looking for food. If deer are a problem in your region, you will want to build your landscape with plants they aren't likely to eat. You might use deer-resistant plants in outlying parts of the landscape and put plants you and the deer both love in hard-to-access areas close to the house — in an enclosed courtyard, perhaps, or up on an elevated deck. "Deer-Resistant Plants for Seashore Gardens" (right) contains a listing of plants that deer are unlikely to eat. But there are no guarantees. When deer are hungry enough, they will eat just about anything. I've known them to chew rugosa roses, which have very thorny stems, nearly to the ground. Deer are usually hungriest at the end of winter, when food is hard to find. You may find them coming onto your property then even if they don't bother you the rest of the year.

The only way to really keep deer out of your garden is to fence it in. And you need a high fence — 8 to 10 feet — or the deer will leap right over it. You may find the best solution is to install black plastic mesh deer fencing all around the perimeter of the property. This kind of fencing can be camouflaged behind tree and shrub plantings, and it really does work. But you'll

DEER-RESISTANT PLANTS FOR SEASHORE GARDENS

Trees and Shrubs

Amelanchier canadensis, shadblow
Aronia spp., chokeberry
Clethra alnifolia, sweet pepperbush
Cotoneaster horizontalis, rockspray cotoneaster
Crataegus spp., hawthorn
Cytisus scoparius, Scotch broom
Ilex spp., holly
Juniperus spp., junipers
Lavandula spp., lavender
Myrica cerifera, wax myrtle
Myrica pensylvanica, bayberry
Picea abies, Norway spruce
Picea pungens var. *glauca,* blue spruce
Pinus densiflora, Japanese red pine
Pinus mugo, mugo pine
Prunus maritima, beach plum
Quercus spp., oak
Spiraea spp., spirea
Thuja plicata, western arborvitae
Viburnum dentatum, arrowwood viburnum
Vitex agnus-castus, chastetree

Perennials

Achillea spp., yarrow
Artemisia spp., artemisia
Asclepias tuberosa, butterfly weed
Aster spp., aster
Astilbe spp., astilbe
Baptisia australis, false indigo
Cerastium tomentosum, snow-in-summer
Cimicifuga spp., snakeroot
Ferns
Gaillardia × *grandiflora,* blanketflower
Hibiscus moscheutos, rose mallow
Iberis sempervirens, perennial candytuft

Kniphofia spp., red-hot poker
Monarda didyma, bee balm
Nepeta × *faassenii,* catmint
Nipponanthemum nipponicum, Montauk daisy
Oenothera spp., evening primrose
Perovskia atriplicifolia, Russian sage
Rudbeckia spp., black-eyed Susan
Salvia spp., sage
Santolina chamaecyparissus, lavender cotton
Solidago spp., goldenrod
Stachys byzantina, lamb's ears
Thalictrum spp., meadow rue
Veronica spp., veronica
Yucca spp., yucca

Annuals

Arctotis venustum, African daisy
Lantana spp., lantana
Lobularia maritima, sweet alyssum
Mirabilis jalapa, four-o'clocks
Pelargonium spp., geranium
Petunia cvs., petunia
Salvia spp., sage
Tagetes spp., marigold
Tropaeolum majus, nasturtium

Ground covers and Vines

Ajuga spp., bugleweed
Arctostaphylos uva-ursi, bearberry
Ceratostigma plumbaginoides, false plumbago
Clematis spp., clematis
Euonymus fortunei, wintercreeper
Hedera helix, English ivy
Lonicera spp., honeysuckle
Thymus spp., thyme
Vinca minor, periwinkle

need tall gates to close the driveway, too, or the deer will stroll right on in.

Another option, if deer are really problematic, is to enclose plants you really prize in cages made of hardware cloth or plastic mesh. It's not an aesthetically pleasing solution, but it will save the plants. Wrap the trunks of young and newly planted trees with tree wrap for protection.

Scent-based repellents can be effective, but you have to reapply them after rain washes them away. Sooner or later the deer will get used to the smell, too, so you have to switch products often. Some people hang bars of deodorant soap in the bushes or suspend bags of hair clippings from tree branches. These methods seem to work well for some gardeners and not at all for others.

OTHER FOUR-LEGGED PESTS

Deer aren't the only four-legged pests you may encounter, although they are usually the most destructive, unless you have a vegetable garden. Rabbits may nibble herbaceous plants, and they also like to eat crocuses and tulips. Groundhogs and raccoons may bother vegetables, if you grow them. A three-foot fence will keep these smaller critters out of beds and borders, or you can sprinkle dried blood over the planting area or spray plants with a deer repellent.

Under the ground, moles and voles devour bulbs (except for narcissus, which they avoid), and sometimes they will eat the roots of perennials and annuals. Chipmunks, too, may get into the garden. If you notice that some plants in the garden die suddenly, and there is no sign of pests or disease, it's possible the roots were eaten by voles or other tunnelers. These creatures are hard to keep out of the garden. One control strategy is to surround entire garden beds with a barrier of hardware cloth sunk two feet into the ground. It might also help to try and eliminate hiding places for them by removing any piled-up brush and other debris that has accumulated in odd corners of the property.

SMALL INVADERS

It's not necessary to drench the garden with insecticide at the first sign of a bug. Indeed, spraying with broad-spectrum insecticides, whether they are of synthetic or organic origin, should be a last resort. Many of these products kill beneficial insects along with the pests, and even organic products are quite toxic when first applied (although they do break down more quickly in the environment than do synthetic insecticides).

This deer-resistant planting of sedum, globe thistle, nepeta, and hyssop also attracts many beneficial insects.

Even plant-based insecticides such as pyrethrum can kill butterflies and beneficial insects along with pests, so use them only when absolutely necessary.

Whatever type of pest-control products you use, always follow package directions explicitly for application, storage, and handling. Dress appropriately — wear long sleeves, long pants, shoes and socks, a respirator mask, and industrial (not kitchen-type) rubber gloves. Don't spray or dust on a windy day, and stand upwind when applying the material. If you need to dispose of leftover, unused insecticides, don't ever pour them down the drain or dump them on the ground. Instead, dispose of them when your town has special hazardous waste disposal times.

Learn to identify beneficial insects in your garden, and leave them alone when you see them. When pests do attack the garden, use the least invasive control measures first. For larger beetles or caterpillars that aren't present in great numbers, put on a pair of gloves and pick them off by hand. Drop them into a can of soapy water. If you spot small pests like aphids and whiteflies, try washing them off plants with a strong spray of water from a hose.

Here are some control measures to take to combat more serious infestations:

- **Insecticidal soap.** Effective on contact for a wide variety of small insects on many kinds of plants. Spray thoroughly so plants are wet. Be sure to spray both tops and bottoms of leaves, leaf axils, and new growth of affected plants. Keep an eye on plants after application; you may need two or more applications of insecticidal soap, several days apart, to control serious infestations.

- **Horticultural oils.** Oils kill pests by smothering them, and are effective for mealybugs, adelgids, scales, and mites. They are mixed with water and sprayed onto affected plants. Some oils (called dormant oils) are applied to trees and shrubs in winter when the plants are dormant. Lighter-weight summer oils are applied during the growing season. Both petroleum-based and vegetable-based oil sprays are available. Monitor plants after application and repeat if necessary.

- **Traps.** Various sorts of traps can catch stubborn pests that are hard to get by other methods. Sticky yellow cards placed among plants can catch whiteflies and other small flying insects. There are also traps available for Japanese beetles and yellow jackets. An old-fashioned way to trap slugs and snails is to sink small containers of beer into the ground so the tops are at ground level (you can also kill them with commercial baits). Rolled-up newspapers or boards laid on the ground can trap earwigs that hide under them.

- **Barriers.** Other kinds of barriers can be useful, too. Some gardeners keep slugs from the garden by edging with copper strips. Diatomaceous earth sprinkled around sensitive plants or the perimeter of beds and borders will keep out caterpillars, slugs, and other soft-bodied pests. Be sure to get diatomaceous earth meant for horticultural use, not the kind used in swimming pool filters.

- **Biological controls.** Biological control means using living organisms to kill pests. Many of these controls are predatory insects or their larvae (praying mantids, green lacewings, ladybird beetle larvae, various kinds of tiny flies and wasps) that are available by mail

Timely pruning can help prevent damage from insects and disease. The leader branch of this old apple tree has split off in a ragged way, leaving an entry point for infection.

and sometimes from local garden centers. A useful biological control for caterpillars is Bt or Btk (*Bacillus thuringiensis* subsp. *kurtaki*). Treating the lawn with milky spore disease (sold under various trade names) will kill Japanese beetle grubs that incubate under the ground and chew on grass roots. Biological controls are not very good as preventive measures, though. If the target pests are not present in your garden, the predators will move on in search of food.

- **Botanical insecticides.** Some very potent insect killers are derived from plants. The best known are rotenone, pyrethrum (look for ingredients listed on labels as pyrethrum or pyrethrins, not pyrethroids, which are synthetic imitations), sabadilla, and neem (which works as both an insecticide and a fungicide). Botanical insecticides break down much more quickly after application and do not linger in the environment like most synthetic (chemical) materials do. They are also less harmful to people, pets, and wildlife when the product dries after application. But they are quite toxic when applied and must be handled with appropriate caution. Follow package directions explicitly.

Some botanical insecticides kill beneficial insects along with pests — they may

Roses are often plagued by black spot. To avoid it, use the "Homemade Disease Prevention" recipe below.

wipe out butterflies and honeybees along with aphids and whiteflies, so use them only as a last resort.

DISEASE CONTROL

The air along the coast is generally humid, and high humidity can promote the development of fungal and bacterial diseases in plants: blights, rusts, rots, mildews, and other nasties. Powdery mildew can be a big troublemaker, attacking roses, lilacs, phlox, zinnias, and bee balm. Although powdery mildew does not usually kill plants, it does disfigure the leaves. Black spot is a notorious plague of rose gardens, and bush roses —hybrid teas, grandifloras, and floribundas — are especially susceptible to it. Shrub roses are less likely to suffer from black spot.

The best way to control plant diseases is to prevent them in the first place. One helpful measure is to allow space between plants so air can circulate freely around them. When plants are crowded together, disease pathogens can collect in the still, humid air.

When and how you water the garden also can influence the likelihood of disease. If possible, water at ground level, with soaker hoses or a drip irrigation system, rather than with overhead sprinklers. If you do use overhead watering, do it in the morning. If you have to water later in the day, do it early enough that the plants dry off before dark. Wet leaves in sticky, still air at night offer an ideal breeding ground for disease pathogens.

Keep the garden clean. Don't let dead leaves and other debris lie on the ground. If you notice any leaves on plants showing signs of disease, pick them off and dispose of them. (Do not put them on the compost pile; even a hot pile is probably not hot enough to destroy all disease pathogens.) If you need to prune to remove diseased stems or branches, remember to dip your shears or loppers in a bleach solution after each cut so you don't spread the infection. Use a solution of one part liquid household chlorine bleach to nine parts water. Mulch the garden, so water droplets that pick up pathogens when they hit the ground won't splash back up onto foliage.

Take care of the plants to keep them healthy. Plants that are weakened or stressed from lack of water or insufficient nutrients are at greater risk of disease. Grow disease-resistant varieties if possible. (The phlox cultivar 'David', for example, is less prone to mildew than others.)

Finally, if you just can't live without some favorite plants, such as hybrid tea roses, even though you know they are susceptible to disease problems, try using the preventive baking soda spray described in "Homemade Disease Prevention" (right). This spray is effective on roses, and may work on other susceptible plants, too. Other preventive measures include dusting plants with sulfur and spraying the foliage with neem oil.

If you do need to use fungicides in the garden, whether you use organic or synthetic products, follow the label directions for handling, application, and storage. Use only as much as the package directs — more is not better. Dress appropriately, as described in the section on pesticides. Dispose of unused fungicides when your town has hazardous waste collection days.

HOMEMADE DISEASE PREVENTION

Use this spray to prevent mildew and black spot on roses. Dissolve one tablespoon of baking soda in one gallon of water. Add a few drops of insecticidal soap, liquid Ivory soap, or horticultural oil to help the spray stick to plant leaves. Spray every four to seven days in summer.

Winterizing the Garden

I**T'S A GOOD IDEA TO PROVIDE SOME** winter protection for plants, especially nonnatives, growing close to the water or in windbreaks or other exposed locations in northern gardens. Trees and shrubs that will be going through their first winter in your garden are also candidates for some extra TLC when the weather gets cold.

As the growing season winds down, make sure garden areas, and individual trees and shrubs, get plenty of water. If the weather has been dry, continue to water regularly until the ground begins to freeze and plants go into dormancy. When the soil freezes, apply a winter mulch as described in the "Mulching" section on page 68. Southern gardeners can lay down a fresh layer of mulch any time during autumn if the soil will not freeze solid over the winter.

CUTTING BACK PLANTS

Perennial gardeners can cut back most of their herbaceous perennials to a few inches from the ground in fall. Some later bloomers, such as perovskia, sedums, and asters, can be allowed to stand in the garden over the winter, then be cut back in early spring before new growth begins. Pull the summer annuals when they stop blooming, or when frost shuts them down. Southern gardeners can replant with winter annuals such as pansies, stocks, larkspur, and calendula.

Ornamental grasses also need to be cut back to within a few inches of the ground once a year. If your grasses are in a location that is sheltered from the wind, you can let them stand in the garden through the winter to bring structure and interest to the landscape. Cut them back in early spring before new growth begins. But in locations that are exposed to winds or winter snows, grasses will be tattered and broken long before spring and are best cut back in late fall. Depending on the size of your grasses, you may need to use hedge clippers, electric hedge shears, or even lopping shears to cut back the tough-stemmed plants.

WINTERBURN PROTECTION

Winter winds are very drying, and bright winter sun can be harmful, too. Broad-leaved evergreens such as hollies and rhododendrons can suffer damaging winterburn to their foliage. Junipers and other conifers also can be damaged. Spraying these plants with an antidesiccant will give them some protection. To shield new trees and shrubs, including hedges, and older woody plants close to the water, you can build little shelters for them. First wrap tree trunks with tree wrap to protect them from sunscald. Stake each tree to keep it upright during storms until it has grown enough roots to be securely anchored. Drive two tall stakes into the ground, one on either side of the trunk, angled into the

The pillar-like yews (*Taxus* sp.) that anchor the arches in this Long Island garden are wrapped in burlap each winter to prevent windburn.

prevailing wind. Tie the tree to the stakes with strips of sturdy fabric, old panty hose, or other soft but strong material. Don't use wire or rope, which could damage the branches when the tree strains against the ties in the wind. Do allow the trunk to have some flex, though. Allowing it to move somewhat in the wind will strengthen the tree.

After the tree is anchored, erect a burlap windscreen around it. Pound four tall stakes into the ground in a ring around the tree several feet out from the trunk. Wrap burlap around the stakes and secure it with twine to form an enclosure. If you are really worried about the tree's survival, fill the enclosure with shredded leaves.

To protect a row of new trees or shrubs, you can erect a windscreen by placing the stakes in a row on the side of the plants facing into the prevailing wind and attaching the burlap to them.

After the first winter, new trees and shrubs should be well enough established that you won't have to provide these shelters in subsequent years.

STORM AFTERCARE

Storms can be intense at the seashore, and they can damage plants in several ways. Strong winds can knock down stems, snap branches, and even topple whole trees. Salt can blow into gardens and settle onto plants, burning foliage. Saltwater may flood lawns and gardens. Taking prompt action after a storm can help to ameliorate the damage.

Any tree branches broken or damaged by storms need to be addressed at once. Prune to remove the damaged wood, or to completely remove broken branches. Trees that are left leaning or even toppled, if the root-ball is still mostly in the ground, may be able to be reset and supported by stakes and cables to hold them upright while they reestablish themselves in the soil. Consult an arborist for advice.

If flooding has occurred, wait until the water has drained away to take any remedial action. Most plants can usually survive an occasional saltwater flooding unless the soil is poorly drained and the salt remains in the garden for an extended time. When the floodwaters recede, get out the hose. Rinse off all your plants, and as high into the trees as you can, with a strong spray of water. Pay particular attention to evergreens, which keep their leaves all year and are thus at greater risk of suffering long-term damage than are deciduous trees and shrubs that lose their leaves each year, or herbaceous perennials that die back to the ground in winter. Deciduous trees and shrubs will sometimes lose their leaves after a severe storm; the salt will cause the leaves to turn brown and fall off. Most of the woodies will recover, however, and produce new leaves the following spring.

To create a protective winter windscreen for an evergreen shrub, surround it with four tall stakes and wrap a length of burlap around them.

WOODY PLANTS THAT TOLERATE SALTWATER

These trees and shrubs can tolerate periodic saltwater flooding.

Acer pseudoplatanus, sycamore maple
Aronia arbutifolia, red chokeberry
Baccharis halimifolia, groundsel bush
Calluna vulgaris, heather
Campsis radicans, trumpet vine
Clematis terniflora, sweet autumn clematis
Clethra alnifolia, sweet pepperbush
Cryptomeria japonica, Japanese cedar
Hibiscus syriacus, rose of Sharon
Ilex glabra, inkberry
Juniperus chinensis 'Pfitzeriana', Pfitzer juniper
Juniperus virginiana, eastern red cedar
Ligustrum amurense, Amur privet
Ligustrum ovalifolium, California privet
Myrica pensylvanica, bayberry
Nyssa sylvatica, tupelo
Parthenocissus tricuspidata, Boston ivy
Picea pungens 'Kosteri', blue spruce
Pinus sylvestris, Scotch pine
Prunus maritima, beach plum
Prunus serotina, chokecherry
Quercus alba, white oak
Rhus spp., sumacs
Rosa cvs., rambler roses
Rosa rugosa, saltspray rose
Rosa virginiana, Virginia rose
Rosa wichuraiana, memorial rose
Vaccinium corymbosum, highbush blueberry
Viburnum dentatum, arrowwood viburnum
Vitis labrusca, fox grape
Wisteria sinensis, Chinese wisteria

Water the soil and lawns thoroughly to wash away excess salt and dilute the concentration of whatever salt is left. If your lawn was flooded with saltwater, flush with freshwater to get rid of as much of the salt as you can. Let the water run until the soil is saturated. Then you may want to spread ground limestone over the lawn, at a rate of 20 to 50 pounds per 1,000 square feet, and water again. Kentucky bluegrass and bent grasses are very susceptible to saltwater damage. But crabgrass, naturally, can easily survive being under saltwater for 24 hours. The lawn may look burned and dry, but if the roots of the grass have survived, new grass blades will emerge next spring. If no new growth appears in spring, the lawn will have to be dug up and replanted.

Trumpet vine, or trumpet creeper (*Campsis radicans*), tolerates saltwater flooding and salty winds, thrives even in poor soils, and attracts hummingbirds.

These hawthorns (*Crataegus* 'Winter King') are very hardy and salt tolerant. Hair grass (*Deschampsia caespitosa*) tumbles about at their feet.

CHAPTER 4

Garden Profiles

GARDENS NEAR THE SEA ARE AS VARIED AS THE GARDENERS and homeowners who create them. Some seashore gardeners succeed in spite of the difficult conditions they face — the English-style perennial border in a seashore town, for example, is a triumph over nature. Other gardeners embrace the seaside's salt and wind to create native plant gardens of a wilder, more natural beauty that do not overcome the limitations of the environment but instead work within them.

The gardens profiled in this chapter represent a variety of styles and ways to solve the problems of coastal conditions. They exist in different settings and climate zones along the Atlantic coastline, from New England to South Carolina. Each garden is unique in its own way, with its own inspired solutions to the challenges of its site.

ABOVE: Along the coast of northern New England, rocky cliffs drop right into the sea.

RIGHT: Gardens tucked into the natural rock ledges on this Maine property anchor the house and unite it with its setting.

Preserving a Historic Garden

SOUTHERN MAINE

In the kitchen garden, hoops made from forsythia prunings support spring plantings of peas. Several kinds of lettuce also grow here, along with other vegetables and herbs.

BRAVE BOAT HARBOR FARM overlooks the ocean on the coast of Maine. A magical place of over 100 acres, the farm has a long history. The land was settled in 1638 as a king's grant, and for the next 300 years it was a subsistence farm. Then, in 1949, the property was purchased by the Hosmer family. Calvin and Cynthia Hosmer live there today, and are the stewards of this beautiful land by the sea.

The gardens are concentrated on approximately three acres immediately surrounding the house. The plantings were begun by Mr. Hosmer's parents. "When my parents-in-law came here in 1949," explains Mrs. Hosmer, "there was a circle of old lilacs here, and the burying ground. Otherwise, what's here they put in." Some of those old lilacs still exist, and have been joined over the years by apple trees, lush vegetable gardens, and magnificent perennial beds. "It's really quite wonderful to see what a mature garden is all about," says Mrs. Hosmer. "It really is the most incredible gift that anyone could be given."

The house is situated some distance above the ocean, with rolling hay fields stretching beyond the landscaped parts of the property toward the sea. Salt wind and spray are seldom a problem for the plants here except during stormy weather. Most of the storms come in from the northeast, and a large grove of hickory trees on that side of the property affords protection.

Deer are present in abundance, and the Hosmers deploy a variety of defensive measures to protect their gardens. Fencing is part of the strategy, as is the use of Milorganite (a fertilizer manufactured from treated sewage sludge) as a deer repellent. "I go around like a fairy godmother in the spring and drop it around," Mrs. Hosmer says with a laugh. Another important part of the deer-repellent program is Daisey May, a two-year-old golden retriever who is a dedicated chaser of the four-hoofed visitors.

The grounds around the house are extensively cultivated, and Mrs. Hosmer does much of the gardening herself, along with the caretaker of 28 years. "He is the

history" of the place, explains Mrs. Hosmer. "He knows everything that's been planted — he can remember planting it."

The lane coming into the yard is lined with crab apple trees. The Hosmers have cleared the brush from the woods and planted rhododendrons and laurels beneath the old beech trees, along with small kousa dogwoods. Preserving the beech trees is an ongoing battle; over the years they've been besieged by a number of imported pests and diseases. The beech woods are extensive, so the Hosmers fight on in the hope of saving as many of the trees as they can.

There are many apple trees on the property — 'McIntosh', 'Cortland', and 'Macoun'. The trees are quite old now, and are pruned to keep them about 15 to 20 feet high, with arced branches that curve downward. "It's very English in that respect," explains Mrs. Hosmer. It takes a week to ten days to prune the trees, and

RIGHT: Oriental and Asiatic lilies grace the perennial garden in summer. The walls are built of stone dug from the property.

LEFT: Stately old arborvitaes, with their lower limbs removed to admit more light, line the drive leading to the house.

pruning is done in August rather than in late winter, when many orchardists prune. By mid-August the trees have completed their new growth, and pruning then allows enough time for tissues to harden before winter sets in. The weather is far more forgiving in late summer than in February, when the nor'easters blow.

Part of what Mr. and Mrs. Hosmer have done since moving to the farm eight years ago is to open up vistas and limb up the trees. The old lilacs were limbed up, rather than cut back, to open up views of the sea.

The gun house (built by Mr. Hosmer's father) faces the sea, offering a relaxing spot for evening cocktails.

The venerable old arborvitaes along the drive also had their lower branches removed. Mrs. Hosmer had wanted to put in a pleached hornbeam hedge there but was advised that it would be too formal to suit the farm. So instead, the arborvitaes were limbed up and trimmed to even out their tops, "and they've become such a wonderful way in here, architecturally," Mrs. Hosmer says.

Near one corner of the house the Hosmers removed some old shadbushes that were tipping over and generally falling apart, and replaced them with a single columnar copper beech that will grow taller over time but remain narrow. "We wanted to have that exclamation point at that corner of the house," says Mrs. Hosmer. "It's a statement unto itself." Enhancing that elegant statement, the English ivy climbing the nearby walls of the house is kept neatly trimmed.

Not far from the copper beech, along the side of the house nearest the driveway, is a kitchen garden. The garden is divided into quadrants, with intersecting paths of stepping-stones. At one end of the main axis path is a white moon gate that frames a view of magnolias beyond. In the center of the garden sits an old millstone upon which rests a large glass ball—it's actually a solar-powered fountain, with the water reservoir in a five-gallon pickle jar buried below.

Plantings are done on the diagonal. In spring there are several kinds of lettuce, including 'Nevada', 'Merveille Quatre Saisons', 'Arctic King', and 'Red Sails', and peas supported on hoops Mrs. Hosmer fashions from forsythia prunings. Parsley grows along the edges of the path. There are broccoli, beans, peppers, and other favorites, too, along with lots of herbs — thymes, basils, and oregano among them. In summer there are luscious raspberries.

Part of the walkway near the moon gate is carpeted with chamomile, which Mrs. Hosmer trims by hand to keep it low and cushiony. Thyme grows in the path, also, both plants releasing their aromatic scents when trodden upon. They are important elements of the garden for Mrs. Hosmer "because sometimes," she says, "I think the sensory pleasure you get from walking through a garden comes from underfoot."

There are cutting flowers in the kitchen garden, too — Oriental poppies, calendulas, salvias, sea holly (*Eryngium*), rubrum lilies, and roses. There are several David Austin varieties, some old roses, and the shrub rose 'Bonica'. All the roses grow on their own roots except for one hybrid tea, 'Tropicana', which "seems to like it here," says Mrs. Hosmer.

In front of the house is a perennial garden enclosed by a stone wall and an old boxwood hedge. The wall — as well as the house, the walkways, and all the walls on the property — is built of stone dug from the ground here. This garden is mostly blues and yellows, with occasional touches of pink. There are golden 'Stella de Oro' daylilies, and lots of Oriental and Asiatic lilies. The fragrant lilies are particular favorites. On hot summer days their delicious scents drift into the house on breezes drawn by a fan placed in a nearby window.

Tall violet monkshood (*Aconitum*) stands in the back of the garden until the weight of its flowers pulls the stems over, then Mrs. Hosmer props them up on the wall and some nearby lilies. Blue delphiniums also supply vertical accents, and the blue spheres of *Allium caeruleum* add substance. A shrub clematis (*Clematis integrifolia*) dangles its blue bells of blossoms. In spring there are pots of tulips in the garden for early color; when the tulips finish, they are removed and replaced with dahlias.

At the end of the day, the Hosmers like to sit near the small stone gun house to enjoy a glass of wine and watch the passing ships. Such moments of leisure are well earned. For Calvin and Cynthia Hosmer, preserving and maintaining the property is a sacred trust, a way of carrying on the family tradition of serving as guardians of this beautiful land. "It is my stewardship and legacy for the rest of my life," says Mrs. Hosmer. The land and its glorious gardens are in good hands.

A moon gate at one end of the kitchen garden frames *Magnolia* 'Elizabeth', part of a collection of magnolias that includes 'Merrill', 'Leonard Messel', 'Butterflies', 'Yellow Bird', and 'Ballerina'.

Tapestry on a Ledge

SOUTHERN MAINE

ABOVE: A seashell planter suggests beach grass and ocean waves with upright *Juncus* 'Quartz Creek', donkeytail spurge (*Euphorbia myrsinites*), and flowering *Laurentia fluviatilis*.

BELOW: Passionflowers follow sweet peas in the formal kitchen garden.

Atop a promontory on the Maine ledge, bordered on three sides by the ocean, sits an elegant stone house that has weathered many storms. Salt spray and wind are constants in the gardens here, and winter winds pose the greatest seasonal challenge of the year. But the plants thrive in a landscape designed to blend the house seamlessly into its breathtaking setting.

The landscape gardener Tony Elliott designed this garden. An agronomist by training, and the proprietor of Snug Harbor Farm, Mr. Elliott has been designing gardens since he was 13. To integrate this house into the site, he created a series of garden rooms that are more formal close to the house and become progressively less formal as one moves outward from the house into the landscape. The informal parts of the garden create a graceful transition to the dramatic natural landscape beyond.

Mr. Elliott amended the soil on the site with dehydrated cow manure, peat moss, and lime to prepare it for planting. The gardens are fertilized with an all-purpose granular 5-10-5 product. Drought is not a problem here; the gardens are irrigated, but even if they were not, says Mr. Elliott, the frequent Maine fogs that roll in would provide adequate moisture for the plants. The moist conditions can encourage disease, however, and plants that develop ailments are removed and replaced with tougher substitutes.

Winter winds pose the biggest challenge to this garden, and the plants must be hardy enough to stand up to them. Mr. Elliott is not a believer in wrapping evergreens and other shrubs to coddle them through the winter. "I'm a do-or-die gardener," he declares. Instead, he chooses plants he believes will be tough enough to withstand the wintry blasts. So far, nothing has been lost. He does, however, make an exception in the case of lacecap hydrangeas, which he finds do better with a winter wrapping of burlap; the wrap goes on in December.

The most formal rooms in this garden are located immediately adjacent to the house. Near the front door is an elegant gathering of blue-flowered lacecap hydrangeas (*Hydrangea macrophylla* 'Mariesii'), one of Mr. Elliott's favorite varieties. Climbing hydrangea (*H. petiolaris*) scales the wall of the house behind them, clinging to the stone with no additional support. Its delicate white lacecap flowers bloom in summer against the glossy, deep green leaves. The hydrangea garden has a serene, elegant feeling that creates a graceful segue into the foyer, a welcome into the home.

Across the walkway from the hydrangea garden is a woodland garden anchored by some old existing junipers that have attained interesting, windswept shapes of the sort bonsai growers aim to re-create.

Along one side of the house, directly off the kitchen, is a formally structured kitchen garden laid out in four square beds, each containing a wooden tuteur to support climbing plants. The vegetable garden is bounded along its outer side by a wall built of local stone to look like it has been in place for many years. In reality, this garden is just four years old. Mr. Elliott regraded the once sloping site better to relate the garden to the house. The wall looks lovely, and is a comfortable height for sitting upon, but it also retains the soil to maintain the level ground for the vegetable garden.

"I wanted a really balanced, formal space" for this garden, explains Mr. Elliott, because it is right next to the house. In designing the vegetable garden, he played off the straight, crisp lines of the house to relate the garden to the building. The beds are edged with antique English garden tiles to emphasize their shape and separate them from the surrounding lawn.

The perennial border, meant to be viewed from the terrace and the master bedroom, is rich with summer color including 'Rocket Red' snapdragons, bee balm (*Monarda* 'Jacob Kline'), astilbe 'Fanal', evening primrose (*Oenothera longifolia* 'Lemon Sunset'), and orange yarrow (*Achillea millefolium* 'Paprika').

The annual garden was designed to look like a tapestry and includes African mallow, perilla, *Lantana* 'Patriot Desert Sunrise', purple tradescantia, *Verbena* 'Superbena Dark Blue', and *Cuphea* 'Tiny Mice'.

The garden produces two crops of radishes a season, as well as two crops of lettuce and a variety of other fast-growing vegetables. There's also a mix of herbs such as tarragon, rosemary, and purple basil. In addition, the garden provides flowers for cutting, including chocolate cosmos and *Salvia patens* 'Blue Angel'. Sweet peas climb the tuteurs in spring, succeeded by passionflowers in summertime. Climbing hydrangea grows on the wall of the house here, too, as well as by the front door. The house and the stone wall provide protection for the plants from salt winds in summer, when the garden is producing its bounty of color.

At the back of the house, with sweeping views of the sea, is a broad stone terrace. At the juncture where terrace meets house is a surprising low hedge of lavender. Mr. Elliott chose lavender for this spot because the stone holds the heat of the summer sun, which releases the intoxicating fragrance of the lavender to float upon the warm air. The cultivar 'Provence' thrives here, having proved itself a better performer than either 'Hidcote' or 'Munstead'.

Tucked against the stone wall at the front edge of the terrace is a small garden of annuals designed to be viewed from the windows of the master bedroom above. The annual garden changes from year to year, but in this season the owner wanted the look of a Persian rug. Mr. Elliott created a tapestry of purples, blues, oranges, and reds with three different salvias, African mallow (*Anisodontea capensis*), eucalyptus, perilla, *Lantana* 'Patriot Desert Sunrise', purple tradescantia, *Verbena* 'Homestead Purple', and a cuphea cultivar called 'Tiny Mice'.

From the terrace, a walkway runs the rest of the way along the back of the house, then around the side. A hedge of rugosa roses on one side of the walkway and a perennial border along the other side create a colorful corridor through which to pass. The rugosa roses flourish here, in part because of the mild maritime climate. "They do incredibly well," says Mr. Elliott.

The perennial border is full of classic flowers and rich with summerlong color. Designed to be viewed from the terrace, the perennial border is home to red bee balm, astilbe, snapdragons, orange yarrow, golden evening primrose, light blue delphiniums, daylilies, and silvery artemisia. Although the straight lines of the border are crisp and formal, the plantings within are looser, beginning the transition to the wilder landscape that lies beyond the gardens.

Outside the confines of the garden, nature rules, as is fitting in a place of such dazzling natural beauty. Down near the water, wildflowers including oxeye daisy and purple loosestrife have colonized among the rocks, moving in from points unknown and establishing themselves in their own home by the sea. Perhaps they, too, are drawn to the beauty of the place.

In the formal kitchen garden, wooden tuteurs support fragrant sweet peas in spring and passionflowers in summer.

Classic Flowers Near the Water's Edge

COHASSET, MASSACHUSETTS

Alongside the pool, cast-iron urns hold tall cannas, trailing sweet potato vine (*Ipomoea batatas* 'Margarita'), calibrachoa, and fountain grass (*Pennisetum setaceum* 'Rubrum').

IN COHASSET, MASSACHUSETTS, IS A house surrounded by water on three sides. The back of the house faces a calm harbor. The front of the property faces the ocean — Massachusetts Bay, to be exact, but the ocean is quite close. A tidal run flows along one side of the property, connecting bay and harbor. The harbor side of the house is protected from the elements, but on the bay side, explains the owner and the garden's creator, Geraldine King, "we're just scoured." That side of the property is buffeted by strong salt-laden winds, and in the winter, fierce nor'easters come roaring in.

Still, this is where Mrs. King wanted to have a perennial garden. She succeeded, admirably. And remarkably, she can grow flowers you'd never expect to see in such an exposed location, like delphiniums, for instance. She does most of the gardening work herself.

The first thing the Kings did after buying their house was to install a privet hedge along the tidal run of the property to create a sheltered environment for the garden. It's all the protection the garden gets, and it works. Privet would not have been Mrs. King's first choice. It's a lot of work to maintain, for one thing. But friends in the area had tried all sorts of other hedges and nothing but privet was able to survive the intense salt wind without burning. So privet it was.

The landscape is laid out in a series of garden rooms that follow changes in grade level. You enter the garden at driveway level. The first room is a formal rose garden with a koi pond in the center. There are 60 or 70 roses in the garden, including hybrid teas, shrubs, floribundas, and David Austin varieties. The garden is magnificent in bloom.

From the rose garden you step down into the next room, a shady hosta garden. Along with hostas there are lady's mantle (*Alchemilla mollis*), astilbes, and dwarf Pia hydrangeas. New Dawn climbing roses are trained on a fence here (but they aren't really thriving, because there's not quite enough sun for them).

An opening from the hosta garden allows a view of the ocean and leads to the pool and the marvelous perennial borders. The perennial garden is about 100 feet long, and sweeps in graceful curves across the front of the property. The Kings brought in lots of compost to create the garden, then installed a drip irrigation system before beginning to plant. More compost is added each year, as needed. The basic structure of the garden comes from a series of low, rounded blue spruces (*Picea pungens* 'Montgomery') backed by red-leaved sand cherries (*Prunus × cistena*). "The dark reds and blues anchor the garden," explains Mrs. King. Hydrangeas also contribute year-round form to the border, and reinforce the blue theme. The rest of the garden is filled with blues, pinks, and some yellow. The protection of the hedge allows her to grow some plants that aren't often seen so close to the ocean. There are blue delphiniums and nepeta, pink carpet roses, soft yellow 'Moonbeam' coreopsis,

RIGHT: A privet hedge affords enough protection for classic perennials such as nepeta, 'Moonbeam' coreopsis, daylilies, delphiniums, and hydrangeas.

LEFT: A few steps lead down from the rose garden to a shady garden full of hostas, lady's mantle (*Alchemilla mollis*), astilbes, and other perennials.

Grass-covered steps lead from the pool to a more
naturalistic garden. The rocky ledge alongside is
planted with sea pinks (*Armeria maritima*), small
junipers, rugosa roses, and other tough plants.

and lots of daylilies, which she plants for their adaptability. "I love those because they grow anywhere," Mrs. King says. "They bloom where nothing else blooms."

A couple of years ago, an especially severe winter killed the buds on all the hydrangeas — that summer they had plenty of foliage but no flowers. Thus the Kings pulled them all out and replaced them with the variety 'Endless Summer', which blooms on both old and new growth, all but guaranteeing at least some flowers even after the hardest winter. So far 'Endless Summer' has done just fine. The white-flowered *Hydrangea arborescens* 'Annabelle', which blooms on new growth, also thrives in this garden.

The perennial border receives a mulch of buckwheat hulls, which Mrs. King highly recommends. "I love it," she says. "It doesn't get slimy, doesn't have any odor. It's attractive, it works into the soil nicely every year, and nonacidic plants love it."

In a reclamation area near the pool, the couple planted natives (in a trade-off with the town to get permission to construct a pool house). Here there are eastern red cedar, highbush and lowbush blueberries, and native azaleas.

At the end of this garden room is a 12-foot-wide gate, and then a descent down some broad, half-round, terraced steps in the lawn. These lead to the lowest part of the garden, which is a very natural area.

"I try to keep my hands off it," says Mrs. King, laughing. "I'm generally a more-is-better person." She has planted the rocky ledge there with tough plants like sea pink, or thrift (*Armeria maritima*), in the cracks, and small junipers in larger crevices in the rock. There are also some small cedars and rugosa roses. This is rocky ground — the entire town is built on ledge. The Kings blasted out rock to create their gardens, and used the stone to build structures on the property.

To hold an embankment in this area, Mrs. King planted bayberries, which she thought would be sure to do well. Inexplicably, they didn't. But rugosa roses did, and now they hold the soil on the exposed slope.

Other plants that thrive in the more exposed parts of the property are rose of Sharon (*Hibiscus syriacus*) and lilacs. "I have really good luck with lilacs," says Mrs. King, "especially 'Miss Kim'."

A gardener through and through, Mrs. King devotes many hours to her plants. Once a week someone comes in to help her, and they work together all day. And Mrs. King works some part of every summer day in the garden. "It's my pleasure to get a cup of coffee in the morning and go outside and work for an hour or so," she says. Spoken like a true gardener. And her love of plants shows in the breathtaking gardens she has created here.

DIE-HARD PLANTS FOR NEW ENGLAND SEASCAPES

Armeria maritima, sea pink, thrift
Hemerocallis spp., daylilies
Hibiscus syriacus, rose of Sharon
Hydrangea arborescens 'Annabelle', hydrangea
Ligustrum japonicum, privet
Picea pungens 'Montgomery', blue spruce
Prunus × *cistena,* sand cherry
Rosa rugosa, rugosa rose
Syringa 'Miss Kim', lilac

The wild, rocky transition from the Kings' garden to the sea.

A Seaside Retreat

NARRAGANSETT BAY, RHODE ISLAND

A riot of colorful annuals surround the entrance to the house.

ALONG THE COAST OF RHODE ISLAND there exists a property like no other. It's the kind of place that needs a very special owner to appreciate the exceptional beauty of its rugged terrain. On this property an extraordinary garden took shape over a period of six years. Created by Oehme, van Sweden and Associates, the principals involved in the project were Sheila Brady, OVS partner in charge of design, and James van Sweden, founding partner.

The property is huge — 85 acres — and when the owner took possession, it was a tangled wilderness of briars and brush and poison ivy. But the owner, born and raised in the city, had long cherished a dream of having a farm by the sea where he could retreat from urban pressures and walk the land. This was the place where he believed his dream would come true.

The property had once been a farm, but the land had not been cultivated for 45 years. Oehme, van Sweden's first year on the job involved a slow process of discovering what was really there underneath all the vines and brambles. Half the property is framed by water, with a classic rugged, rocky New England shoreline. Craggy outcrops of shale drop sharply to the water. It is undoubtedly, says Sheila Brady, one of the most extraordinary pieces of land she has worked with in her 25 years as a landscape architect.

First the team set about removing the thickets of briars and scrub. They uncovered groves of tall, native eastern red cedars (*Juniperus virginiana*) whose trunks had not even been visible. They found big old highbush blueberries (*Vaccinium corymbosum*) that had been twisted by the wind into compelling, gnarled forms.

When they found the remains of the old stone walls surrounding former farm fields, they decided to use them as an organizing principle for the landscape. When the strangling brushy and weedy growth was cleared away, the incredible beauty of the site revealed itself, and the design team worked with it.

Key to Oehme, van Sweden's success with coastal gardens is their understanding of the soil in each location. They work with a skilled and extremely knowledgeable soil scientist, Dr. Frank Gouin, who studies the parent soil on each site, performing extensive testing to determine what sorts of amendments are needed to support a sustainable landscape that will not require the addition of fertilizers or other foreign materials. Before planting, they work with the soil, incorporating compost specially formulated with local materials for each site, such as a crab-based compost or a cranberry bog compost. The goal is to work with the parent soil rather than disturb it. Compaction is broken up, then compost is tilled in to create a balanced, self-sustaining growing medium for plants that are native or naturally suited to the site. The result is a sustainable landscape that requires no synthetic fertilizers or pesticides.

On the Rhode Island property, the team replaced the old broken stone walls with a series of low retaining walls built mostly of stone found on the property, to provide an organizing framework for the design. The walls divided the land into a series of precincts through which visitors pass as they enter the property and proceed toward the house. A long, winding entrance drive weaves through these precincts until it reaches the house, which is situated at a high point.

Following the drive feels suspenseful and mysterious — you don't know what's around the next bend. The first precinct you encounter is the inland meadow, which was probably the most recently farmed part of the property. No trees or shrubs grew here, and the design team cleared the old fields and allowed the meadow to come back naturally. From there, a series of low stone walls announce the transition into the evergreen woodland collection, the groves of cedars. The trees here were limbed up to admit more light and air, and the ground beneath them was planted with grasses mowed to a height of six to eight inches. This area is quiet and green, a textural and visual contrast to the sunny openness of the inland meadow. The next precinct is a deciduous seaside woodland

An ancient highbush blueberry, uncovered as the property was being cleared of overgrown vines and brambles.

The winding drive creates a sense of mystery as it passes through each precinct of the property. When visitors reach the seaside meadow, the bay is revealed.

with trees and shrubs, such as yellowwood, carefully chosen to enhance that theme. From there the drive enters the eight-acre seaside meadow, where at last the sea becomes visible. Finally, the drive arrives at the expansive three-acre garden surrounding the house.

Passing through the fluid, graceful transitions from one precinct to the next enables owner and visitor alike to shed the stresses and tensions of city life in anticipation of the rest and solitude of this remarkable seaside retreat.

The designers carved a series of walking trails through the property, including three that lead to ocean overlooks. Working with the shoreline was a challenge, because the Rhode Island Coastal Resource Council strictly regulates a 200-foot buffer zone along the waterfront. The buffer of natural vegetation had to remain intact except for the three overlooks where access to the shoreline was permitted. Oehme, van Sweden turned that potential liability into an asset by siting the house, drives, and walking trails on high ground to take advantage

of the breathtaking view. "You actually have the feeling of being surrounded by water," says Ms. Brady. Had the house been set closer to the shoreline, the view would have been lost behind the buffer vegetation.

Close to the house the gardens are rich with color and texture, alive with the movement of plants in the wind and the interplay of light and shadow. The plantings here are a tapestry of texture, light, and color. It's a painterly approach to design that resonates with Ms. Brady's fine arts background. The ground plane is her canvas, the plants a composition of light and shadow, mass and space, form and texture, patterns of color. All the elements here and throughout the property combine to express the spirit of this most special place, a landscape and garden united with their setting.

RIGHT: A series of walking trails lead to ocean overlooks and allow an intimate experience of the beauty of the landscape.

BELOW: Long drifts of foxtailed *Pennisetum alopecuroides* and lavender-blue Russian sage (*Perovskia atriplicifolia*) sway in the passing breezes, forming dynamic patterns of color, texture, light, and shadow.

STRATEGIES FOR SUSTAINABLE DESIGN

- Organize a large, open landscape around existing features, such as old stone walls, highbush blueberries, and red cedars.
- In areas where natural vegetation will be preserved, create a series of scenic overlooks instead of one sweeping vista.
- Improve and maintain existing soil using local materials, such as crab and cranberry waste.

Making the Most of a Narrow Lot

MARTHA'S VINEYARD, MASSACHUSETTS

The heart of the garden is a small pool surrounded by cut bluestone, in perfect scale with the narrow property.

On one side of the property, a pink rose of Sharon (*Hibiscus syriacus*) screens a utility area from view.

FOR MANY LANDSCAPE DESIGNERS, THE most rewarding kinds of projects are those in which they help a homeowner realize his or her vision for the garden. This New England garden is the result of such a partnership. Landscape designer Robbie Hutchison, of Donaroma's Nursery and Landscape Services in Edgartown, Massachusetts, worked with the owner to create a garden that combines elegant structure with lots of multiseason color.

The house is located on Martha's Vineyard, in a historic district full of old whalers' houses. Space was the greatest challenge posed by the site. The houses here are close together on narrow lots, so privacy is a major consideration. Another issue is getting access for equipment onto the property; the design team had to plan construction carefully. They started work behind the main house and worked their way to the back edge of the property. The environment was less of a limiting factor here than it is in many seaside gardens.

This house is not directly on the water; the nearest water is a harbor located behind the houses across the street from this one. Although deer and direct salt winds do not trouble the garden, it is nonetheless a windy place, and that had to be taken into account. But there are sheltered nooks and crannies that are used to good advantage.

The landscape here began with the pool. The owner had found a picture of a small pool — really a large spa — that spoke to her. And she had made a sketch showing paths weaving through the property. That was the genesis of the design, with the pool as a focal point in a series of interlocking paths. The owner, explains Ms. Hutchison, "had this great bubble of an idea, and we just helped her organize it, to make it more real." The owner had a vision of what she wanted in the landscape, Ms. Hutchison goes on, "and I think we captured it for her."

In the backyard the homeowner wanted a similar small pool with space around it for chaise longues. It left plenty of room for gardens. "I commend her for that," declares Ms. Hutchison. Many people

A moon gate near one end of the garden frames a view of the pool and pool house with its vine-covered arbor, and the back of the main house. In the foreground is one of the brick circles edged with boxwood.

would tend to want to put in a big swimming pool, then cram some landscaping around it. But the pool here is on a scale that's very comfortable for the property.

An elegant bluestone patio surrounds the pool. An existing shed was transformed into the pool house. An arbor built onto the front of the pool house is planted with wisteria and trumpet vine (*Campsis radicans*), which climb up the framework to the roof, forming a leafy canopy in summer. The white columns supporting this structure are repeated in a freestanding arbor marking the junction of the patio with one of the paths.

The paths arc away from the patio in pairs — two heading toward the main house at the front of the property and two more toward the garage and guesthouse at the rear. The paths are made of unmortared brick set into the lawn, and they have a lovely antique charm. Together, all the paths form a series of ellipses that flow down the length of the property. Where the paths intersect, Ms. Hutchison created circular areas of brick pavement ringed by two varieties of dwarf boxwood on either side of a taller variety, all of them kept neatly clipped. On each brick circle is displayed an elegant antique urn full of flowers. The plants are changed seasonally and the urn overflows with color. In summer there are lush combinations of annuals; in winter there are cut evergreens. The urns

A focal point of the garden is an antique urn of annuals including Persian shield (*Strobilanthes dyerianus*), coleus, scaevola, 'Margarita' and 'Blackie' sweet potato vines, and angelonia.

provide yet another opportunity for color, as well as focal points that help to break up the long, narrow stretch of the lot.

Another thing the homeowner wanted in her garden was color — and there is an abundance of it. When you walk through the gate into the yard, says Ms. Hutchison, you feel like you're in the original version of *The Wizard of Oz*, where suddenly everything is in color. Magnificent borders run along the sides of the property. These plantings were designed by Janice Donaroma, owner of the nursery. They are full of classic perennials — delphinium, Shasta daisy (*Leucanthemum × superbum*), foxglove (*Digitalis*), bee balm (*Monarda didyma*), catmint (*Nepeta × faassenii*), and black-eyed Susan (*Rudbeckia* spp.). In shadier areas there are astilbes and heucheras, along with annuals like coleus and impatiens. The borders gain structure from shrubs, including Tardiva hydrangea, chastetree (*Vitex agnus-castus*), and blue mist (*Caryopteris × clandonensis*).

Close to the house a row of pink and white rose of Sharon (*Hibiscus syriacus*) screens a small utility area. Nearby, under a cryptomeria limbed up to let in more light, the pink and white are echoed in mounds of impatiens edging a shady part of the border. The colorful borders and overflowing urns and window boxes soften the controlled, elegant structural elements of the landscape.

For Ms. Hutchison, designing this landscape was a most rewarding and satisfying collaboration with the homeowner. "What I really enjoyed," she says, "is that she had a vision and she wanted to participate. To me that's rewarding. Now I feel like I know her."

Indeed, the goal for any good garden is to express the spirit and sensibility of the gardener or homeowner. The ability to capture that essence is part of the landscape designer's art.

In the perennial border, late-summer flowers blooming in front of white Tardiva hydrangea include black-eyed Susans (*Rudbeckia hirta*), Shasta daisies (*Leucanthemum × superbum*), sunflowers, pink cosmos, red bee balm (*Monarda didyma*), and blue-mist shrub (*Caryopteris × clandonensis*).

One Garden, Many Styles

LONG ISLAND, NEW YORK

In the walled garden, Indian architectural elements are a focal point at the end of the brick path. A venerable agave that is overwintered in a greenhouse provides dramatic punctuation below.

ON THE EASTERN END OF LONG ISLAND, between the Atlantic Ocean and a saltwater pond, is a uniquely beautiful garden that's a blend of formal elements and a wilder kind of informality. Designed by Ryan Gainey, the garden evolves and changes each year, in an ongoing collaboration among the designer, the homeowners, and head gardener John Hill. Here's one example of the juxtaposition of formal and informal style in this garden: a row of large yews that are kept neatly clipped look very classical and English, but nasturtiums climb all over them, adding a wild look. The yews anchor a border of perennials and annuals that is lush and overflowing with rambunctious boltonia, dahlia, agastache, and other flowers. There are also some large old boxwoods (*Buxus sempervirens* 'Suffruticosa') on the property — another nod to traditional English garden style.

It's a very exposed site here, with sandy soil and lots of deer and rabbits. But despite

A comfortable seating area, surrounded by cosmos, in front of the guesthouse.

the challenges posed by the site, the entire garden is managed in a highly ecological way — the method is almost 100 percent organic. The organic approach here is not simply a matter of using organic products; it's a mind-set as well. There's a willingness to coexist with wildlife, using fences and repellents to keep them away from the plants. There are beehives on the property, and birdhouses to attract the purple martins that are part of the pest-control program.

The sandy soil is lean and low in nutrients, and Mr. Hill has put in place an ongoing amendment program. Before planting, he brought in soil that is a mix of equal parts topsoil, compost, and sand. Each year the gardens are top-dressed with compost in winter and during the growing season, and more compost is mixed into the soil. In addition, Mr. Hill uses chicken manure, which he gets from a local farm six months before he plans to use it. By the time the manure is applied to the garden, it is well rotted and ready to release its nutrients into the soil. Mr. Hill has also been experimenting with compost teas. And an organic plant care company comes in to do root feeding with microbial products intended to boost the population of beneficial microorganisms in the soil and foster their work. (Mr. Hill has been experimenting, too, with fish emulsion as a foliar feed, but he can't yet say for sure whether it has been effective.)

Salt wind is a great challenge in this garden. When the winds come off the ocean — from the south rather than the east, on the spit of land upon which this property lies — they strike the oceanfront side of the house, hitting the dunes and flowing up and over them, then slamming down hard onto the lower part of the property. In winter, the winds whip across the property from the pond. "They're relentless," says Mr. Hill.

The house itself, sitting on the crest of the dunes, protects the gardens behind it, especially in summer. From this high spot, the grade level drops about 20 feet as the property slopes down toward the pond on the opposite side. One part of the garden is enclosed by walls. A hedgerow of yews (*Taxus* species) also shelters the gardens. Heroic measures are taken to protect some of the plants. "We didn't go out of our way to choose salt-resistant plants," explains Mr. Hill, "but we do go to extraordinary lengths to get the plants to succeed" in the difficult environment.

A canal in the formal walled garden serves as an axis in the design. Lotus grow in the water, and carefully shaped yews edge the canal. Potted 'Meyer' lemon trees trained as standards mark the intersection of the canal and the main brick path.

The lush, informal perennial borders are given structure from a series of clipped columnar yews anchoring arches made of copper tubing.

In late summer there are masses of white boltonia, and the nasturtiums begin to show renewed vigor after a midsummer slump.

In winter they wrap all the yews and other sensitive plants with burlap. "It looks like [Dr. Seuss's] Whoville," Mr. Hill says. The wrappings go on right after Christmas and remain in place until the weather starts to moderate in spring, usually around the beginning of April. Antidesiccant sprays are applied to evergreens in fall, before the wrapping occurs. During the growing season, especially after storms in the autumn hurricane season, the garden staff wash down the evergreens with water to rinse salt from the foliage.

Other plants are wind sheared and never attain their full growth potential, but the owners are willing to put up with that for the particular visual contribution the plants make to the garden at a specific time. For example, there's a photinia whose perfect moment comes when its branches spill over a wall in an especially beguiling way. The rest of the season the wind takes its toll, but by then the photinia has already had its time to shine.

On the lower parts of the property, the blend of formal and informal elements is beautifully orchestrated in the garden. Leading to the guesthouse, a series of arches made of copper tubing mark a mown grass path that runs between a pair of colorful borders. A series of clipped, flat-topped, columnar yews march alongside the arches. This formal structure is engulfed by masses of perennials and annuals that spill onto the path. Annual nasturtiums (which are started from seed in three successions two weeks apart) clamber up the yews. 'American Pillar' and other roses climb the arches.

The walled garden is also formally structured, then softened with lush plantings. Brick walls enclose a classically laid-out space with a brick walkway forming the main axis of the garden, bisected by a canal that serves as the secondary axis. Lotus and papyrus grow in the canal, and there are fish. Cone-shaped yews (cleverly tied and clipped into that form) punctuate the garden with a series of vertical spires. Neatly pruned 'Meyer' lemon trees in large pots provide additional vertical accents. One year they tried planting Italian cypress in this garden; the trees looked great for a season, but perished in winter, despite their best efforts. One exotic plant that does last here is a 'Brown Turkey' fig, which has grown to eight feet tall. How do they get it through the winter? "We build a little house around it," says Mr. Hill.

Tender plants such as agave and rosemary lend exotic touches to the garden in summer, and they overwinter in a cool greenhouse. Asian and Indian architectural elements enhance the air of faraway places that infuses this garden.

Like most seaside gardens, this one continues to develop. It's an ongoing process of growth and change, and with each passing year the garden becomes more fully integrated with the special piece of land it occupies. It's a unique blend of sophisticated design and cutting-edge horticultural technique.

PROTECTING PLANTS FROM THE ELEMENTS

- Offer delicate plants more protection by siting them on the leeward side of a building or hedge. Spray salt-sensitive evergreens with an antidesiccant product, then wrap them with burlap for the winter.
- After storms, hose down evergreens that haven't been wrapped in burlap, to remove salt residue.
- Overwinter tender plants like agaves, rosemary, and fig trees indoors, or cover individual plants with a large cold frame.

Capturing a View

LONG ISLAND, NEW YORK

Looking back at the house from the meadow. In late summer, the mown grass path is bordered by native goldenrod and the airy panicles of an ornamental grass, *Miscanthus sinensis* 'Gracillimus'.

RIGHT: An intimate dining area overlooks the meadow full of goldenrod with a view of the pond. In the distance at the horizon is the ocean.

ON THIS EASTERN LONG ISLAND PROPERTY, the goal of the landscape design is to take maximum advantage of the expansive view in a very low-maintenance way. Landscape designer Edwina von Gal used native plants and ornamental grasses to reveal and enhance the innate character of the land. The result is a casual, simple landscape that requires very little in the way of maintenance, allowing the homeowners to relax and enjoy the magnificent natural surroundings.

From the property there is a view across a somewhat brackish pond to the ocean in the distance. The soil is classic "Bridgehampton loam," as it is called in these parts — three to eight feet of clay loam over sand. It is some of the best farmland in the country, and it supports a varied community of plants. The mix of soils on the eastern end of Long Island is one of the most interesting aspects of the landscape. Unlike many regions, not all the soil here is sandy. The area is, geologically speaking, a terminal moraine, where retreating glaciers left behind rock and soil carried here during the last ice age. Despite relentless development, there are still a few places where you can look across fields of potatoes growing in rich loam to see rolling sand dunes and the ocean beyond. It is a place of breathtaking beauty, and this property exemplifies the unique grandeur of the place.

Ms. von Gal's mission was to leave the view undisturbed and to bring aspects of the ocean view back into the landscape nearer the house. "You can't plant in front of an incredible view," Ms. von Gal told the owners. There are massive clumps of bayberry (*Myrica pensylvanica*) out on the distant dunes, so she planted bayberry on the property to connect it to the view. The repetition of plants visually annexes the ocean to the property, making the entire view part of this landscape. The result is a sense of expansive openness that is both majestic and serene. It's a sight you feel you could take in forever.

On the farther, more exposed reaches of the property there were areas in need of screening, and autumn olive (*Elaeagnus umbellata*) was planted. This tree is controversial because it spreads so vigorously

Grass paths mown regularly along with the lawn bring definition to the landscape. This path leads to a bench placed for viewing the pond, a vista that connects this property to the natural landscape beyond.

In an area of lawn near the house, wisteria frames a pair of swings. The soil here is excellent — several feet of clay-loam over sand.

that it has become invasive. But it is extremely tough, and many landscape designers feel it still has its uses in harsh seaside environments where little else will grow. It also provides food and good habitat for birds. In this landscape, the trees are prevented from spreading because self-sown seedlings are cut down when the adjacent meadow is mowed.

Although it does not front on the ocean, this property is close enough that salt-tolerant plants are an important component of the landscape. There are bayberries and native wild cherries. "Once you have bayberries," says Ms. von Gal, "you'll get more if you have the right conditions." London plane tree (*Platanus* × *hispanica*) was planted too. It is not a native, but it can take quite a bit of salt as long as it's not right on the beach. Butterfly bushes (*Buddleia*) also thrive here despite the salt winds that sweep across the property.

In one area the owners needed screening plants to replace Japanese black pines that had died. Ms. von Gal put in Hinoki cypresses (*Chamaecyparis obtusa*), which have flourished. "They're remarkably salt tolerant," she observes.

A portion of the property is devoted to an expansive meadow of goldenrod, through which paths are mowed for strolling and benches are placed for contemplating and observing the landscape. As with all else in this garden, the meadow

was achieved very simply — by mowing. "There was an old field, and we just mow it," Ms. von Gal explains. "If you time the mowing right, you can encourage what you want. In this case we got goldenrod, and that's fine."

Some wild cherries and bayberries were allowed to come up in the meadow. Although we generally think of bayberries as dune plants, they do quite well in the loamy soil here. The only regular maintenance the meadow receives is a twice-yearly mowing, to keep down unwanted woody plants. The bayberries and cherries are allowed to stay.

Paths through the meadow are kept mowed by the lawn service. The paths are an important structural component of the garden. "I think paths are one of the best and easiest ways to landscape," says Ms. von Gal. "The areas you don't mow are defined by the areas you do."

One thing that does trouble her about the meadow is the emergence of miscanthus seedlings coming up from seeds blown in from nearby plantings. The seedlings in the meadow are coarser and less attractive than the *Miscanthus* 'Gracillimus' planted in the garden, and mowing the meadow doesn't really slow them down (they are, after all, grass). "I'm worried that at the rate they're seeding in, they might be a new invasive," she says. When asked if she thought the miscanthus might

outcompete and overwhelm the golden-rod, Ms. von Gal said she believes they may be evenly matched. Time will tell.

Bordering the meadow closer to the house are plantings of *Miscanthus* 'Gracil-limus', pennisetum, and mugo pine. Mugo pine is another plant that does quite well here. Several were used to screen the pool from the house, as they are high enough to serve that purpose.

Elsewhere are a number of Kwanzan cherries that are lovely when they bloom in spring. There's also a grove of hawthorns with a carpet of fine-textured hair grass (*Deschampsia caespitosa*) underneath. Several existing hawthorns on the property were thriving, so Ms. von Gal decided to add more to create a grove. She was told the existing trees were 'Winter King' hawthorn, which is reputed to be highly salt tolerant, so 'Winter King' was planted. Alas, the old hawthorns are doing better than the new ones, and they were apparently not, after all, 'Winter King.' "I wish I could find out what they are," Ms. von Gal says. "But once you find out what they are, it doesn't mean you'll be able to find them." In any case, there's a mystery hawthorn growing in this garden that's remarkably salt tolerant.

That kind of adaptability is the key to this landscape. It's a paragon of subtle, low-maintenance design that lets the natural beauty of the site shine through.

SALT-TOLERANT LANDSCAPE PLANTS

Buddleia spp., butterfly bush
Chamaecyparis obtusa, Hinoki cypress
Crataegus 'Winter King', hawthorn
Deschampsia caespitosa, hair grass
Myrica pensylvanica, northern bayberry
Pinus mugo, mugo pine
Platanus × hispanica, London plane tree
Solidago spp., goldenrod

In late summer and early autumn, the low, slanting rays of the sun illuminate the bottlebrush inflorescences of fountain grass (*Pennisetum* sp.) in the foreground and the fanlike plumes of *Miscanthus sinensis* 'Gracillimus' farther back.

A Secret Garden by the Sea

REHOBOTH, DELAWARE

Assorted culinary herbs —golden oregano, red-veined dock (*Rumex sanguineus*), and French tarragon — thrive in pots on the sunny patio.

FROM THE BEACH, THIS REHOBOTH house looks like a quintessential beach house with a typical garden. There's a boardwalk heading toward the sea. Beach grass grows in the sand. Low pots of wind- and salt-tolerant annuals line the brick wall around the patio. But from other angles, surprises abound. The other side of the house, which faces a quiet lake, looks elegant and traditional, even English. Some of the brick walls enclose a hidden courtyard that is home to plenty of plants you'd never expect to see at the beach. The lady of the house, Meredith Marshall, is an accomplished gardener who has had a passion for gardening since her childhood.

Mrs. Marshall comes from a gardening family — both her mother and grandmother were gardeners, too. "My grandmother had a beautiful kitchen garden," she says, "with roses, larkspur, sweet William, and bachelor's buttons — plants that reseeded — and a huge vegetable garden." Carrying on the family tradition, Mrs. Marshall has created an amazingly lush and colorful courtyard garden near the beach. The garden is the summer home of Mrs. Marshall's prized plant collection, including award-winning myrtle topiaries. It's also a peaceful haven, offering respite from the busyness of the beach and the crash and boom of the nearby ocean waves.

The Marshalls' landscape was designed by landscape architect Mario Nievera, of Mario Nievera Designs, based in Palm Beach, Florida. Mr. Nievera used structural elements — walls, walkways and other hardscape elements, and large old trees — to anchor the design and organize the outdoor space. The courtyard is the quiet heart of the property. It is full of deliciously fragrant plants — sweet-smelling

An enclosed courtyard offers a protected environment for a host of plants not usually associated with seashore gardens, including topiaries trained by Mrs. Marshall.

Like all beachfront gardens, this one is exposed to strong winds and salt. In this case, the house itself provides protection for the gardens that grow behind it.

daphnes, aromatic herbs, lightly fragrant butterfly bushes — along with junipers and camellias and a variety of perennials. The myrtle topiaries, which Mrs. Marshall trains herself, travel back and forth with her between their winter home in Florida and their summer home in Delaware.

A garden had existed in the courtyard when the Marshalls bought the house, but they made modifications to the space to make it their own. Mr. Nievera removed a large old crape myrtle and took out some of the brick flooring to open up more space for plants. He also opened up part of one wall to create access to a terrace with a swimming pool. This also allowed a view of the lake, which couldn't be seen from the house before. The courtyard wall was constructed with small openings that allow wind to pass through as the wall greatly slows its force; a solid wall would have created strong wind eddies and currents that could have damaged the plants behind it.

The pool is lined with many pots of colorful annuals and complemented by beds of shrubs. Annuals play a big part in the Marshalls' garden, too, filling it with loads of color all summer. The Marshalls plant all the pots themselves, and the flowers change every year. Mr. Marshall is usually in charge of buying annuals. "You name it, whatever is in the garden center that particular year, he'll try," laughs Mrs. Marshall.

From the pool terrace, a gate leads through a board-on-board fence (an ideal design for a windy site) and between terraced beds of roses, daylilies, ornamental grasses, and creeping junipers. Mrs. Marshall grows lots of roses. David Austin English roses thrive here, and she's also fond of 'Just Joey', 'Tropicana', and especially 'Albertine', which grows on the front fence facing the lake.

On this side, the property slopes down toward the lake. Perennial borders curve across the face of the slope and are full of summer color from classic flowers like nepeta, perovskia, Shasta daisy, bee balm, roses, and agastache.

Mrs. Marshall looks forward each year to the time when the roses and peonies and clematis are in bloom — but she

Pots of colorful annuals change every year, according to what looks good at the local garden center. This year there are snapdragons, phlox, marigolds, salvia, and nicotiana, among others.

Lacecap hydrangeas thrive near the swimming pool (foreground) near a pot of agapanthus. The brick wall acts as both windbreak and enclosure for the courtyard.

doesn't play favorites among her plants. As she says, "I think if you're a gardener, you love everything."

Despite the protection afforded by the courtyard walls and the house itself for the lake side of the property, gardening here is still a challenge. The soil is almost pure sand, and before any gardening could be done, a better growing medium had to be provided. The Marshalls brought in truckloads of topsoil, and mixed manure and peat to amend the soil and create a deep, rich, loamy blend. Soil building went on for several years, and they still top-dress from time to time.

Wind and salt are constant problems. Inevitably, plants are lost and have to be replaced. The worst weather calamity to befall the garden so far, says Mrs. Marshall, was a dry nor'easter that blew salt on the garden for three straight days. Many plants had to be cut back. The hollies dropped their leaves. The annuals in all the pots died. "It was pretty depressing," she says. It has taken the plants two or three years to recover.

And so the Marshalls continue to garden, as true gardeners always do. Gardening "is either in your blood or it isn't," Mrs. Marshall says. Gardening is most definitely in the blood of these seaside homeowners, and the extraordinary beauty of their landscape is a testament to their skill and passion.

Floating on a Meadow

CHESAPEAKE BAY, MARYLAND

A naturalistic meadow visually connects the house to the Chesapeake Bay. Large windows take advantage of the view and help to bring the outdoors in.

FOR MOST OF US, A DREAM OF FLOATING would involve a boat and water or a magical ability to ride a current of air through the sky. But renowned landscape architect James van Sweden, one of the founders of Oehme, van Sweden & Associates, had a dream of a house that floated over a meadow. Several years ago he realized that dream, building on the eastern shore of the Chesapeake Bay a house that is surrounded by a meadow. The meadow runs right up to the house — there's no lawn, and no traditional garden beds and borders. "I wanted an ugly garden," he says.

His garden *isn't*, in fact, ugly, though it is vastly different from a standard perennial garden. This landscape has a rugged natural beauty that unites the house with the site and captures the spirit of the shoreline.

The garden blends grasses, shrubs and trees, native perennials (and varieties bred from them), and aquatic plants in a quiet but compelling composition of texture and form. It blends seamlessly into its surroundings. Mr. van Sweden didn't want a conventional garden: "I didn't want pretty flowers," he declares. He wanted the garden to look tough, not delicate. And tough it is.

The property is coastal plain, "flat as a pancake," he says. Although it's brackish, there's not the sort of searing salt wind that besieges oceanfront gardens. He didn't specifically put in a lot of salt-resistant plants, but the natives are naturally salt tolerant; groundsel bush (*Baccharis halimifolia*) and wax myrtle (*Myrica cerifera*), two very durable, salt-resistant natives, grow near the house. When a hurricane struck in 2004, saltwater came 70 feet inland, flooding part of the meadow, but none of the plants was permanently damaged, and all have recovered.

Not only is this garden tough; it's a positive benefit to the environment. No chemical fertilizers or pesticides are used to maintain the garden, so it does not contribute to the fertilizer runoff that has become so problematic for the Chesapeake, as for so many of our coastal waters. The water draining from this property into

the bay is clean. Indeed, says Mr. van Sweden, "I see my garden, which has no lawn and uses no chemicals, as one huge filter for the water that runs across it going to the bay."

The meadow also attracts its share of wildlife; black snakes, rabbits, and, of course, deer are common, but they don't bother the plants. The ornamental grasses and most of the other plants in the garden are deer resistant. Plants that are susceptible to deer browsing, such as oakleaf hydrangea and viburnum, get sprayed periodically with a garlic mixture that has proved sufficient to keep away the deer.

The only other regular maintenance required is some weeding. The garden is well established now, and the plants shade out a lot of the weeds. The poison ivy that grew on the property initially is gone now. The worst problem is Canada thistle, but it is removed as soon as it pops up. The yellow-flowered compass plant (*Silphium*

RIGHT: Hackberry trees (*Celtis occidentalis*) punctuate a tapestry of lower plants that includes blocks of *Aster oblongifolius* and *Eupatorium hyssopifolium* near the pond and wild rice (*Zinzania latifolia*) and *Thalia dealbata* in the water.

LEFT: A planting of *Schizachyrium scoparium* and *Coreopsis tripteris* connects the house to the bay.

Paths maintain the natural look of the rest of the property; they are surfaced with crushed oyster shells, a traditional paving material along the East Coast in times past when oysters were plentiful in the waters.

laciniatum), a prairie native, is a prolific self-sower that has become invasive, so unwanted seedlings have to be pulled every year. The silphium that remains is striking, however; in some places it is nine feet tall.

The three-acre property had once been a soybean field. When Mr. van Sweden took possession, he planted soybeans once more but did not fertilize them. After the soybeans were gone, he left the land alone, and horsetail came up. The horsetail was gone the next year. Then 50 pounds of panicum and schizachyrium seed were planted with a seed drill. Then there was a drought and none of the grass came up. Finally, though, the rains came and then the grasses grew.

Closer to the house, sturdy perennials such as giant black-eyed Susan (*Rudbeckia maxima*), asters, and grasses including broom sedge (*Andropogon virginicus*), wild oats (*Chasmanthium latifolium*), and little bluestem (*Schizachyrium scoparium*) were planted in bands and blocks and then allowed to go their own way. Paths through the garden are made of flagstones set in crushed oyster shells — a traditional paving material at the seashore that, these days, is difficult to come by.

Like all gardens, this one has evolved over time. Even a meadow requires a certain amount of experimentation and revision to arrive at the ideal mix of plants.

Switchgrass (*Panicum virgatum* 'Cloud Nine') planted right off the deck grew quickly to eight feet high and blocked the view of the bay from the expansive windows of the house. It was moved and replaced with *Pycnanthemum muticum,* a lower-growing perennial with aromatic, minty foliage.

In and around the pond, Mr. van Sweden planted Asian wild rice (*Zinzania latifolia*), butterbur (*Petasites japonicus*), rose mallow (*Hibiscus moscheutos*), and *Thalia dealbata.* Cattails (*Typha* sp.) have to be weeded out to prevent them from taking over and crowding out the other plants.

Hedgerows run along the property lines and they were overgrown with poison ivy, which was removed. Poison ivy is tenacious, but repeated pulling or mowing will eventually get rid of it without the need for herbicides. Native eastern red cedars populate the hedgerows (and don't burn from salt wind, as they often do near the ocean) and produce new seedlings. Mr. van Sweden has added desirable trees such as *Oxydendrum arboreum* and *Magnolia grandiflora* to the hedgerows, as well.

Another tree that grows in the garden is hackberry (*Celtis occidentalis*). The eminent tree authority Donald Wyman said the hackberry had no landscape value whatsoever, but Mr. van Sweden's business partner, Wolfgang Oehme, likes the tree, so several found their way into the land-

scape. As Mr. van Sweden describes them, hackberries are not pretty, they have no fall color, and they don't have nice flowers — that is, they fit his criterion of not having pretty plants in his garden. But the birds like them, he says. And they are very tough.

Mr. van Sweden's Chesapeake retreat demonstrates that a naturalistic landscape can have a positive effect on the environment that surrounds it and still be attractive (even when "pretty" flowers aren't employed).

RIGHT: Hackberry trees, while not conventionally beautiful, are tough and resilient, and they provide habitat for birds, so they have earned their place in this landscape.

BELOW: Because it uses no chemical inputs and relies largely on native plants, this garden helps in its own small way to preserve the incomparable beauty of the Chesapeake Bay.

TOUGH PLANTS FOR A NATURALISTIC LANDSCAPE

Andropogon virginicus, broom sedge
Baccharis halimifolia, groundsel bush
Celtis occidentalis, hackberry
Magnolia grandiflora, southern magnolia
Pycnanthemum muticum, mountain mint
Rudbeckia maxima, giant black-eyed Susan
Schizachyrium scoparium, little bluestem

Designing with Nature

KIAWAH ISLAND, SOUTH CAROLINA

ON A BARRIER ISLAND OFF THE SOUTH Carolina coast, there's a wonderful example of how native plants can be used to integrate a seaside house into a beautiful natural setting and create a landscape that is sophisticated yet low maintenance.

The house is built of wood and stone; it's natural and rustic, yet elegant and stylish. To take advantage of the unspoiled character of the maritime forest site, landscape architect Clyde Timmons, of DesignWorks, LC, in Charleston, created a garden that relies heavily on native plants to fit the house comfortably into its surroundings.

To reach the house, you travel along a winding drive paved with crunchy, dark crushed slag through a woodland planted with ferns and dwarf palms. The natural environment here is so beautiful that the designer and the owners agreed they wanted a landscape that blended into its surroundings, with some added touches of color and texture.

As a starting point, they decided to preserve the magnificent huge old live oaks (*Quercus virginiana*) that graced the property. The architecture of the house already embraced the trees — the outstanding feature of the house is a circular glass block tower with a spiral staircase that is located right under one of the live oaks. Climbing the stairs feels like walking through the branches of the tree.

There were also native wax myrtles (*Myrica cerifera*), yaupon hollies (*Ilex vomitoria*), and palmettos (*Sabal palmetto*). The natural vegetation was enhanced with additional plantings on the grounds just beyond the house. Once established, these natives need little in the way of maintenance, tolerating drought, heat, and the salt winds off the river that flows behind the property. Another plus is that the plentiful deer population leaves the plants alone. Needle palm (*Rhapidophyllum hystrix*), a hardy and shade-tolerant native, was added here for greater textural contrast.

Close by the river at the rear of the property is a marsh dominated by a native cordgrass, *Spartina alternifolia*. Along the edge of the marsh, Mr. Timmons and his team planted another native marsh cordgrass, *Spartina patens*, which can tolerate periodic saltwater flooding.

Closer to the house, the plantings combine with striking architectural features to create a more controlled, elegant, but still natural look. The house itself is actually two separate buildings linked by a courtyard. Here there is a rectangular lap pool surrounded by a terrace of cut bluestone, which is bordered with rippling bands of rounded river stone alternating with dwarf mondo grass (*Ophiopogon japonicus*) that reinforce the linear feeling but create an interesting contrast of textures. In a bit of serendipity, the homeowners had chosen tiles with a wavy pattern to run down the

A winding driveway paved with crushed slag ends in a parking area near the house. Here, the soaring branches of old live oaks create a cathedral effect. Sandanqua viburnum (*Viburnum suspensum*) and dwarf palmetto (*Sabal minor*) grow beneath the oaks.

ABOVE: Saw palmetto (*Serenoa repens*) is hardy and resilient in this garden, tolerating salt, wind, and drought, and it's not tempting to deer.

RIGHT: The crisp lines of the courtyard and lap pool are softened with plantings of sago palm, and Confederate jasmine climbing the pillars. Dwarf mondo grass planted in undulating lines echoes the wavy tile pattern down the center of the pool.

The fragrant white flowers of Confederate jasmine (*Trachelospermum jasminoides*) perfume the courtyard in spring. The sago palm (*Cycas revoluta*) below grows very slowly but can eventually reach an impressive size.

center of the bottom of the pool, a perfect complement to the pattern of the mondo grass and river stone. Designer and owners were thinking on the same plane, which made for a very successful collaboration.

For the plantings in this area, the design team amended the naturally quite sandy soil with compost, peat moss, and fertilizer to support a wider range of plants. Along the sides of the pool, magnificent columns of Confederate jasmine (*Trachelospermum jasminoides*) scale the posts supporting the roof. When the fragrant jasmine flowers in the spring, the effect is intoxicating, but there's still plenty of interest when the jasmine is not in bloom. In the river stone below are several sago palms (*Cycas revoluta*), which can eventually become quite large but grow very, very slowly. Here at the northernmost limit of its hardiness range, the palm can burn in a very severe winter, but it has so far done just fine. Taller windmill palm (*Trachycarpus fortunei*) is not a native, but it is hardy.

Perennials and annuals in the courtyard bloom at different times of year. The garden includes agapanthus, plumbago (*Plumbago auriculata*), gaura, and crocosmia, along with pink lantana. All of them do well there.

Behind the house a series of terraced planters step down toward the marsh. The strong architectural lines of the planters are softened with native sweetgrass (*Muh-*

lenbergia filipes), which is used locally to make sweetgrass baskets. "It has a beautiful little pinkish purple bloom in late summer and fall," says Mr. Timmons. He also used saw palmetto (*Serenoa repens*) in the planters. This is about as far north as it can grow, but there are some natural stands of it on the island, and it is fairly low growing. He also used some creeping rosemary in the planters, a plant he likes because "it takes the salt, takes the dryness, takes the winds." Plants here are mulched with local pine straw to help retain moisture.

In front of the house, the driveway ends in a parking area that's an architecturally strong space, again blending house and garden. The main houses, the guesthouse, the garage, and some tall live oaks with their overhanging branches combine to form three sides of this cathedral-like space. One feels a sense of both enclosure and verticality. "The live oaks are absolutely beautiful," says Mr. Timmons. The plantings simply reinforced the structure that was already there. Beneath the live oaks are palmetto (*Sabal palmetto*), *Viburnum suspensum* (which, although not native, has a natura-

listic feel and tolerates the shady conditions under the trees), evergreen giant liriope (*Liriope muscari*), and a redbud tree (*Cercis canadensis* 'Forest Pansy').

The sensitive design and use of native plant materials unite this remarkable house with the unspoiled natural environment that surrounds it. The courtyard plantings reinforce the architectural lines of the house while adding color and texture. It's an ideal marriage of house and landscape.

Behind the house, a series of terraced planters are filled with native sweetgrass (*Muhlenbergia filipes*), trailing rosemary, creeping fig (*Ficus pumila*) and saw palm (*Serenoa repens*).

Inspired by Frank Lloyd Wright

KIAWAH ISLAND, SOUTH CAROLINA

Planters near the house contain ornamental grasses, palms, and a creeping shore juniper (*Juniperus conferta* 'Blue Pacific') that drapes itself over the edges.

FRANK LLOYD WRIGHT BELIEVED THAT landscape and architecture should connect to each other; his houses were all designed to fit into their surroundings, with landscaping to enhance the connection. Many of his houses are low to the ground, to blend with their flat prairie sites. The owners of this property on a barrier island off South Carolina wanted a house and landscape in the spirit of Frank Lloyd Wright. But this house had to be tall — there were setback and flood requirements, and the owners wanted to have enough space and a good view. The verticality of the house made it more challenging for landscape architect Clyde Timmons, of DesignWorks, LC, in Charleston, South Carolina, to tie together the landscape and house. But he employed a number of creative design strategies to accomplish the goal.

There were also a number of landscape challenges presented by the site. The property is buffeted by strong salt winds coming off the ocean. There are plenty of hungry deer in residence. The house sits on a flag lot, and a driveway had to be constructed in a narrow corridor lined with live oaks (*Quercus virginiana*) that both designer and homeowners wanted to preserve. There is a range of soils, from sand to muck, each with different watering needs. In addition, the property lies in a swale between two dune fields, and water naturally collects there. The water table is only three feet down, even in dry weather. Local development has channeled ever more water into the swale — there's no place for it to run off. The water problem exists on the landward side of the property (the sandy beachfront side drains well). The design team solved the water problem by building up mounds of soil to improve drainage. They created a berm to accommodate plantings near the street, graded

Terraces and porches help to unite the house with the landscape, and their horizontal lines evoke the feeling of Frank Lloyd Wright's prairie style of architecture.

carefully, and made raised planting areas with drainage pipes installed underneath.

In the end, the owners wanted a low-maintenance landscape that was respectful of and appropriate to the environment — and they got it. First, they left intact as much of the indigenous vegetation as was practical, and added some new, primarily native, plants. On the seaward side of the house, they used dune and beach plants. They added some grasses and palms that are visually compatible although not necessarily native. They also added a few gingers to strike a tropical note. A few unhealthy loblolly pines were removed on the beach side, and they selectively pruned the remaining pines and oaks to frame views of the ocean that had been blocked. A boardwalk leading to the beach was carefully located to wind through the existing vegetation, making a stroll to the beach visually more interesting while still protecting the dunes and plants.

On the landward side of the house, Mr. Timmons relied on plants suited to the maritime forest. Along the driveway, most of the existing vegetation, including wax

The boardwalk leading to the beach is carefully designed to wind through the existing vegetation, protecting the dunes and the plants.

myrtle (*Myrica cerifera*), yaupon holly (*Ilex vomitoria*), redbay (*Persea borbonia*), and *Magnolia grandiflora*, remained in place, with just some cleanup and pruning, and some new plants were added to provide better screening and more textural interest.

A second design strategy was to bring some dune plants close to the house. Mr. Timmons installed palms and dune grasses in terraced planters off the first floor. Conditions were different from one planter to another — wind exposure and amount of sunlight varied — and the plants had to be suited to the particular environment. Another consideration was not to block the view with plants. To evoke the spirit of Frank Lloyd Wright, who liked to use trailing plants and vines in his own landscape designs, Mr. Timmons included trailing rosemary in the planters.

The planters hold a variety of ornamental grasses — sweetgrass (*Muhlenbergia filipes*), maidengrass (*Miscanthus sinensis* 'Gracillimus'), and pennisetum. Dwarf yaupon holly, which forms a large mound that can be clipped to keep it small or left to assume its natural form, also figures in the planters. (The holly is, says Mr. Timmons, tough and durable as well as attractive — an all-around good, versatile plant.)

More planters grace the broad porches that forge another link between house and landscape. Here the grasses are joined by yellow lantana, aspidistra, variegated ginger, and a creeping shore juniper (*Juniperus conferta* 'Blue Pacific').

Mr. Timmons connected the landscape to the house by pulling architectural materials into the landscape; he also made design recommendations for creating a covered walkway or breezeway leading to the front door. He designed angular retaining walls that reach out into the landscape in front of the house to create terraced planting areas right alongside the building. In these beds are holly fern (*Cyrtomium falcatum*), the finer-textured autumn fern (*Dryopteris erythrosora*), and yellow lantana for color. To introduce a vertical line close to the wall of the house there are cast-iron plants (*Aspidistra elatior*), which are very

The pool and spa offer a view down the boardwalk to the beach. Native loblolly pines were selectively pruned to frame the vista.

Angular planters are sided with wood to match the house, bringing an architectural element into the landscape. At the base, native sweetgrass is mulched with local pine straw, connecting planted areas to the surrounding natural landscape.

tough and can take a lot of shade. Close to the breezeway is a trident maple (*Acer buergerianum*), planted to lighten up the brick wall against which it is seen. Red maple was rejected for this space because it is too large, and Japanese maple was considered too fragile for the seaside environment.

A higher wall, sided with wood like the house, creates a second, elevated level for planting. Masses of Confederate jasmine (*Trachelospermum jasminoides*) spill over the edges of this higher wall, in another nod to the style of Frank Lloyd Wright.

Altogether, this landscape achieves its aim — that of uniting a well-conceived and beautifully detailed home with a wonderful seaside setting.

STRATEGIES FOR UNITING HOUSE AND LANDSCAPE

• Leave existing vegetation intact as much as possible; prune selectively and replace damaged specimens with healthy plants.

• Select native (or native-looking) plants to mix effectively into the existing landscape.

• Use plants close to the house that also occur in the distant landscape.

• Repeat architectural elements from the house in the landscape, in the form of paths, beds, breezeways, and retaining walls.

CHAPTER 5

Top Seaside Plants

THIS SECTION IS A CONCISE GUIDE TO MORE THAN 100 plants that do well in seaside gardens. There are many more plants suited to seashore conditions than can be described here, so don't be afraid to experiment. Some of the plants in this chapter will grow in beachfront gardens, and some will work near the beach if sheltered by a windbreak or the house itself. Others have less tolerance for salt or wind, and are best located away from the beach.

ABOVE: *Dahlia* 'Caboose'

RIGHT: Astilbes, hostas, and ferns thrive in a protected, shady spot on the rocky coast of Mane.

Understanding Environmental Conditions

Growing conditions vary widely near the beach. If you have shade, it is important to understand its density and duration.

WHEN CHOOSING PLANTS FOR YOUR seaside garden, it is essential that you have a very clear understanding of the environmental conditions they will face in your garden or in their particular spot in your garden. Seashore conditions vary significantly from one property to another. The closer you are to the beach, the greater the variation can be. At the beach, growing conditions just a thousand feet apart can be totally different from one another.

To select plants that will thrive in your garden, it is important to know the direction from which the prevailing winds blow in summer and in winter. Find out when the stormiest weather usually occurs.

Sun exposure is another critical factor. You will need to know how many hours of direct sun the garden will receive each day, and how the sun shifts in the sky over the course of the growing season, which will alter the patterns of light and shadow across the property. If you have shade, be realistic about the type and degree of shade it is. Sun-loving plants will just not thrive in the shade. But there are plenty of plants that will. See "Kinds of Shade" (below) for more information.

KINDS OF SHADE

The quality of shade varies greatly, and understanding what constitutes partial shade or full shade will help you make better plant choices for your garden.

Partial shade, semi-shade, or half shade. A partially shady location receives two to six hours of sun, either in the morning or in the afternoon. It can also refer to a full day of dappled sunlight. Partial shade is usually cast to the east or west of a relatively solid body, such as a wall, building, or thick hedge, or beneath an arbor or lattice.

Light or thin shade. This can be found under young trees, or mature trees with a light, lacy canopy. Light shade can also be cast by trees or buildings at some distance from the garden. While not sunny, this environment is still bright and airy.

A lightly shaded garden may receive only an hour or two of direct sun during the day, but it is bright enough the rest of the time to allow a variety of plants to thrive. The thin canopy creates shifting patterns of light and shadow, or intermittent shade, as some of the sun's rays pass through spaces between the leaves.

Full shade. This is found under mature trees that have dense, spreading foliage. Unpruned oaks and maples cast this kind of shade in summer. A fully shaded location is fine for woodland plants.

Heavy shade. Cast by tall buildings and mature evergreens, heavy shade is too dim, and often too dry, for all but a few plants.

The other key factors are soil and moisture. Don't automatically assume your soil is sandy — not all seashore gardens are. If you do have sandy soil, how sandy is it? How well does the soil drain and how long does it retain moisture? What is the pH? What are nutrient levels like? Have a good soil test done. In addition to providing test results, USDA county Cooperative Extension offices and good private testing labs will make recommendations on amending and improving your soil.

The answers to all these environmental questions will guide you both in your choice of plants and in how you manage the plants in the garden. If you work with nature and choose plants that are naturally suited to the growing conditions present on your property, your chances of success will be much greater. You'll also have to do less work to coddle and nurse them along. Use this chapter as a guide to help you find plants that will work in your garden.

Beach grass and bayberry, like other native plants, are adapted to seashore conditions and will do well with little help.

Making Good Choices

Beach peas are among the few plants that thrive in the harsh dune environment.

HOMEOWNERS LIVING NEAR A BAY often have more leeway in terms of plant choices than do oceanfront dwellers, especially if the property is elevated on a bluff. Farther away from the water, the choices become even broader.

Still, seaside gardening is always a process of trial and error, and you have to resign yourself to losing plants. Over time, you'll find out which ones work in your garden and which ones don't. But unusually severe winters and hard storms can wipe out plants that have done well in your garden for years. It's part of life at the shore, and you don't have much choice but to accept it. Still, for those of us who live near the sea, the trials and tribulations of seashore gardening are worth it.

For each of the plants in this chapter you will find a quick capsule of information on its hardiness, sun and shade requirements, and approximate degree of salt tolerance. You will also find out whether the plant tolerates drought, and if deer are likely to eat it. There is a description of the plant, suggestions on how to use it in the garden, and, where applicable, recommended varieties.

There is also basic information on how to grow and care for the plant. Just bear in mind that plants do not perform the same way in all gardens, especially at the shore. So many different environmental factors come into play that it is really difficult to make generalizations about how plants will perform. Use the information in this chapter as a basic guide, but observe your plants carefully and get to know the growing environment that exists on your property. And remember: Never, never stop experimenting!

Trees and Shrubs

Amelanchier species
Shadbush, serviceberry

Zones: 4–8

Exposure: Full sun to partial shade

Salt Tolerance: Good

Drought Tolerance: Poor

Deer Resistance: Good

There are actually two woody plants called shadbush — *Amelanchier canadensis* and *Amelanchier arborea* (also known as downy serviceberry). The two are often confused, and are used in similar ways. Both are natives, and both may take the form of a large, dense, clump-forming shrub. Downy serviceberry may also grow as a small tree with an oval to rounded crown, and is a bit taller, growing to 25 feet high. *Amelanchier canadensis* reaches about 20 feet with a 10-foot spread.

Serviceberries, also known as shadbush, have oval, toothed leaves and clusters of white flowers in spring. In early summer they produce juicy, purple-black berries that can be used for pies and jellies, if the birds don't get to them first. Fall color is mostly yellow in *Amelanchier canadensis* and ranges from yellow to orange and sometimes red in downy serviceberry. Their light grayish bark is attractive in winter.

Shadbush prefers moist but well-drained soil with an acid pH. It grows wild in boggy areas up and down the coast from Maine to South Carolina, but it adapts to a range of soils. These trees can tolerate dry soil, but need watering during prolonged spells of dry weather. They look best in a naturalistic or informal garden. Plant at the edge of a woodland or alongside a pond, or in a shrub border. Shadbush is sometimes affected by scale, fire blight, or black spot.

Amelanchier species

Aronia species
Chokeberry

Zones: 5–9

Exposure: Full sun to light shade

Salt Tolerance: Good

Drought Tolerance: Moderate

Deer Resistance: Good

Red chokeberry (*Aronia arbutifolia*) is a leggy, upright shrub with arching stems that spreads by suckers to form a clump. It grows 8 to 10 feet high and may be 5 feet or more across. Leaves are oval, finely toothed, and dark green. They turn rich red in fall. Large clusters of small, fragrant white flowers bloom in spring, then from fall into winter the plants are covered with bright red berrylike fruits. The cultivar 'Brilliantissima' has spectacular autumn foliage and larger, shinier fruits than the species.

Red chokeberry grows well in full sun to light shade. It adapts to a range of soils from wet to dry. Moderate fertility suits it well, but it will grow in poor soils, too.

Black chokeberry (*Aronia melanocarpa*) is similar to the red species but bears dark purple-black fruits; the cultivar 'Autumn Magic' has especially large, glossy fruits. It is a bit smaller than red chokeberry (growing to six feet high), and its fall foliage is usually a deep purplish red. Like red chokeberry, this species adapts to a range of soils.

Both chokeberries are best grown in a shrub border or massed together.

Aronia arbutifolia 'Brilliantissima'

Baccharis halimifolia

Baccharis halimifolia
Groundsel bush, saltbush, salt myrtle

Zones: 3–8
Exposure: Full sun
Salt Tolerance: Excellent
Drought Tolerance: Good
Deer Resistance: Fair

This bushy deciduous shrub is rather weedy looking, but it's extremely tough. Saltbush stands up to salt spray, strong winds, and dry, sandy soil with no problem, and it's not bothered by saltwater flooding. It grows wild along the East Coast in a variety of habitats from sandy to marshy.

Groundsel bush grows to about 5 feet high at the beach, but will reach 10 or 11 feet in less exposed locations, with a spread of about 12 feet. The leaves are leathery and grayish green, oblong and coarsely toothed, and poisonous. Large clusters of white to yellowish white flowers appear on female plants in late summer and fall, and are followed by ornamental, foamy-looking, thistle-like seed heads. The plant self-sows and spreads; its vigor can be problematic in good soils.

Give saltbush a location in full sun, with very well-drained soil. It is useful in windbreaks at the beach, for screening in exposed locations, and to hold soil and control erosion on dunes and slopes. Away from the beach, it can fill space in poor soil where few other plants would thrive. Space plants two to three feet apart in a windbreak or other screen planting, or set them three feet apart in a double row. Cut back plants occasionally to promote bushier growth.

Buddleia species
Butterfly bush

Zones: 5–9
Exposure: Full sun to partial shade
Salt Tolerance: Fair
Drought Tolerance: Fair
Deer Resistance: Good

Butterfly bushes are lovely additions to gardens. They are adaptable and easy to grow, and their wands of little flowers bloom for a long time and are magnets for butterflies. Butterfly bushes prefer full sun, although cultivars with variegated leaves will do better with some afternoon shade in southern gardens. *Buddleia davidii* has some salt tolerance, but all species need protection from salt spray and strong winds.

Butterfly bushes thrive in soil that is well drained and reasonably fertile, but they can tolerate poorer soils, too, although they won't bloom as well. Deadhead plants to prolong flowering. Prune once a year if you want to limit their size.

Common butterfly bush (*Buddleia davidii*) grows to 20 feet if left unpruned, and can be cut back to the ground in early spring to rejuvenate old bushes or keep plants shorter. It has lance-shaped, grayish green leaves. Its fat, conical spikes of lightly fragrant flowers bloom in late summer and fall in shades of purple, violet, pink, burgundy, and white. This butterfly bush holds up well in dry conditions but needs some water during periods of prolonged drought.

Fountain buddleia (*B. alternifolia*) is a more graceful plant, with arching stems lined with narrow, dark green leaves. In late spring its branches are lined with dense clusters of light purple flowers that from a distance look like long wands of bloom. Fountain buddleia grows 10 to 15 feet high when unpruned, but can be pruned right after it finishes blooming to control its size.

Buddleia davidii

Calluna vulgaris
Scotch heather

Zones: 4–7
Exposure: Full sun
Salt Tolerance: Fair
Drought Tolerance: Fair
Deer Resistance: Good

This small evergreen shrub grows just two feet high with an equal spread, and forms a low mat. The thin, needlelike leaves are a rich medium green in summer and may take on a bronze cast in winter. From midsummer into fall plants produce long clusters of tiny bell-shaped flowers of deep purple-red, rosy pink, or white, which bees love.

Shear back plants after blooming to remove the old flowers, or prune occasionally to keep plants looking neat.

Heather needs plenty of sun and moist but

Calluna vulgaris

very well-drained soil with a mildly acid pH. It grows well in poor, infertile soil, but it can dry out in an exposed, windy location. Water well during periods of dry weather.

Heather can be used in a number of ways — in a rock garden, on a slope, or as a ground cover in an area that does not get foot traffic.

Caragana arborescens
Siberian peashrub

Zones: 2–7
Exposure: Full sun
Salt Tolerance: Good
Drought Tolerance: Good
Deer Resistance: Good

Siberian peashrub is an upright deciduous shrub to 20 feet high, with a spread of about 15 feet. Its compound leaves are composed of pairs of bright green oval leaflets with spiny tips. Clusters of bright yellow flowers bloom in spring, and pealike brown seedpods follow in mid- to late summer. Like legumes, Siberian peashrub fixes nitrogen in the soil.

Although not a terribly ornamental plant, Siberian peashrub is deep rooted, very cold

Caragana arborescens

hardy, and easy to grow. It tolerates salt, stands up well in strong winds, and can take poor soils and alkaline pH. Use it in a windbreak or screen near a bay beach or in other difficult sites. If you start with young plants, they will likely adapt to conditions near the ocean, too.

Clethra alnifolia
Sweet pepperbush

Zones: 4–9
Exposure: Partial to light shade
Salt Tolerance: Fair
Drought Tolerance: Poor
Deer Resistance: Poor

Sweet pepperbush offers its wands of fragrant white flowers in late summer to early fall, when they are especially welcome. Native to the eastern United States, this deciduous shrub forms a clump of stems about eight feet high and spreads by means of suckers but is not invasive. Leaves are oval and medium green in color, turning bright yellow in autumn. Dwarf and pink-flowered cultivars are also available.

Grow sweet pepperbush in a sheltered, partly shaded spot. Reliable and easy to grow, it does best in moist but well-drained, humusy soil that is reasonably fertile and has an acid pH, but it can adapt to a range of soils. Although it is not considered deer resistant, deer have not touched it in my garden.

Sweet pepperbush works well in informal shady borders away from the water.

Clethra alnifolia

Cryptomeria japonica
Japanese cedar

Zones: 6–9	
Exposure: Full sun to partial shade	
Salt Tolerance: Fair	
Drought Tolerance: Fair	
Deer Resistance: Poor	

Cryptomeria japonica 'Sekkan-sugi'

This stately evergreen is a tough, attractive plant for seashore gardens. It can grow 60 to 80 feet high, but many cultivars are available, in a range of heights. Some varieties are conical in form, others narrow and columnar, still others rounded and dense. Sprays of soft, medium to deep green needles turn bronze or brownish in winter in cooler climates. The bark is an attractive reddish brown and peels in strips.

Japanese cedar thrives in moist but well-drained soil that is fertile and rich in organic matter, but it will tolerate a range of soils as long as they are well drained. It is reasonably salt tolerant, but the foliage will burn right at the beach. Though generally a tough plant, the tree is sometimes attacked by leaf spot and blight.

Use Japanese cedar for screening or as a specimen tree in a lawn, where its attributes can be fully appreciated. It is best used away from the ocean, but will do reasonably well near a bay.

× Cupressocyparis leylandii
Leyland cypress

× *Cupressocyparis leylandii*

Zones: 6–10	
Exposure: Full sun to partial shade	
Salt Tolerance: Good	
Drought Tolerance: Moderate	
Deer Resistance: Poor	

This tough, fast-growing, pyramidal evergreen is widely used for hedges and screening. Leyland cypress can grow to 60 or 70 feet in home landscapes, with a spread of 10 to 15 feet, but it can be kept smaller with pruning. A graceful, handsome plant, Leyland cypress has feathery, scalelike, dark green foliage and reddish brown bark.

Leyland cypress is most often used in screens and informal hedges, but it can be sheared for a more formal look. It can also be planted in pairs flanking an entry or at the end of a driveway, or as a single specimen.

Leyland cypress needs well-drained soil, and it will tolerate poor, infertile soil. The tree can withstand salt spray and wind, and survives in difficult locations. It works well near a bay.

The best spot for Leyland cypress is a location in full sun. It will also grow in partial shade, but it won't be as dense. A quick grower even in poor soil, this plant will grow even faster in moist but well-drained, fertile soil. Pests and diseases seldom trouble it. If you prune or shear the tree for a hedge, do not cut back so far that you slice into old wood. Some gardeners find that touching the foliage irritates their skin, so wear gloves to work around the plant if you are sensitive.

RECOMMENDED CULTIVARS
- 'Gold Nugget' — golden foliage
- 'Naylor's Blue' — blue-green foliage
- 'Silver Dust' — white splotches on the foliage

Cytisus scoparius
Scotch broom

Zones: 5–8
Exposure: Full sun
Salt Tolerance: Good
Drought Resistance: Good
Deer Resistance: Good

In California, Scotch broom is an invasive nuisance, but along the East Coast it's a useful plant for sandy seaside gardens. Not a candidate for formal gardens, Scotch broom is a deciduous shrub to five or six feet high, with a mass of slender, upright, light green stems that arch over at the ends. The leaves are small and oblong, and masses of small, bright yellow flowers bloom along the stems in spring. A more compact variety with light yellow flowers is 'Moonlight'. There are also varieties with garnet red or red-violet flowers available in the nursery trade.

Grow this plant in full sun. It is not fussy about soil, so long as it has good drainage. In fact, broom does best in light, sandy soils of low fertility. Rich, wet soil will kill it. It also tolerates a range of pH levels. Scotch broom is susceptible to blight and leaf spot, which can kill the plant. It is reputedly difficult to transplant, but starting with young plants will reduce the risk of transplant shock. If you need to prune the plant, do it soon after it finishes blooming.

A word of caution: Scotch broom often self-sows. Be sure to pull up any unwanted seedlings.

Cytisus scoparius

Erica carnea

Erica carnea
Spring heath

Zones: (5) 6–8
Exposure: Full sun to partial shade
Salt Tolerance: Good
Drought Tolerance: Fair
Deer Resistance: Poor

A familiar plant to rock gardeners, spring heath has a place at the seashore, too. Low and spreading, it's a good addition to a sunny bed or border, or perhaps massed on a bank. Or you can use it as a ground cover in low-traffic areas.

Spring heath has dark green, needlelike, evergreen leaves. In late winter to early spring, depending on your location, it bears masses of tiny, tubular, rosy purple flowers. There are many cultivars in various shades of pink and purple, plus white. Some varieties also have golden foliage, which adds another season of color.

This heath grows just 8 to 12 inches high, forming a low mat or mound, and needs well-drained soil. Like other ericaceous plants, spring heath thrives in acid soil, but unlike many of its relatives, it will also tolerate alkaline soils. It is seldom bothered by salt or wind—they just blow right over it.

RECOMMENDED CULTIVARS
- 'December Red' — deep rose-pink flowers
- 'King George' — dark pink flowers, early blooming
- 'Myretown Ruby' — flowers open pink and darken to ruby red as they age
- 'Springwood Pink' — profuse, clear pink flowers; plant has a trailing habit
- 'Springwood White' — masses of white flowers on trailing plants

Zones: *E. fortunei,* 5–9; *E. japonicus,* 7–9
Exposure: Full sun to full shade
Salt Tolerance: Fair to good
Drought Tolerance: Poor
Deer Resistance: Poor

These two members of a large and varied genus are both evergreen and able to stand up to salt winds to varying degrees. They grow in sun or shade, and tolerate a range of soils. If your soil is mostly sand, though, amend it with compost and topsoil before planting euonymus, to provide nutrients and help hold moisture for the plants. Fertilize annually with a balanced organic fertilizer, or with an all-purpose synthetic according to package directions.

Evergreen euonymus is more salt tolerant but less hardy than wintercreeper, which generally does best behind a windbreak near the beach. Evergreen euonymus can stand direct hits from salty wind. Its stems will swell from water buildup in very salty conditions, but the plant will generally keep on growing anyway.

Most kinds of euonymus are, unfortunately, subject to scale, and may also be bothered by mildew, galls, leaf spots, or aphids. Deer will eat them, too.

Euonymus fortunei 'Emerald Gaiety'

Euonymus fortunei
Wintercreeper

This woody vine has small, oval, leathery, dark green leaves with serrated edges. Plants form roots at nodes along the stem and sprawl across the ground or climb, clinging to walls and tree trunks. When left unsupported, the plants become rather shrubby. In fall, they sport small reddish fruits that open to reveal orange seeds.

You can use wintercreeper as a ground cover under shrubs or trees, in a mixed border, or to prevent erosion on a slope. Clip the plants as needed. Space plants 1½ to 2 feet apart.

RECOMMENDED CULTIVARS
- *E. f.* var. *coloratus* — glossy deep green leaves that turn reddish or purplish in winter
- 'Emerald Gaiety' — grows three to four feet high, with white-edged leaves
- 'Emerald 'n' Gold' — a low-growing, shrubby form to two feet high and three feet across, with yellow-edged green leaves
- 'Green Lane' — with glossy, thick leaves said to resist windburn
- 'Harlequin' —green leaves splashed with pink and white
- 'Kewensis' — a low-growing ground hugger just a few inches high, with small, dense leaves

Euonymus japonicus
Evergreen euonymus

An upright shrub growing 8 to 10 feet high and 4 to 6 feet wide, evergreen euonymus has leathery, glossy, oval leaves with slightly toothed edges. Clusters of tiny white flowers bloom in late spring and are followed in autumn by orange-red fruits. Less hardy than wintercreeper, this species is rated to Zone 6, but it doesn't do well where I live on the south shore of Long Island (Zone 7). It is a better choice for southern gardens.

Use evergreen euonymus in a windbreak, as a hedge or screen (spacing plants three feet apart), or in a mixed border. It takes shearing well.

RECOMMENDED CULTIVARS
- 'Aureo-variegata' — a compact variety 5 to 10 feet high, with yellow-splotched leaves
- 'Grandifolia' — a dense variety to eight feet high that has larger leaves
- 'Microphyllus Albovariegatus' — tiny leaves resemble those of boxwood and are edged in white
- 'Silver King' — upright grower to about six feet high, with leaves edged in white

Euonymus japonicus

Fatsia japonica
Japanese fatsia

Zones: 8–10
Exposure: Partial to full shade
Salt Tolerance: Fair
Drought Resistance: Fair
Deer Resistance: Fair

Northerners know fatsia as a houseplant, but homeowners in warm climates can grow it outdoors as a bold accent plant or to bring a tropical note to shady beds and borders. It also creates a striking effect when massed in front of a wall or next to the house.

This large-leaved shrub grows about three to six feet high near the water. Its leathery evergreen leaves are dark green and divided into seven to nine pointed segments with wavy edges splayed around a central point. The leaves can be more than a foot across. In fall, spherical clusters of tiny white flowers bloom on thin, branched stems and are followed by blue-black berries.

Fatsia has moderate resistance to salt spray, but it does best behind a windbreak at the beach. Its large leaves will turn brownish in sunny, windy locations and can become damaged and tattered in extremely windy spots. Cold, drying winds will also take their toll. The plant is fairly vigorous and prefers humusy, moist, well-drained soils, but will tolerate sandy soils. Give it a shady location where it will receive a couple of hours of sun a day. Fertilize plants with an all-purpose organic fertilizer at the beginning of the season, or once a month with a soluble fertilizer while the plant is growing actively. Cut back on watering during the winter to let the plant rest.

Northern gardeners who want to use fatsia for a tropical effect in the garden can grow it in a large container and move it indoors to a bright location to spend the winter.

Fatsia japonica

Gleditsia triacanthos var. *inermis*
Thornless honey locust

Zones: 4–9
Exposure: Full sun
Salt Tolerance: Good
Drought Tolerance: Good
Deer Resistance: Poor

The species *Gleditsia triacanthos* is native to the eastern and central United States. It has sharp thorns along the trunk, so most homeowners prefer the thornless variety, *inermis*. This medium-size tree has been widely planted around the country, and it can be useful in seashore gardens, too, planted in an open space or close to garden beds and borders.

Honey locust varies in size with the particular variety and the growing conditions, ranging from 30 to 60 or more feet high, with a spreading crown. The graceful leaves are bright green and lacy looking, made up of pairs of small, oblong leaflets. They cast a dappled shade, which is hospitable to shade-tolerant perennials and annuals or lawn grasses that are planted near the tree. Small yellow-green flowers in late spring are extremely fragrant but not very showy, and are followed by brown seedpods.

Honey locust is shallow rooted but will stand up well in wind once it becomes established. Stake it during its first year or two in the garden. Tough and adaptable, honey locust will grow in a range of soils. Fertile, moist but well-drained soil with a neutral to mildly alkaline pH will promote maximum growth, but the tree will also grow in poor, sandy soil. It is quite salt tolerant.

Unfortunately, honey locust sometimes can be troubled by webworms, borers, and spider mites, as well as a variety of diseases including leaf spot, rust, powdery mildew, and cankers. All of these conditions are less likely to occur, however, if only a few trees are present.

RECOMMENDED CULTIVARS

- 'Elegantissima' — shrubby and dense, grows 15 feet high and equally wide
- 'Aurea' — grows 30 to 40 feet high, with leaves that emerge bright yellow-green in spring and deepen to dark green in summer
- 'Rubylace' — leaves start out burgundy in spring and turn deep green by late summer

Gleditsia triacanthos var. *inermis* 'Sunburst'

Hibiscus syriacus
Rose of Sharon

Zones: 5–9

Exposure: Full sun

Salt Tolerance: Fair

Drought Tolerance: Fair

Deer Resistance: Poor

Easy to grow and adaptable, rose of Sharon is an upright shrub with prominent-stamened, single or double flowers of pink, lavender-blue, white, or red in midsummer to early fall. You can treat rose of Sharon like a small tree and prune to keep it neat and limited in size. Or grow it in a row along a driveway, as an informal screen, or in a mixed border.

Rose of Sharon grows 6 to 12 feet high and half as wide, but can be kept smaller with an annual pruning. Give it a sunny location and it will thrive in a range of well-drained soils, even poor ones. Plants need regular watering until they are established, but can tolerate some drought after that. They have some tolerance to salt but generally do best behind a windbreak near the beach or in a spot farther away from the water. Rose of Sharon is seldom troubled by pests or diseases, although deer may nibble on it. Its biggest drawback is that it self-sows and produces a lot of seedlings that you'll have to pull up.

RECOMMENDED CULTIVARS

- 'Aphrodite' — rich rose-pink flowers with a red central eye; does not self-sow
- 'Blue Bird' — lavender-blue flowers with a red eye
- 'Diana' — large, pure white flowers
- 'Lucy' — deep red, double flowers
- 'Minerva' — lavender-pink flowers with a dark red eye

Hibiscus syriacus

Hippophäe rhamnoides
Sea buckthorn

Zones: 3–8

Exposure: Full sun

Salt Tolerance: Good to excellent

Drought Tolerance: Good

Deer Resistance: Good

This bushy, spiny-stemmed shrub handles salt spray, wind, and sand with aplomb. Use it in a windbreak near the beach, to hold soil on the back of the dunes, as an informal hedge or screen, or as a barrier along property boundaries. It would also be at home in a very informal or naturalistic bed or border near the water.

Sea buckthorn grows as a clump of upright, thorny stems to 20 feet high and wide, lined with narrow, silvery green leaves somewhat similar to willow leaves. If both males and females are planted, females will follow their tiny yellow-green spring flowers with orange berrylike fruits in autumn, which persist and brighten winter landscapes (they are very acidic, and birds will pass them by). The plants take shearing and pruning well, and they spread by means of suckers to form colonies.

Plant sea buckthorn in a sunny location in light, well-drained, preferably sandy soil with a neutral to alkaline pH. High fertility will probably kill the plant, so fertilize only lightly, if at all. If you need to prune or clip the plant to improve its shape or limit its size, fall is the best time.

RECOMMENDED CULTIVAR

- 'Sprite' — a dwarf, grows just three to four feet high

Hippophäe rhamnoides

Hydrangea macrophylla

Hydrangea macrophylla
Bigleaf hydrangea

Zones: 6–9	
Exposure: Full sun to light shade	
Salt Tolerance: Fair	
Drought Tolerance: Poor	
Deer Resistance: Poor	

The big round or flat-topped flower heads of hydrangea are synonymous with summer in most East Coast seashore towns. Although they have only a modest tolerance for salt spray, when planted behind a windbreak or away from the water hydrangeas are lovely additions to mixed beds, foundation plantings, screens and space dividers, and borders along drives and walkways. You can also use them as specimen plants or in groupings in a lawn.

Bigleaf hydrangea grows three to four feet high near the beach and to six feet or taller farther inland. Size varies somewhat with cultivar, however. The large leaves are glossy green and broadly oval with toothed edges. The summer flowers may be full, round "snowball," "mophead," or "hortensia" types, or flattened, more delicate "lacecap" flowers with tiny fertile flowers in the center surrounded by a ring of larger, petal-like sterile flowers.

Blue-flowered varieties will be blue in acid soil but will turn pink in alkaline soil. White-flowered varieties do not change their color with soil pH. Grow hydrangeas in full sun to partial or light shade; afternoon shade is particularly helpful in southern gardens. The ideal soil for hydrangeas is moist but well drained and rich in organic matter. Amend very sandy soils with lots of compost before planting. To encourage blue flowers in neutral or perhaps mildly alkaline soil, add sulfur to the soil. For pink flowers in neutral to very slightly acid soil, work in lime or phosphate.

The plants bloom on old wood, setting their buds for next year's flowers after they finish blooming. If you need to prune your hydrangeas for reasons other than removing damaged or diseased growth, prune right after the plants finish blooming or you will remove some of next year's flower buds. But it's better not to prune hydrangeas if you don't have to. Leave them alone and they'll be happy.

Hydrangeas are cold sensitive — or at least their buds are. Cold winters or late frosts that strike when plants have broken dormancy in spring can kill the developing flower buds and eliminate this year's crop of flowers.

Hydrangeas don't usually suffer a lot of pest and disease problems, although the leaves may develop small burned spots where droplets of water sat on them in the sunlight.

RECOMMENDED CULTIVARS
- 'All Summer Beauty' — long blooming and compact, three to four feet high, with blue mophead flowers that form on the current season's growth
- 'Ayesha' — unusual pale lilac-pink mophead
- 'Blue Wave' — lacecap type with big heads of tiny blue or pinkish fertile flowers surrounded by lilac to white sterile florets
- 'Endless Summer' — blooms all summer on both new and old wood, so there's less chance of losing the flowers by pruning at the wrong time or from a late frost that nips the buds; deadhead to encourage continued production of blue (or pink) flowers
- 'Forever Pink' — pink flowers that deepen to rose in cool weather, on three-foot plants; early blooming
- 'Lanarth White' — compact, three to four feet high with lacecap fertile flowers of blue or pink surrounded by white sterile flowers
- 'Mariesii' — to four feet high, with blue to pink lacecap flowers
- 'Nikko Blue' — considered the most salt-tolerant variety by many gardeners and widely grown; big flower heads of rich, true blue (in acid soil)
- 'Pia' — dwarf variety just one to two feet high, with rosy pink flowers in any soil pH

Ilex species

Zones: Vary with species

Exposure: Full sun to light shade, varies with species

Salt Tolerance: Varies with species

Drought Tolerance: Varies

Deer Resistance: Good

Many of us associate holly with Christmas wreaths, but the genus includes trees and shrubs of varying sizes, forms, and leaf types, and not all of them are evergreen. One characteristic shared by all hollies is that only female plants bear the berrylike fruits that are so brightly colorful in many *Ilex* species, and they need a male nearby to pollinate them. Birds love the berries, too. Hollies come in a host of sizes and growth habits, from dense and globelike, to pyramidal, to narrowly upright.

The hollies discussed here are all good choices for seaside gardens. They each have some degree of salt tolerance; how much varies from one species to another. Some make good hedges or screens, others are useful in windbreaks, and some are striking as specimen plants displayed on a lawn or used as accents in mixed borders.

Moist but well-drained soil of average fertility will suit many hollies, but some will grow in dry, very sandy ground and others will tolerate wet, almost boggy, conditions. A location in full sun to partial or light shade is best, although light needs do vary somewhat among the species.

Ilex crenata
Japanese holly

This is a dense, slow-growing shrub with small, oval, leathery, glossy dark green leaves. It looks rather like boxwood and is used in much the same way: for sheared formal hedges or informal plant screens; in mixed borders or foundation plantings; or massed along a driveway or walk.

Japanese holly grows in sun or shade, as much as 15 feet high (although many cultivars are much smaller) and does best in light, moist but well-drained soil with a mildly acid pH. It has slight resistance to salt spray but is best planted behind a windbreak or in another protected spot at the beach. Female plants produce small, glossy black berrylike fruits. Although considered hardy in Zones 5 to 8, Japanese holly generally does best in Zones 5 to 7. Plants take clipping and shearing well, and older plants can be pruned severely to rejuvenate them. Spider mites and black knot disease are sometimes a problem.

RECOMMENDED CULTIVARS

- 'Beehive' — male pollinator, dense and mounded, to four feet high
- 'Compacta' — densely branched dwarf, four to six feet high and equally wide; good choice for an informal, unclipped screen
- 'Glory' — another male, grows four to six feet high and has small leaves
- 'Golden Gem' — has golden leaves and grows five feet tall
- 'Lemon Gem' — has golden leaves in spring that deepen to chartreuse by summer
- 'Helleri' — a dwarf, just one and a half feet high by three feet wide, with very small leaves
- 'Hetzii' — a pyramidal form growing four to five feet high and equally wide
- 'Sky Pencil' — very narrow and upright; it grows fast, takes shearing, and works well in a hedge

Ilex crenata 'Sky Pencil'

Ilex glabra
Inkberry

A native of eastern North America, inkberry is a more informal plant that is an excellent choice for a natural screen or divider in a difficult location. It also can be clipped for a hedge, or massed along a driveway or walk, or included in a foundation planting or mixed border.

Inkberry grows to about eight feet high and equally wide, with glossy, lance-shaped, dark green evergreen leaves. Shiny black berries appear in fall. It is hardy in Zones 5 to 9. The plant will grow in sun or shade, in a range of soils. In the wild it is found in swamps, where it spreads by underground stems to form thickets. Inkberry has good resistance to salt spray but is best with a bit of protection in northern gardens near the beach. The leaves may winterburn in exposed, windy locations. Inkberry grows best in sun but also thrives in light shade in moist, acid soils. It will tolerate alkaline soil, too. After a time the foliage tends to become sparse around the bottom of the stems. Older plants can be cut back severely to rejuvenate them.

RECOMMENDED CULTIVARS

- 'Compacta' — grows only about four feet high and wide when left unpruned, or can be kept as low as two feet when clipped as a hedge
- 'Nigra' — reaches 8 to 10 feet; leaves take on a purplish tone in winter; good salt tolerance; works well as a formal clipped hedge or an informal screen planting

Ilex glabra

Ilex opaca
American holly

Ilex opaca

This is a classic upright, evergreen holly. An American native, it grows as a small tree but often tends to take a shrubby form at the beach. The oval leaves are dark green and leathery, with spiny teeth. Female plants produce red berries when a male pollinator is nearby. The tree grows slowly to 20 to 30 feet high and up to 20 feet wide, and has gray bark.

Use American holly as an accent or specimen plant or in groupings. It needs full sun to partial shade and adapts to a range of soils from sandy to humusy. It is moderately salt tolerant but does best when given some protection from salt winds. (In some areas, including the eastern end of Long Island, American holly grows naturally in the swales between dunes.) Transplant carefully to avoid injuring the root system. Older plants can be pruned hard to rejuvenate them.

American holly is more likely to suffer pest and disease problems than are the other species discussed here. Leaf miners, scales, and other insects can attack, as can a variety of leaf spots, cankers, blights, and other ailments.

RECOMMENDED CULTIVARS

- 'Canary' — growing slowly to 10 feet or more, pyramidal when young and more open and irregular later; produces yellow berries
- 'Cardinal' — grows slowly to 15 to 20 feet high, with small, dark green leaves and abundant red fruit
- 'Carnival' — dense and slow growing, to 50 feet, with very bright orange-red fruit
- 'Old Heavy Berry' — a vigorous grower that produces lots of fruit
- 'Jersey Knight' — a male pollinator variety growing to 30 feet

Ilex pedunculosa
Longstalk holly

Hardy in Zones 6 to 8, longstalk holly is an upright evergreen that takes the form of a large shrub or small tree. Its oblong, shiny, dark green leaves are not spiny and sometimes turn yellowish in winter. Longstalk holly grows 15 to 20 feet high by about 22 feet wide, at a slow to medium rate. Female plants produce bright red fruits. Less well known than many other hollies, this one is very hardy, with good salt tolerance. It is a good choice for northern gardens but doesn't always do well in Zone 8. Longstalk holly is seldom troubled by pests or diseases.

Ilex pedunculosa

Ilex verticillata
Winterberry

A deciduous, rounded shrub with toothed and pointed, bright green, oblong leaves, its best feature is the masses of bright red berries that decorate the plants in fall and remain most of the winter (if the birds don't eat them all). Native to eastern North America, winterberry can grow to 10 feet high and just as wide, although most cultivars stay somewhat smaller. The plant is hardy from Zones 3 to 9, and spreads by means of suckers to form clumps.

Ilex verticillata 'Winter Red'

Winterberry can be part of a shrub border, or you can plant it en masse near the edge of a pond or in another wet place. It will grow in sun or shade and does best in moist, humusy soil with an acidic pH. In alkaline soil winterberry is likely to develop chlorosis (yellowing of leaves). It occasionally suffers mildew or leaf spot.

RECOMMENDED CULTIVARS
- 'Autumn Glow' — compact shrub six to eight feet high, with the typical red fruit and, in some years, warm-colored fall foliage
- 'Berry Nice' — grows six to eight feet high with very bright red fruit; resists mildew
- 'Jim Dandy' — a male variety that can pollinate early-blooming females such as 'Autumn Glow' and 'Red Sprite'
- 'Nana' — just four feet high, with lots of fruit
- 'Southern Gentleman' — a male cultivar; can pollinate late-blooming females including 'Berry Nice' and 'Winter Red'
- 'Winter Red' — grows to 10 feet high and wide, with deep green leaves and very red berries that persist throughout the winter

Ilex vomitoria
Yaupon holly

This is a tough, adaptable species for southern gardens in Zones 7 to 10. It is very salt tolerant, adapts to both wet and dry soils, and is a good choice for windbreaks and screens in exposed locations or wet places. It also can be sheared for a more formal look, or it can be planted as an accent or specimen.

Yaupon holly grows at a moderate pace as an upright evergreen shrub or a small tree to 20 feet high and about 10 feet wide. It has small oval, toothed, glossy deep green leaves. Females bear red fruits, and the plant's attractive light gray bark is another notable feature. This species is native to the eastern United States from Long Island to Florida and the Gulf states. Birds love the berries. Be aware, though, that deer will sometimes eat the leaves.

If you plan to plant yaupon holly in sand, add compost or good topsoil before planting.

RECOMMENDED CULTIVARS
- 'Jewel' — compact and rounded in habit, with abundant fruit
- 'Nana' — a dwarf, mounded form growing three to five feet high
- 'Pendula' — weeping habit, to 20 feet high

Ilex vomitoria

Juniperus species

Zones: Vary with species

Exposure: Full sun

Salt Tolerance: Good

Drought Tolerance: Good

Deer Resistance: Good

The juniper clan is large and varied, and several of its members are good choices for seaside gardens. As a group, junipers are tough, adaptable plants. Hardy, tolerant of many soil types, and unattractive to deer, they often will grow where few other plants can survive. As long as they get plenty of sun, they can grow practically anywhere.

When you plant junipers, as when you plant any other tree or shrub, be sure to allow enough space in the garden for them to comfortably reach their full mature size.

Junipers take many forms, from low, sprawling ground covers, to pyramidal, wide-spreading, globe-shaped, or densely columnar shrubs, to conical or pyramid-shaped trees. They have flat, needlelike leaves that may be light green, rich deep green, golden, blue-green, or silvery, depending on the cultivar. Their small cones look more like berries (they are called juniper berries) and may be brown or blue to blue-black, with a whitish bloom on the surface.

Junipers grow best in well-drained soil. They need lots of sun, and will look ratty in more than very light shade. They need little pruning except to remove branches damaged by storms. Junipers are resilient plants, although rust, blights, and bagworms can sometimes cause problems. Cedar apple rust and cedar hawthorn rust can be spread between some junipers and hawthorns or apple trees, so do not plant these species near one another. Bagworms, if they are too numerous, can destroy the foliage and are most problematic in warmer climates.

Junipers can play a variety of roles in seaside gardens, according to their size and shape. Tall, dense ones are good in wind-breaks and screen plantings that create a sheltered area downwind for perennials and other garden plants. Narrow, upright plants work well as hedges, since junipers can take the regular pruning and shaping that keep a hedge looking neat. Some junipers, such as the sculptural Hollywood juniper (*Juniperus chinensis* 'Torulosa'), make interesting specimen plants or vertical accents, and low-growing spreaders such as creeping juniper (*J. horizontalis*) are durable, low-maintenance ground covers for areas that don't get foot traffic.

The junipers described below can withstand the windy conditions, sandy soil, and salty air that typify the seashore environment.

Juniperus chinensis

Juniperus chinensis
Chinese juniper

This species of juniper varies widely in height and shape among its many cultivars, although the most typical form is a rather narrow, upright, egg-shaped to conical tree. Needles range in color from green to gray-green to bluish. Chinese junipers have attractive peeling brown bark. There are dozens of cultivars, most hardy in Zones 4 to 9.

RECOMMENDED CULTIVARS

- 'Aurea' — columnar, to 35 feet high, with golden foliage
- 'Blue Point' — pyramidal, to eight or more feet high, blue-green foliage
- 'Hetzii' — upright, to 15 feet high and wide, silvery foliage; 'Hetzii Columnaris' is narrower and good for screens and hedges
- 'Torulosa' or 'Kaizuka' — Hollywood juniper, has interesting, twisted branches and grows to about 15 feet high, sculptural and dramatic
- 'Milky Way' — spreading, three to four feet high; dark green foliage splashed with white
- 'Pfitzeriana' — Pfitzer juniper, one of the most widely grown; wide spreading, to 5 or more feet high and 10 or more feet wide, with drooping branch tips; various cultivars bred from it are yellowish, bluish, or more compact
- *J. c.* var. *sargentii* — low and spreading, to two feet high and eight feet across, with bluish green foliage; makes a good ground cover
- 'Sea Green' — compact and vase shaped, to six feet high and six to eight feet wide, with bright green foliage

Juniperus conferta
Shore juniper

Hardy in Zones 6 to 9, shore juniper is low and spreading, growing slowly to one and a half or two feet high and reaching eight feet wide. The prickly needles are blue-green, turning bronzy in winter. Shore juniper can be planted to help stabilize dunes. It can take shade better than most junipers, but cannot stand wet soil.

RECOMMENDED CULTIVARS

- 'Blue Pacific' — bluer and smaller than the species, just one foot high or less, and holds its color better in winter
- 'Boulevard' — grayish green and hugs the ground
- 'Silver Mist' — compact, with a silvery cast to its blue-green needles

Juniperus conferta

Juniperus horizontalis
Creeping juniper

Hardy in Zones 3 to 9, creeping juniper stays low and spreads to form a mat to two feet high and eight feet wide. Its soft-textured foliage is silvery

Juniperus horizontalis

or bluish green and turns purplish in winter. Creeping juniper makes a good ground cover.

RECOMMENDED CULTIVARS

- 'Bar Harbor' — discovered growing along rocky bluffs overlooking the sea in Maine, grows just a foot high, with prickly bluish green needles; very tolerant of salt spray
- 'Douglasii' — Waukegan juniper, has trailing branches with blue-green foliage and grows rather quickly to and and a half feet high; does well in very sandy soil
- 'Plumosa' — Andorra juniper, is dense and wide spreading, to 2 feet high and as much as 10 feet wide, with grayish green foliage; widely grown but sometimes suffers from blight
- 'Wiltonii' — blue rug juniper, grows just six inches high and six or more feet wide, with silvery blue foliage; tolerates cold but also grows well in the South

Juniperus virginiana
Eastern red cedar

This is the source of the aromatic wood used to make storage chests and closets. Native to eastern and central North America, it is hardy in Zones 2 to 9 and is often found colonizing fields and meadows. The tree is dense and pyramid shaped when young, but the branches of older trees often droop at the ends. The peeling bark is reddish brown or grayish. This species is good for screening, planting in groups, and naturalizing.

Eastern red cedar makes a good windbreak, but it can sometimes windburn in beachfront gardens. Smaller trees of five feet or less acclimate better to the conditions and are less likely to burn, so start with small plants. Female trees generally do better than males, and offer the advantage (if you are trying to populate the dunes) that birds will eat the berries and spread the seeds through their droppings.

One cautionary note: Eastern red cedar is susceptible to cedar apple rust and cedar hawthorn rust. If you have it in your garden, do not plant it near hawthorns (apple trees are not generally a good choice for seashore gardens).

RECOMMENDED CULTIVARS

- 'Glauca' — narrow and columnar, to 25 feet high, with foliage that is bluish in spring, silvery green in summer
- 'Grey Owl' — three feet high and six feet wide; grayish green foliage
- 'Pendula' — weeping red cedar, to about 40 feet high, with spreading branches from which the branchlets droop
- 'Pyramidalis' — a name used for various pyramidal forms of the plant; height and spread vary; foliage turns purple in winter
- 'Silver Spreader' — two or three feet high and twice as broad; silvery foliage

Ligustrum species

Zones:	Vary with species
Exposure:	Full sun to light shade
Salt Tolerance:	Good to moderate
Drought Tolerance:	Good
Deer Resistance:	Good

Privet is ubiquitous up and down the East Coast, and with good reason. It makes a dense, high hedge that can be sheared into neat green walls (angled slightly outward for best plant growth). There are both evergreen and deciduous species, and even a deciduous hedge is effective in winter because of its dense growth. At the seashore, privet hedges protect gardens from salt and wind, although they're not usually tough enough to serve as a first line of defense. The garden profiled on page 96, however, relies on a privet hedge for its protection. Behind the dunes, or as a second line of defense, privet is very effective.

Privet isn't limited to hedging, although that's how most people use it. For a different look, consider planting privet as a billowy, informal, unclipped screen.

The plants are sturdy and adaptable with good tolerance for salt. They grow well in full sun to light shade. They will adapt to a range of soils, except for very wet, soggy ones, and are easy to grow. Both deciduous and evergreen species have dark green oval leaves and, in summer, sprays of highly scented white flowers that are pleasantly fragrant or headache inducing, depending upon your point of view. Privets are occasionally plagued by leaf diseases or attacked by aphids, scale, or other pests, but for the most part you can expect them to be healthy and trouble-free.

Set plants about two feet apart when planting a formal hedge, or three to four feet apart for an unclipped screen planting. Older hedges periodically need to be severely pruned to rejuvenate them. Clipping the hedge so the sides slope slightly outward will allow all the leaves to receive good light and will prolong the time a hedge can grow before needing rejuvenation.

Ligustrum japonicum
Japanese privet

An evergreen shrub, Japanese privet grows vigorously to 12 feet high and about 6 feet wide. The oval leaves are glossy and very deep green, and flowers bloom in spring. Small, shiny black berries appear in late fall and remain into winter. Hardy in Zones 7 to 10, Japanese privet is moderately salt tolerant, but needs some protection from salt wind, especially in the North.

RECOMMENDED CULTIVARS
- 'Texanum'— a compact six to eight feet high and four to six feet wide
- 'Texanum Silver Star'— a slower grower with white-edged leaves
- 'Variegatum'— with leaves edged and splotched with white

Ligustrum japonicum hedge

Ligustrum ovalifolium
California privet

This is shrub that may be deciduous, semievergreen, or evergreen, depending on the climate. It is considered hardy in Zones 6 to 8 and tends to be deciduous in the northern part of its range and evergreen in the south. Vigorous and dense, California privet makes a good salt barrier, although southern gardeners have reported it as being less salt tolerant for them than Japanese privet. On Long Island, it affords good protection, and holds on to its leaves until the end of December in most winters. The glossy, dark green leaves turn purplish in winter in locations where the plant is evergreen. The sprays of tiny, white, late-spring flowers are followed by small black fruits in fall.

RECOMMENDED CULTIVARS
- 'Argenteum'— white-edged leaves
- 'Aureum'— leaves have a broad golden border surrounding a green center
- *L. o.* var. *regelianum* — regal privet; a low and dense, rounded form growing five to six feet high and equally wide

Zones: *M. pensylvanica, 3–6; M. cerifera, 6–9*
Exposure: Full sun to partial shade
Salt Tolerance: Good to excellent
Drought Tolerance: Good
Deer Resistance: Good

Both these plants can be used for informal screening and to help control erosion on dunes after beach grass or sea oats have become established. Bayberry is an excellent addition to beachfront windbreaks, and it can also be useful for screening farther from the water. Wax myrtle tends to do best in the lee of the dunes, and it also makes a good specimen or accent plant when pruned as a small tree. Both species tolerate a range of soils and have good tolerance for both salt and drought. Bayberry is arguably the tougher of the two, adapting to soils from dry sand dunes to moist and almost marshy or clayey situations.

Myrica pensylvanica
Northern bayberry

Though considered semievergreen, bayberry can lose all its leaves in a hard winter. Plants grow to 10 feet high and spread by suckers to form colonies. The leaves are oblong, two to four inches long, and deep green. They are wonderfully aromatic when crushed.

In fall female plants bear clusters of grayish white berries, which can be used to make candles. They also attract birds — in fall along the beaches of southern New Jersey, great flocks of tree swallows descend on the dunes to eat the bayberries.

Like wax myrtle, bayberry can fix nitrogen in the soil. It will grow in practically any soil from sand dune to wetland. It's a tough, adaptable plant, a good choice for a windbreak at the beach, to stabilize dunes once beach grass is established, and for low-maintenance beds and borders. It combines well with broad-leaved evergreens. Bayberry can take salt and drought, and isn't bothered by strong winds. In a screen or windbreak, space plants two to three feet apart. Otherwise, set them four to five feet apart.

Myrica cerifera
Wax myrtle

This broad-leaved evergreen shrub or small tree grows from 10 to 15 feet high or taller. The variety *pumila* is just three feet tall. Its leathery, narrowly oblong leaves are yellowish green, and aromatic when crushed. Its light gray bark is attractive. In fall, female plants produce clusters of small, waxy white berries (if a male plant grows nearby) that can be used in making candles. Birds like them, too.

The roots of wax myrtle fix nitrogen in the soil like legumes do, enabling the plant to grow in poor soils. It tolerates drought and salt wind, although it does best behind the dunes where it receives a little protection. It is sensitive to cold, and the leaves will turn brown or fall when the mercury hits zero. In the wild, wax myrtle inhabits the swales between dunes, where the soil is a bit moister than higher up on the dunes. Leaf diseases are sometimes a problem.

Use wax myrtle as a hedge or screen, spacing plants three to four feet apart. Otherwise, space plants five or six feet apart. Or prune its lower limbs to turn it into a small tree and use it as a specimen or accent plant. Wax myrtle combines well in the landscape with junipers and other evergreens. It is also useful for controlling erosion on the lee side of dunes.

Myrica pensylvanica

Myrica cerifera

Nerium oleander
Oleander

Zones: 8–10	
Exposure: Full sun to partial shade	
Salt Tolerance: Good	
Drought Tolerance: Good	
Deer Resistance: Good	

This warm-climate evergreen is an upright shrub that generally grows quickly to 6 to 10 feet high near the beach and to 15 feet away from the water in protected locations. It has a spread of up to 10 feet. The lance-shaped leaves are dark green. In summer, plants bear clusters of single or double flowers in shades of pink, red, and yellow, as well as white, at the tips of the stems. Red-flowered varieties are said to be hardiest. All parts of the plant are poisonous if eaten, or if burned and the smoke is inhaled. Handle it with care.

Oleander has good tolerance to salt wind, and is reasonably drought tolerant. Give it well-drained, moderately fertile soil. Fertilize monthly with an all-purpose fertilizer when plants are growing actively, or two or three times during the growing season with an all-purpose organic fertilizer. The most common pests are scale, aphids, and mealybugs.

Oleander makes a lovely clipped hedge or informal screen; space plants three to four feet apart. It is a nice addition to mixed borders and back-of-the-garden plantings, and makes a handsome specimen or accent plant. You can also grow it in a tub or other large container.

RECOMMENDED CULTIVARS
- 'Algiers' — dark red, single flowers
- 'Casablanca' — single white flowers
- 'Hardy Pink' — single, salmon pink blossoms
- 'Isle of Capri' — single, soft yellow flowers
- 'Ruby Lace' — large, ruby red flowers with wavy edges

Nerium oleander

Nyssa sylvatica
Black tupelo

Zones: 4 to 9	
Exposure: Full sun to partial shade	
Salt Tolerance: Fair	
Drought Tolerance: Poor	
Deer Resistance: Poor	

A native of eastern North America, the black tupelo can be found growing in the wild in woodlands and swamps. It's a handsome tree, growing as tall as 50 feet or so, with a spread of 20 to 30 feet. It is pyramid shaped when young, but becomes more spreading with age. At the seashore it may take the form of a multi-stemmed tree without a central leader. The lower branches tend to droop. Black tupelo's greatest asset, ornamentally speaking, is its brilliant autumn color. The three- to five-inch-long oval leaves, which are leathery and glossy dark green in summer, turn rich shades of yellow, orange, red, and even purple in fall. Female trees produce small blue fruits in fall.

Black tupelo grows well in full sun to partial shade. The ideal soil is rich and moist but well drained, with an acidic pH, but the tree is somewhat adaptable. It has a fair degree of salt tolerance, but does best with the protection of a windbreak near the beach.

Trees adapt best if planted when still small; larger trees are difficult to transplant because of the large taproot. Black tupelo sometimes suffers dieback of branch tips, scale, or leaf miners, but these are not usually major problems. Fall is the best time to do any necessary pruning.

Nyssa sylvatica

Zones: *P. abies,* 2–7; *P. pungens* var. *glauca,* 3–8
Exposure: Full sun to partial shade
Salt Tolerance: Fair
Drought Tolerance: Poor
Deer Resistance: Good

The stately spruces are mostly big trees and belong to the cooler regions of the Northern Hemisphere. Some of them are good choices for seashore gardens in Zone 7 and north, with some protection from a windbreak or dune or away from the water. The root system is spreading and fairly shallow, so give new trees good support until they become well established in the garden. Spruces tolerate a range of soils, although they thrive in moist but well-drained, sandy soil with an acid pH. They need water during dry weather, especially during their first few years in the garden. Spruces sometimes suffer from spider mites, spruce gall aphids (which cause branch tips to die), and spruce budworm.

Spruces, especially blue spruce, make interesting specimen trees. Dwarf varieties can add year-round interest to beds and borders or rock gardens, or you can plant them behind a retaining wall or in a foundation planting.

Picea abies

Picea abies
Norway spruce

Pyramidal in form, Norway spruce grows 40 to 60 feet high and 25 or so feet wide. Its needles are rich green, and the cones are slender and brown, up to six inches long.

RECOMMENDED CULTIVARS
- 'Argenteospicata' — has white-tipped branches
- 'Aurea' — new needles are golden, then deepen to yellow-green
- 'Flat Top' — just one foot tall and three feet across; forms a dense, flat-topped mound
- 'Inversa' or 'Pendula' — weeping Norway spruce, forms a large, low mound that will tumble over a wall or rocks, or can be staked and trained to grow upright with weeping branches
- 'Nidiformis' — bird's nest spruce, forms a dense, spreading mound with branches in horizontal layers and a hollow central "nest," two feet high and three feet across
- 'Pumila' — globe-shaped dwarf variety three to four feet high with an equal spread

Picea pungens var. *glauca*
Blue spruce

Known for its blue-green color, blue spruce is quite tough and durable at the seashore. The tree grows 30 to 40 feet high, with a spread of 10 to 15 feet, and numerous cultivars have been bred from it. Blue spruce is pyramidal in form and has oblong brown cones two to four inches long. It does best in full sun and can tolerate drought better than does Norway spruce.

RECOMMENDED CULTIVARS
- 'Fat Albert' — broadly pyramidal, 10 to 12 feet high and 7 to 8 feet wide, with good blue-green color
- 'Globosa' — round and shrublike with a flat top, to three feet high and four to five feet wide
- 'Hoopsii' — silvery blue, especially new needles, pyramidal form, to 30 or more feet tall and 5 feet wide
- 'Montgomery' — broadly pyramidal; dwarf to five feet high and four to six feet wide
- 'R. H. Montgomery' — popular older variety with very blue needles, grows to six feet tall and five feet wide

Picea pungens var. *glauca*

Pinus species

Zones: Vary with species
Exposure: Full sun
Salt Tolerance: Varies with species
Drought Tolerance: Fair to good
Deer Resistance: Good

Windswept pines have long been part of seashore landscapes. Japanese black pine (*Pinus thunbergii,* or *thunbergiana*) has been widely planted along the East Coast because of its resilience in the face of salt spray, wind, and dry, sandy conditions. It has survived where many other trees would fail. Now, however, the black pines are dying, the victims of beetles and disease. Scotch pine (*P. sylvestris*) and red pine (*P. densiflora*) are also at risk.

Other pines popular among gardeners, such as white pine (*P. strobus*) and Japanese red pine (*P. parviflora*), can't handle salt very well, although white pine is widely planted for screening away from the water.

Still, there are a number of pines that are good choices for seashore landscapes.

Among the toughest are mugo pine (*P. mugo*) and pitch pine (*P. rigida*). In the Southeast, the native loblolly pine (*P. taeda*) holds up well. Bosnian pine (*P. leucodermis*) is being planted as a replacement for Japanese black pine.

There are lots of uses for pines in the landscape. Plant them in groups or use them to mark boundaries, or to provide a backdrop for gardens. Dwarf varieties find a place in mixed beds and borders, rock gardens, and foundation plantings.

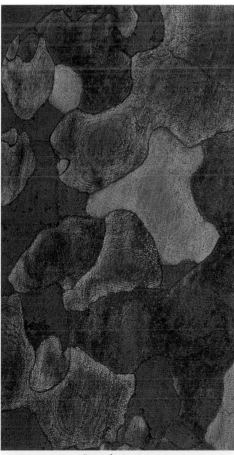

Pinus bungeana

Pinus bungeana
Lacebark pine

This pine has striking bark that peels away in patches of cream, green, and reddish to grayish brown. Pyramidal to rounded and spreading in form, it grows slowly to 30 to 50 feet high with a spread of 20 to 25 feet. It often grows as a multi-trunked tree. If necessary, remove some of the lower branches to reveal more of the bark. Lacebark pine is hardy in Zones 4 to 8. Although it is native to China, this handsome tree does well in gardens along the Atlantic coast. Give it a location away from the beach, with full sun and well-drained soil.

Like all other evergreens, lacebark pine adds interest to the landscape year-round. Its beautiful bark is especially attractive in winter. Lacebark pine makes a handsome specimen tree; site it where you can easily see the bark.

Pinus leucodermis
Bosnian pine

Touted in some quarters as a potential substitute for Japanese black pine, Bosnian pine is tough and drought tolerant. It grows slowly to 40 or 50 feet high and 25 to 30 feet wide. It is pyramidal and dense, with small cones that are blue at first, and gray bark. Bosnian pine has good salt tolerance and is hardy in Zones 5 to 8.

Pinus leucodermis

Pinus mugo
Mugo pine

It's difficult to typify the mugo pine, because so many varied forms are available. The tree may be broad, pyramidal, and upright, to ground hugging and spreading, to small and round. But all of them are extremely tough, and well able to handle salty wind and drought. The size ranges from 2-foot-high by 6- to 8-foot-wide dwarfs up to 20-foot trees. Mugo pines are hardy in Zones 2 to 7.

The taller mugo pines can help protect gardens from salty winds near the beach; plant them behind the dunes. Or use them in windbreaks or screens. Dwarf types are good additions to mixed borders, rock gardens, and foundation plantings, or you can plant them in groups.

RECOMMENDED CULTIVARS
- 'Mops' — round dwarf about three feet high and three feet wide
- *P. m.* var. *mugo* — low grower less than eight feet high and twice as wide, but very variable
- *P. m.* var. *pumilio* — also dwarf, also quite variable, but generally bushy, low, and spreading, two to four feet high and six feet across

Pinus mugo

Pinus nigra

Pinus nigra
Austrian pine

A dense and pyramidal tree, Austrian pine becomes more open and spreading with age, fast growing to 50 to 60 feet high and 20 to 25 feet wide. It has rather attractive ridged bark. Hardy in Zones 4 to 7, Austrian pine tolerates heat and some drought, and adapts to a range of soils, especially if it receives moisture regularly. Pine nematodes can, unfortunately, kill the tree. If nematodes are a problem in your area, don't plant this pine in your landscape. Use Austrian pine in a windbreak or screen away from the beach, or plant it in groups.

RECOMMENDED CULTIVAR
- 'Hornibrookiana' — a compact, slower-growing form to about five feet high

Pinus rigida
Pitch pine

This is a good one for beachfront properties. It is scrubby looking, but can become dramatically gnarled and windswept near the water. Native to eastern North America, pitch pine has excellent tolerance for salt, wind, and sand. Use it in a windbreak for oceanfront property. The tree is hardy in Zones 4 to 7, and grows to about 50 feet high (or less near the beach) and up to 30 feet wide. It thrives in light, sandy, moist but well-drained, acidic soil, given its druthers. But it is tough and adaptable.

Pinus rigida

Pinus taeda
Loblolly pine

Native to the mid-Atlantic and southeastern regions, loblolly pine grows rather quickly to about 50 feet high and 40 feet wide, with long needles, furrowed bark, and resinous wood. The tree is cone shaped when young but becomes broader, looser, and more oval in time. It is widely grown for use as lumber. Loblolly pine is hardy in Zones 6 to 9, and best suited to southern gardens. It prefers acid soil but otherwise adapts to many soil conditions. Loblolly pine is easy to transplant, and it develops a wide-ranging system of lateral roots that provide good anchorage.

This pine is often planted to create a quick screen. For a small property, look for the dwarf form, 'Nana'.

Pinus taeda

Pittosporum tobira
Japanese pittosporum

Zones: 8–10	
Exposure: Sun or shade	
Salt Tolerance: Excellent	
Drought Tolerance: Good	
Deer Resistance: Poor	

Northerners know pittosporum as a houseplant, but in the South it is found in outdoor gardens. Its ability to withstand direct exposure to salt winds and spray makes it an excellent choice for seaside gardens.

Pittosporum is a broad-leaved evergreen shrub 6 to 10 feet high, with an equal spread. Its glossy, leathery, dark green, oblong leaves are arranged in whorls around the stem. In spring there are clusters of fragrant, bell-shaped white flowers, and brown fruits with orange-red seeds follow in autumn. Pittosporum is vigorous and grows fairly quickly in full sun to almost full shade when given loose, well-drained soil. If you are planting at the beach, amend the sand with compost first. Fertilize annually with a high-nitrogen fertilizer to maintain good leaf color.

Pittosporum makes an attractive informal screen, with plants set four feet apart. It works well as a hedge, too; plant two feet apart. To include pittosporum in a windbreak, set plants three feet apart for good coverage.

Pittosporum tobira

Zones: *P. caroliniana*, 7–10; *P. maritima*, 3–6
Exposure: Full sun
Salt Tolerance: Fair, but varies
Drought Tolerance: Varies
Deer Resistance: Good (*P. maritima*)

This genus contains cherries, peaches, and plums, along with a variety of ornamental trees and shrubs, including some evergreens. Two species, both native to eastern North America, can often be found in seashore gardens.

Prunus caroliniana
Carolina cherry laurel

An evergreen shrub or small tree, Carolina cherry laurel grows to 20 or more feet high, but near the beach is usually kept pruned to 10 to 15 feet. It has oblong, pointed, glossy dark green leaves two to four inches long, and clusters of small, white, intensely fragrant flowers in spring. Shiny little black fruits follow in fall and provide food for birds. The stems give off a scent of cherries when they are broken or bruised. Native to the Southeast, Carolina cherry laurel is hardy in Zones 7 to 10.

Plants have some salt tolerance, but need to be grown behind a windbreak or in another sheltered location close to the beach. Amend very sandy soil with compost before planting.

Many homeowners plant Carolina cherry laurel as a high, clipped hedge (space plants about three feet apart) or as an informal screen (with plants spaced eight feet apart). You can also plant a row of them along a driveway or property boundary, or use them as single specimens.

RECOMMENDED CULTIVAR

- 'Bright 'n Tight' — compact, to 10 feet high and 6 to 8 feet wide.

Prunus maritima
Beach plum

This deciduous shrub grows wild in dune fields along the coast and has become a garden plant, too. Hardy in Zones 3 to 6, it has excellent tolerance for salt and wind. Plants grow to six feet high or more, with oblong leaves, fragrant white flowers in spring, and purple to reddish fruits in late summer that can be used to make jam. Beach plum spreads to form a clump.

Because of its tolerance for wind and salt, beach plum can be part of a windbreak or shelterbelt at the beach. It will help to hold sand in the dunes. Beach plum also works in low-maintenance beds and borders.

Prunus maritima

Prunus caroliniana

Quercus species

Zones: Vary with species	
Exposure: Full sun	
Salt Tolerance: Varies	
Drought Tolerance: Fair	
Deer Resistance: Good	

Oaks are valued for their hard wood, the shade they cast, and the acorns that feed wildlife. Many of them would have a hard time at the seashore, but the ones discussed here can handle the conditions. Near the beach they are best planted behind a windbreak or in another sheltered location. Live oak can take more salt than the others. Away from the water you have more leeway. In seashore landscapes, oaks can serve as shade trees or specimens in a lawn or other large space.

Quercus virginiana

Quercus alba
White oak

This big, sturdy tree grows slowly to 60 feet or higher (taller inland), with a rounded, spreading crown. It has the lobed leaves typical of many oaks, and these turn deep burgundy in fall. Native to the eastern United States, white oak is hardy in Zones 4 to 9. It prefers seashore conditions when the sandy soil is amended with compost. Oaks in general are subject to a host of pest and disease problems, but white oaks seem to be seldom bothered by them.

Quercus marilandica
Blackjack oak

A southeastern native, blackjack oak is a shrubby tree with a low, spreading habit. It has glossy, leathery, dark green leaves and rough dark bark. Blackjack oak can grow as high as 40 feet, but it is usually smaller and shrubbier at the shore. It is hardy in Zones 6 to 9.

Blackjack oak has good tolerance for salt and wind. It also grows naturally in poor, often sandy, acidic soils. Blackjack oaks aren't widely sold in nurseries, although they are available. If you have them on your property, think twice before getting rid of them in favor of showier species.

Quercus alba

Quercus virginiana
Live oak

This is another native that has become a southern classic. Hardy in Zones 8 to 10, live oak is tall and stately inland with wide-spreading branches that come almost to the ground. At the seashore, though, it is often more shrubby, kept lower by the fierce salt winds. But older specimens can be magnificent even near the beach. They can be anywhere from 6 to 40 feet high, depending on conditions.

Live oak grows very slowly and sends a large taproot deep into the ground in search of moisture and nutrients. As the taproot develops, live oak is slow to become established in the garden — it can take three or four years for it to settle in. Live oak needs good drainage and will grow in poor, sandy soil. Fertilize each year in spring with an all-purpose fertilizer. Trees have moderate to good tolerance for salt spray and wind, but generally they do best behind the dunes or at a modest distance back from the water. Live oak can also be planted on the lee side of a dune to help control erosion.

Zones: Vary with species	
Exposure: Full sun	
Salt Tolerance: Good	
Drought Tolerance: Good	
Deer Resistance: Good	

Sumacs are wild-looking shrubs most at home in naturalistic or informal gardens. Their brilliant autumn color is arguably their most ornamental feature. They are very tough, and able to tolerate salt wind and spray. They adapt to a range of soils, although their preference is for moist but well-drained soil of reasonable fertility. Sumacs are spreaders and not for small gardens. Use them in windbreaks, to hold soil on a bank or slope, or in dry, stony soil. One note of caution: Make sure you do not bring into your garden poison sumac (*Rhus vernix*), which has whitish fruits. It causes a nasty skin rash in susceptible people. The following sumacs are all natives and are good choices for seaside gardens.

Rhus copallina
Flameleaf sumac

The aptly named flameleaf sumac has glorious autumn foliage of bright scarlet and red. Hardy in Zones 4 to 9, it grows in the wild as a shrub or small tree in acidic, poor soils in the Southeast. It grows to 10 feet high at the seashore, with an interesting spreading form. The compound leaves are divided into up to 21 oblong leaflets that are shiny and dark green in summer and brilliant in fall. Clusters of red fruits are produced on female plants in fall and attract birds.

Flameleaf sumac spreads by suckers to form vigorous colonies and can be a pest in the South. It prefers some moisture but will get by in poor, dry soil. This sumac is less salt tolerant than the others described here and needs some protection from salt wind or the foliage may burn. That said, it can be used to control erosion on the lee side of dunes. Set plants six to eight feet apart.

Rhus typhina

Rhus glabra
Smooth sumac

Hardy in Zones 4 to 9, smooth sumac grows as an upright shrub or small tree to 12 feet high and wide. Its compound green leaves, composed of oblong, toothed leaflets, turn bright orange, red, and purple in fall. Scarlet fruits hang on female plants into winter if the local wildlife doesn't get to them first. This species is good for planting in groups or even masses in poor, dry soil.

RECOMMENDED CULTIVAR
- 'Laciniata' — finely dissected leaflets

Rhus glabra

Rhus typhina
Staghorn sumac

This sumac was named for the resemblance its branches bear to deer antlers. Hardy in Zones 3 to 8, it grows to about 15 feet high and wide. It grows as an open, spreading shrub, or sometimes a small tree. The compound leaves are made up of oblong leaflets with toothed edges. The velvety stems are covered with soft hairs.

Staghorn sumac adapts to many kinds of soil as long as it is well drained; it can't stand soggy ground. It tolerates a good amount of drought. Like other sumacs, this one is not seriously bothered by pests or disease. You can rejuvenate old, overgrown plants by cutting them back to the ground in late winter. Plant staghorn sumac in groups or masses; it is especially useful where little else will grow.

Rosa species

Zones:	Vary with type
Exposure:	Full sun
Salt Resistance:	Varies
Drought Tolerance:	Poor, except *R. rugosa*
Deer Resistance:	Poor

Roses are part of many seashore gardens. With good protection from salt spray and wind, and in soil well amended with compost, many kinds of roses will thrive. Which kinds are right for your garden depends upon your location and the amount of time and effort you want to devote to them.

TYPES OF ROSES

Shrub roses take up the most space but require the least amount of effort from the gardener. Just deadhead them to remove faded flowers and prune as needed to remove dead or damaged growth. Look for stems that are pale and dry and snap when bent, or canes that are shriveled, not firm. Shrub roses make lovely additions to mixed beds and borders.

Hybrid teas are harder to mix with other plants, so many gardeners like to grow them in beds of their own. Low, sprawling perennials such as nepeta, perennial candytuft, dianthus, and lamb's ears and annuals like sweet alyssum and Wave petunias make good companions for hybrid teas and other bush roses. Just don't let them get too close to the base of a rosebush. Clematis is lovely trained with climbing roses or clambering over shrub roses.

Train climbing roses on trellises, arches, and arbors for beautiful architectural accents in the garden. Rambler roses are lovely trained on a fence or allowed to scramble over the ground.

Hybrid tea roses (hardy in Zones 5 to 10) and climbers (hardy in Zones 4 to 10) need special protection close to the ocean in winter. They also need pruning, and climbers need training, too. Prune hybrid teas in spring, when the weather has settled and they begin to break their buds. For the greatest vigor, remove all but the strongest four or five canes, and cut those back to about eight inches. On climbing roses, cut back to the ground old, woody canes on older plants that have developed bark. Lightly prune other canes, cutting them back by just a few inches.

WINTER PROTECTION

In northern areas, gardeners near the beach may want to protect hybrid teas over the winter by covering them with a loose mulch of salt hay or shredded leaves and surrounding the bed with a burlap windscreen. Climbers can be wrapped in burlap and left on their supports where winter temperatures do not drop below −5°F. In colder areas, carefully remove canes of climbers from their support and lay them on the ground. Cover with a loose mulch at least six inches deep, and cover with burlap.

PESTS AND DISEASE

One thing all kinds of roses need by the seaside is good air circulation. Roses are prone to disease, especially black spot and mildew. The heavy, humid summer air and frequent fogs along the coast can provide the perfect environment for disease pathogens to develop. Although some gardeners believe the salty air actually discourages disease, it is wise to allow plenty of room between plants so air can circulate freely. Space hybrid teas, climbers, and ramblers two to three feet apart, and shrub roses four to five feet apart. Use the larger spacing in warm parts of Zone 7 and south.

If Japanese beetles are a problem in your area, be on the lookout for them and take appropriate measures if they appear. Treating lawns with milky spore helps prevent future infestations by killing the larvae that develop under the lawn.

Rosa banksiae

Rosa banksiae
Lady Banks' rose

Southern gardeners in Zones 8 and 9 can grow Lady Banks' rose. This vigorous semievergreen rambler can grow to 15 feet with proper support. Left to its own devices, the thornless stems will ascend to four or five feet, then arch over to trail on the ground. In late spring, plants produce clusters of fragrant, single or double yellow or white flowers.

Lady Banks' rose has some resistance to salt spray, but needs the protection of a windbreak at the beach. It will grow in full sun or partial shade. Some gardeners train it on a trellis or let it climb a tree; others let it spill over a wall. The only pruning it needs is the removal of old stems. Provide mulch or other protection in winter.

Rosa rugosa
Saltspray rose

One of the absolute best roses for the seaside is the saltspray or beach rose, *Rosa rugosa*. Rugosas, hardy in Zones 3 to 10, bloom through much of the summer with gloriously fragrant magenta, pink, white, or yellow flowers. Pink and magenta varieties are generally the most vigorous, yellows the least. The plants are robust, very thorny shrubs to six feet high that tolerate salt and will grow in very sandy soil. They spread by means of suckers and can become a bit of a pest. In fall, large, orange-red hips decorate the plants. Rugosas make a good barrier or screen, and can be planted on the lee side of dunes or on slopes and banks to help control erosion.

RECOMMENDED CULTIVAR
- 'Thérèse Bugnet' — double pink blossoms

Rosa rugosa

Memorial rose

Rosa wichuraiana
Memorial rose

Hardy in Zones 5 to 9, memorial rose is a semi-evergreen shrub with long, vinelike stems that can reach 20 feet. It can be trained on a trellis or fence, or allowed to ramble over the ground as a low, mounded ground cover. The stems will root where they touch the ground if you cover them with soil. In summer, plants bear fragrant, single white flowers with golden stamens. In fall there are red hips. Memorial rose needs some protection from salt winds, but it can take sandy, infertile soil and a fair amount of drought. Try it on a bank or slope.

Ramblers

Rambler roses, with their clusters of small, full flowers, also have good tolerance for wind and salt. Plants produce slender stems 15 or more feet long and are hardy in Zones 5 to 10. You can train ramblers on a fence or use them to cover swales and banks — the stems will root where they touch the ground. They are not fussy about soil. Ramblers bloom on stems produced the previous year. Prune them in spring to remove thin canes that crowd together in the center of the plant. After blooming, cut off at least some of the canes that produced flowers to make room for the stems that will bloom next year. Fasten those new stems into place.

RECOMMENDED CULTIVARS
- 'American Pillar' — deep pink with a white eye
- 'Goldfinch' — yellow
- 'May Queen' — pink
- 'Seagull' — white, fragrant
- 'Veilchenblau' — purple and white

Ramblers

Sabal palmetto
Cabbage palmetto

Zones: 8–11
Exposure: Full sun to partial shade
Salt Tolerance: Good to excellent
Drought Tolerance: Good
Deer Resistance: Good

The state tree of North Carolina, cabbage palmetto grows as far north as about Wilmington, North Carolina, although it is sometimes damaged by cold temperatures in the northernmost parts of its range. This native palm grows slowly to 10 to 20 feet high near the beach and can reach 30 or more feet inland. Its large, fan-shaped, evergreen leaves, each a cluster of narrow, five- to six-foot-long blades, are gathered into a rounded clump atop a straight, narrow trunk. The bases of old leaf stems remain on the trunk as the tree grows, giving the trunk a classic palm tree look. In summer, palmetto bears clusters of creamy white flowers that are followed by small black fruits.

A tough, adaptable plant, cabbage palmetto brings a tropical look to warm-climate landscapes. It can tolerate salt spray, high winds, drought, and sand. It will grow in sand dunes, but does best there if given some fertilizer. Plant the tree as a specimen or accent, or in a row along a driveway or property boundary. Space trees 8 to 10 feet apart.

Cabbage palmetto may need to be staked at planting time, especially in exposed, windy locations, until the roots become well established. Fertilize with a balanced, all-purpose fertilizer at planting time. Water regularly until you see signs of new growth, indicating that the tree has sent new roots into the soil.

Sabal palmetto

Spiraea species

Zones: 4–8	
Exposure: Full sun to partial shade	
Salt Resistance: Fair	
Drought Tolerance: Good	
Deer Resistance: Good	

Spireas are adaptable, easy-to-grow deciduous shrubs that bloom beautifully in summer.

They thrive in moist but well-drained soil that is reasonably fertile, but will tolerate poorer, drier soils, too. Give them a location in full sun to partial shade and provide some water during extended periods of drought. Spireas have some tolerance for salt, but need the protection of a windbreak near the beach. Use spireas in beds and borders, massed alongside a driveway, or as an informal screen or space divider. Dwarf varieties are nice in rock gardens. Like other plants in the rose family, spireas are sometimes subject to diseases such as mildew and leaf spots and pests including aphids and scales. In my experience, however, both species described here are mostly trouble-free.

Spiraea japonica 'Anthony Watereri'

Spiraea japonica
Japanese spirea

This is a highly variable species, encompassing a range of sizes from two or three to five or six feet high and wide. Plants sometimes listed as a separate species, *S.* × *bumalda*, are now classified by taxonomists as belonging to this one. You may find them for sale under either name. The plants have oblong leaves with toothed edges and in mid- to late summer, flat-topped clusters of small pink or white flowers appear at the ends of the stems.

RECOMMENDED CULTIVARS
- 'Anthony Watereri' — three to four feet high; has raspberry pink flowers and leaves sometimes edged with cream
- 'Fire Light' — three to four feet high; has pink flowers in summer and red fall foliage
- 'Goldflame' — dwarf, to two and a half feet high; has young leaves that start out reddish, turn golden, then yellowish green, and, finally, orange, red, and yellow in autumn; pink flowers
- 'Little Princess' — dwarf, two to three feet high and four to five feet wide, with pink flowers and red fall foliage

Spiraea × *vanhouttei*
Bridalwreath spirea

Hardy in Zones 3 to 8, bridalwreath spirea is a tougher plant than Japanese spirea, and just as easy to grow. It forms a tall mound five to six feet high, with graceful, fountainlike stems that arch over toward the ground. In midspring the plants are covered with clusters of tiny white flowers. This species is especially lovely as an informal hedge or screen.

RECOMMENDED CULTIVAR
- 'Pink Ice' — leaves that are pink at first and then change to green and white

Spiraea × *vanhouttei*

Tamarix ramosissima
Tamarisk

Zones: 3–8
Exposure: Full sun
Salt Tolerance: Excellent
Drought Tolerance: Good
Deer Resistance: Good

Tamarisk is among the most rugged of seashore plants, with excellent tolerance for salt spray, drought, wind, and sand. It prefers poor, infertile soil and will even grow in sand. Reaching to about 15 feet high and 8 to 10 feet wide at the shore, tamarisk has tiny, feathery, aromatic, light green leaves on graceful arching stems. The leaves have glands that secrete salt absorbed by the plant. In early to late summer, depending upon your location, tamarisk produces long, feathery plumes of soft, rosy pink flowers. Tamarisk is fast growing and can take very strong sun. The only quality that argues against it is that in winter, when the leaves are gone, the plant can look awfully weedy.

Tamarisk works well in windbreaks at the beach or as an informal hedge. Space plants three feet apart. Give tamarisk a spot in full sun, in practically any well-drained soil, ideally with an acid pH. Tamarisk blooms on new growth, so do any necessary pruning in early spring.

RECOMMENDED CULTIVARS
- 'Cheyenne Red' — darker pink flowers
- 'Pink Cascade' — vigorous grower with flowers of rich, rosy pink
- 'Rosea' — very hardy, later blooming, rose-pink flowers
- 'Rubra' — rich pink blossoms

Tamarix ramosissima

Taxus cuspidata
Japanese yew

Zones: 4–7
Exposure: Sun or shade
Salt Tolerance: Fair
Drought Tolerance: Moderate
Deer Resistance: Good

Yews are generally somewhat sensitive to salt and wind close to the beach, but this species does better than the rest of them at the seashore. I have seen a row of them growing just feet from the back of the dunes (in improved soil, of course). Nevertheless, Japanese yew is best planted behind a windbreak. Without protection, it will sometimes burn under fierce salt winds, on the side facing into the wind, close to the beach. In time, plants usually recover. Farther from the beach burning is much less of a problem. Japanese yew can take all the pruning and shearing you care to give it, which is why it's traditionally used in formal gardens. Use Japanese yew as a hedge or informal screen, as a specimen plant, in groups, or in a foundation planting or mixed border.

An upright evergreen shrub with soft, needle-like, evergreen leaves, the form varies with cultivar, from columnar to pyramidal, to broad and flattened. Size varies, too. Japanese yew grows slowly. Female plants produce a hard brown seed inside a fleshy red aril.

Japanese yew will grow in sun or shade. It prefers moist but well-drained, sandy loam soil but adapts to a range of soils as long as there is excellent drainage. In cool climates it is moderately drought tolerant; in hot climates it needs summer moisture. One thing this plant will not tolerate is wet feet. It has no serious pest or disease problems. If you grow it as a hedge, trim it in summer and again in early fall.

Taxus cuspidata, trained as pillars

RECOMMENDED CULTIVARS
- 'Bright Gold' — to three feet high, mounding; young needles turn from golden to green
- 'Nana' — to three feet high and six feet wide, dark green needles
- 'North Coast' — round form three to four feet high, six to eight feet wide; drought resistant, olive green needles
- 'Silver Queen' — spreading semidwarf, white-edged new needles appear silvery

Thuja occidentalis
American arborvitae

Zones: 2–7
Exposure: Full sun
Salt Tolerance: Fair
Drought Tolerance: Good
Deer Resistance: Good

Native to eastern North America, arborvitaes are among the most widely planted of evergreens. At the seashore, they hold up well if given some protection from salt spray and wind near the beach. Use arborvitae as a specimen plant or as a hedge or screen. Size and form vary with cultivar. It grows at a slow to moderate rate.

Plants grow best in full sun, in moist but well-drained soil. Once it is established, arborvitae can tolerate drought and heat. If you grow it as a hedge, clip it in spring and again in late summer. Bagworms and spider mites can cause problems.

RECOMMENDED CULTIVARS
- 'Aurea' — small globe or broad cone to three feet high and wide, golden yellow leaves; hardy to Zone 4
- 'Wintergreen' — pyramidal to 30 feet high and 10 feet wide; holds its color well in winter

Thuja occidentalis 'Degroot's Spire'

Zones: *V. angustifolium*, 2–6; *V. corymbosum*, 3–7
Exposure: Full sun to partial shade
Salt Tolerance: Fair
Drought Tolerance: Poor
Deer Resistance: Poor

The two species of blueberries described here can be found in the wild in eastern North America, and offer the rewards of edible fruit and fiery fall color. Both must have acid soil or they will not thrive.

Vaccinium angustifolium

Vaccinium angustifolium
Lowbush blueberry

A low, spreading shrub to two feet high and wide, lowbush blueberry bears clusters of small white flowers in spring and petite sweet berries in summer — the famous Maine blueberries. Hardy in Zones 2 to 5 or possibly 6, lowbush blueberry does well in poor, dry soil as long as the pH is acid. If you can find plants for sale, use them for massing or ground cover in an open space, or include them in informal mixed beds and borders.

Vaccinium corymbosum

Vaccinium corymbosum
Highbush blueberry

This is the blueberry that's widely grown commercially, with different varieties suited to northern or southern gardens. Check with your county Cooperative Extension office to see which varieties are recommended for your area. Plants are dense, compact, and rounded, growing slowly to 6 to 12 feet high and 8 to 12 feet wide. The dark green oval leaves turn yellow, orange, and red in fall. There are clusters of small white flowers in spring, and the berries follow in summer. The ideal soil is humusy, moist but well drained, and acidic. In the wild, highbush blueberry is found in wet, swampy places, but it does well in sandy soil as long as the pH is quite acid. Mulch to conserve moisture. Prune, if needed, after the fruit is picked.

Zones: *V. dentatum, 2–8; V. tinus, 7–10*	
Exposure: Varies	
Salt Tolerance: Good to excellent	
Drought Tolerance: Poor	
Deer Resistance: Good	

These two viburnums are good choices for seashore gardens. Both have good to excellent salt tolerance and are attractive landscape plants. Use them in groups or masses, in mixed beds and borders, or for an informal hedge or screen planting.

Viburnum dentatum
Arrowwood viburnum

Hardy in Zones 2 to 8, arrowwood viburnum is a big, rounded shrub growing to 8 feet or so high and up to 15 feet wide. A native of eastern North America, it has glossy, dark green, toothed oval leaves that turn yellow, red, or red-purple in fall and flat-topped clusters of tiny white flowers in late spring. In fall, plants produce lots of little blue-black fruits that birds love. Give it a location in full sun to partial or light shade. It adapts to a range of well-drained soils. At the beach, grow arrowwood viburnum behind a windbreak.

Viburnum dentatum

RECOMMENDED CULTIVARS
- 'Blue Muffin' — compact, five to seven feet high, rounded form; fruits are rich blue
- 'Chicago Lustre' — rounded, to 10 feet high, glossy leaves turn red-purple in autumn
- 'Northern Burgundy' — upright, 10 to 12 feet high, burgundy leaves

Viburnum tinus
Laurustinus

Hardy in Zones 7 to 10, laurustinus is an evergreen growing about 10 feet high and wide, with glossy, deep green, oval leaves. Small white flowers open from pink buds in winter and are followed by small blue fruits that turn black when they ripen; birds love them. Laurustinus tolerates sun to light or medium shade, and grows best in well-drained, humusy soil, although it is drought tolerant once established.

Viburnum tinus

Vitex agnus castus

Vitex agnus-castus
Chastetree

Zones: 6–9	
Exposure: Full sun	
Salt Tolerance: Fair	
Drought Tolerance: Good	
Deer Resistance: Good	

This lovely shrub deserves to be better known. In the northern part of its range, it dies back to the ground in winter like herbaceous perennials do. In the South, it may take the form of a small tree. It grows 6 to 10 feet high and as wide, with aromatic (when crushed), dark grayish green compound leaves composed of five to seven oblong leaflets splayed around a central point. In mid- to late summer the plant bears many long, slender wands of fragrant lavender-blue flowers. White and pink varieties are available, but they are less robust than the species.

Give chastetree a location in full sun, protected by a windbreak near the beach, with moist but well-drained soil of reasonable fertility. Amend very sandy soil with compost before planting. Fertilize with an all-purpose fertilizer after planting, and annually in spring thereafter.

Chastetree makes an elegant specimen plant, or you can incorporate it into a mixed border.

Perennials

Achillea cultivars
Yarrow

Zones: 3–9	
Exposure: Full sun	
Salt Tolerance: Fair	
Drought Tolerance: Fair	
Deer Resistance: Good	

Yarrow is grown for its flat-topped clusters of small flowers in warm shades of yellow, orange, red, and pink, as well as white. Flowers bloom in early to midsummer, and regular deadheading extends flowering of some varieties. The gray-green leaves are ferny and finely divided. Heights range from one and a half to four feet. Good companions are salvia, nepeta, artemisia, daylilies, coreopsis, echinacea, and perovskia.

Yarrow prefers a well-drained, loamy soil of average fertility, but it adapts to a range of soils including dry, sandy ones, as long as drainage is good. Plants need full sun. They hold up well in the wind, but are best behind a windbreak at the beach. Achillea needs little fertilizing; once a year in spring with an all-purpose product should be fine. Yarrow can tolerate heat and a fair degree of drought once it is established, but it appreciates some water during extended spells of dry weather. Cut back plants to the basal mound of foliage after they finish blooming.

RECOMMENDED CULTIVARS
- 'Coronation Gold' — bright gold flowers on two- to three-foot plants
- *A. filipendula* 'Gold Plate' — bright gold flowers on taller plants, to four or five feet
- 'Moonshine' — soft yellow flowers on one-and-a-half- to two-foot plants; does better in northern than in southern gardens; needs some protection from salt winds
- *A. millefolium* 'Cerise Queen' — deep rosy pink flowers; plants spread to form clumps
- *A. millefolium* 'Paprika' — bright orange-red flowers

Achillea cultivar

Armeria maritima
Sea pink, thrift

Zones: 3–9	
Exposure: Full sun	
Salt Tolerance: Fair	
Drought Tolerance: Good	
Deer Resistance: Poor	

Sea pink is a small, clump-forming perennial about eight inches high, with a basal mound of narrow, grassy, dark green leaves. In late spring and early summer, plants send out many spherical heads of rose-pink, pink, or white flowers on stiff, slender stems (regular deadheading will keep them blooming longer). Sea pink grows well in a rock garden or at the front of a bed or border. It's a good companion for small sedums, rock cresses (*Arabis* and *Aubrieta*), perennial candytuft (*Iberis sempervirens*), and basket-of-gold (*Aurinia saxatilis*).

This diminutive plant needs well-drained soil of average to poor fertility and does fine in sandy soils. Sea pink will not thrive in heavy, wet soil — it will suffer crown rot. Wind doesn't bother the plant, and while it can tolerate some salt, it is best behind a windbreak near the beach. Otherwise, it's a good choice for coastal gardens.

Armeria maritima

Artemisia species

Zones: 4–9, varies with species	
Exposure: Full sun	
Salt Tolerance: Fair to excellent, depending on species	
Drought Tolerance: Good	
Deer Resistance: Good	

The silvery leaves of artemisias are an asset to flower gardens, where the foliage serves as a foil or a softener for the colors of annuals and other perennials. Planting artemisias with pink and blue flowers gives the garden a soft, misty look, especially in northern climes where the sun is less glaring than it is in the South. Surrounding hot red, orange, and yellow flowers with artemisias produces a cooling effect, toning down some of the flowers' intensity. In a garden of many colors, artemisias can soften strong contrasts and make the garden look more unified. The leaves of many artemisias are lacy or feathery, finely cut or dissected, and contribute textural interest as well. Artemisias produce small white or yellow flowers in summer, but many gardeners feel the flowers detract from the plants' appearance and cut them off.

Artemisias range in size from one to three or more feet high, and their leaves are strongly aromatic. They need full sun and well-drained soil of average fertility. Sandy soil suits them just fine. Very good drainage is critical to their success in southern gardens. What they don't like is heavy, soggy soil and continual high humidity. Plants may become floppy or straggly looking in hot, humid weather; if this happens in your garden, cut them back by half to clean them up and to encourage fresh growth. Large artemisias, if you have a lot of them, can be pruned and shaped with hedge shears if they become weedy, but do not cut into the woody base of a plant or you could injure or even kill it.

Most artemisias are moderately salt tolerant, but one species, *A. stelleriana*, is native to sand dunes along the East Coast and has excellent salt tolerance.

Artemisia 'Powis Castle'

This hybrid is very fine textured, forming a two-foot-high clump of feathery, finely dissected silver leaves. It's a beauty, but a vigorous grower; trim it if needed to keep it neat. It does best in Zones 5 to 8.

Artemisia 'Powis Castle'

Artemisia abrotanum

Artemisia abrotanum
Southernwood

Hardy in Zones 5 to 9, southernwood is a four-foot-tall, back-of-the-garden plant. Its divided, ferny leaves are greener than those of many other artemisias but are still grayish.

Artemisia stelleriana
Beach wormwood

This artemisia can be seen growing on the dunes at the beach. It is hardy and adaptable, flourishing in Zones 4 to 9, and is an excellent choice for oceanfront gardens. Plants vary in size from 1 to 2½ feet high, and spread by means of rhizomes to form a mat. The leaves are deeply cut and very silver. This tough customer can handle poor soil, sand, salt, and drought. 'Boughton Silver' and 'Silver Lace' are two attractive cultivars.

Artemisia stelleriana

Artemisia ludoviciana
White sage

White sage, a tall species, can grow four feet high, with narrow, lance-shaped silver leaves. Its salt tolerance is moderate to good. Allow some space for it to spread in the garden.

RECOMMENDED CULTIVARS

- *A. l.* var. *albula* has a fuzzy silver-white leaves
- 'Silver King' — grows two to three feet high, with lance-shaped, silvery leaves; it's a good choice for southern gardens
- 'Silver Queen' — is similar, growing about two and a half feet high and with slightly larger leaves
- 'Valerie Finnis' — also does well in the South, is two feet tall, and its silver-gray leaves have deeply cut edges

Artemisia ludoviciana 'Silver King'

Asclepias tuberosa
Butterfly weed

Zones: 4–9	
Exposure: Full sun	
Salt Tolerance: Fair	
Drought Tolerance: Good	
Deer Resistance: Good	

Butterfly weed (*Asclepias tuberosa*), a relative to milkweed, really does attract butterflies. It's a nectar source for monarchs, among others. It can be a bit weedy looking and is best for an informal garden, but the plant is easy to grow and its brightly colored flowers enliven summer beds and borders or meadow gardens. Possible garden companions for butterfly weed are black-eyed Susan (*Rudbeckia* species), goldenrod (*Solidago* species), asters, purple coneflower (*Echinacea purpurea*), and smaller ornamental grasses.

Butterfly weed grows two to three feet high, with lance-shaped leaves and clusters of yellow-orange to reddish orange flowers in midsummer. Deadhead spent flowers to encourage another round of bloom in late summer.

Give butterfly weed a location in full sun; it can take a bit of shade in southern gardens. As you would expect of a plant native to the midwestern prairies, butterfly weed needs well-drained soil and can withstand a fair degree of drought. It has some salt tolerance and will grow near the beach if given a little protection.

Plants often self-sow, so deadhead them before the fruits mature and drop their seeds to prevent lots of volunteer seedlings. Butterfly weed is late to come up in spring; you might want to mark its location so you remember where it is. Once the plant is established, it does not take kindly to transplanting, so try not to move it.

Two good cultivars to look for are 'Gay Butterflies', with a mix of red, orange, and yellow flowers, and 'Hello Yellow', with bright yellow blossoms.

Asclepias tuberosa

Aster species

Zones:	(4) 5–8
Exposure:	Full sun
Salt Tolerance:	Fair
Drought Tolerance:	Fair
Deer Resistance:	Good

Asters are a terrific source of late-season color for seashore gardens. Easier to grow and more reliably perennial than the ubiquitous chrysanthemum, asters have a casual look that's well suited to an informal bed or border. The daisylike flowers come in a range of pinks, blues, and purples, along with white. Plants have narrow, linear leaves. Asters look fine with ornamental grasses, goldenrod (*Solidago* species), boltonia, black-eyed Susan (*Rudbeckia* species), 'Autumn Joy' sedum, and *Eupatorium*.

Give asters a sunny location with well-drained soil. To encourage bushier, more compact plants, you can cut or pinch back taller varieties in early summer. Be sure to allow for plenty of air circulation around your asters — crowded plants are prone to mildew and other leaf diseases. Cutting back the plants once — or, in southern gardens, twice — as they grow can also help them avoid mildew problems. But don't cut back after mid- to late July unless you want the plants to bloom later than usual.

Aster carolinianus
Climbing aster

As its common name implies, this southeastern native has vining stems that can grow 10 to 15 feet long. Plants bear yellow-centered lavender flowers in late fall, and may continue blooming into winter in mild southern locations. Hardy in Zones 7 to 10, climbing aster is best suited to mild climates. Cut back the plants in early spring to make way for the new season's growth.

Aster carolinianus

Aster laevis

Aster laevis
Smooth aster

This aster is vase shaped and forms clumps of nonbranching stems 3½ to 4 feet high, with grayish green oblong leaves up to 5 inches long. In late summer and into fall, plants bear clusters of lavender-blue flowers with yellow centers. Hardy in Zones 4 to 9, it is native to the eastern and central United States.

Like other members of the clan, smooth aster brings color to the garden when most other perennials have finished blooming.

Aster novae-angliae 'Fanny'

Aster novae-angliae
New England aster

Another native species, New England aster was long overlooked here, but English plant breeders took to it and developed lots of cultivars, calling them Michaelmas daisies. Now there are New England asters in shades of pink-rose, red, purple, and violet, along with white. Plants grow one to five feet high, depending on the cultivar. They can take partial shade in the South. Hardy in Zones 4 to 8.

Baptisia species
False indigo

Zones: 4–9

Exposure: Full sun

Salt Tolerance: Fair to good

Drought Tolerance: Good

Deer Resistance: Good

False indigos provide the look of shrubs in the garden, but they are really herbaceous perennials that die back to the ground in winter. The plants grow as a bushy clump of upright stems to four feet high, and bear loose spikes of pealike flowers in spring or early summer, depending on the climate. The plants have oblong leaves of bluish green. They are attractive additions to beds and borders of ample size, where they will not look crowded into the space. False indigo can be at home in a garden with yarrow (*Achillea* species), coreopsis, Shasta daisy (*Leucanthemum super-*

bum), bearded or Siberian iris, and Russian sage (*Perovskia atriplicifolia*).

Both species discussed here are natives, and grow well in loose, well-drained, sandy soil. To grow them near the beach, though, add some compost to soil that is very sandy before planting. False indigo has decent salt tolerance and can withstand salt wind as long as it is set back from the beach. False indigos tolerate partial shade in warmer climates. To keep the plants from becoming loose and floppy, you can cut back the stems by a foot or so after they finish blooming.

White false indigo (*Baptisia alba*) bears white flowers. Blue false indigo (*B. australis*) has deep blue flowers that are followed by dark, rattling seedpods. This species may take several years to really settle in, but once it does, it's impressive.

Baptisia species

Cerastium tomentosum
Snow-in-summer

Zones: 3–7

Exposure: Full sun

Salt Tolerance: Fair

Drought Tolerance: Good

Deer Resistance: Good

Snow-in-summer is a low-growing spreader that can be a real pest in decent soil, but it's useful in poor, dry soils and windy, exposed locations. The plant forms a low mat of leaves only a few inches high. The leaves are small, narrow, and grayish green, and there are lots of small white flowers in late spring and early summer.

You can use snow-in-summer in the front of beds and borders, to spill over a retaining wall,

or in a rock garden. It will cover a bank or slope, too. In the garden it can keep company with small sedums, perennial candytuft (*Iberis sempervirens*), sea pinks (*Armeria maritima*), and plumbago (*Ceratostigma plumbaginoides*).

Give snow-in-summer plenty of sun and well-drained soil. Wet soil and high humidity can cause it to rot. At the beach it does best behind a windbreak or other protection. Shear back plants when they finish blooming to keep them looking neat and to keep the centers of the plants dense and full. Wait until spring, before new growth really gets started, to cut back the plants close to the ground.

Cerastium tomentosum

Coreopsis species

Zones: (4) 5 9
Exposure: Full sun
Salt Tolerance: Slight to moderate
Drought Tolerant: Fair
Deer Resistant: Good

Perennial garden favorites and for good reason, coreopsis are easy to grow, adaptable, and long blooming; many will flower right through the summer and into autumn if you deadhead them regularly. Most coreopsis are yellow, although there are now also pink- and red-flowered forms, which in my experience are less resilient and not as long lived as the ones described here. All coreopsis tend to be longer lived in northern gardens than in southern ones.

Depending on the depth of your bed or border and the sizes of the other plants in it, coreopsis can go in the middle or near the front of the garden. Good companions are salvia, veronica, nepeta, bee balm (*Monarda*), daylilies (*Hemerocallis*), Siberian irises (*Iris sibirica*), perovskia, and many other perennials and annuals.

Plant coreopsis in full sun, or perhaps partial shade in the South. They need well-drained soil that is not too rich. Coreopsis thrives in hot sun and tolerates a fair degree of drought, although it will need water during prolonged periods of dry weather.

Coreopsis grandiflora

Hardy in Zones 4 to 9, this coreopsis forms a clump of oblong leaves above which rise daisy-like flowers of rich golden yellow, 1½ to 3 feet high. 'Early Sunrise', also grown as an annual, is 1½ feet high, with semidouble flowers; 'Goldfink' is a dwarf, just 8 to 10 inches high; 'Sunburst' has full, double flowers.

Coreopsis grandiflora 'Early Sunrise'

Coreopsis verticillata

Coreopsis verticillata
Threadleaf coreopsis

This is an airy, delicate-looking plant with thin, threadlike leaves on slender, branching stems and daisylike flowers about two inches across. Threadleaf coreopsis keeps on blooming well into autumn.

RECOMMENDED CULTIVARS

- 'Crème Brûlée' — has large, pale yellow flowers on bushy, mounded plants
- 'Golden Shower' — has rich yellow flowers
- 'Moonbeam' — has lovely, soft yellow flowers that mix beautifully with many other flowers in the garden
- 'Zagreb' — has bright golden flowers

Eryngium amethystinum
Amethyst sea holly

Zones: 3–8
Exposure: Full sun
Salt Tolerance: Good
Drought Tolerance: Good
Deer Resistance: Good

Sea hollies are unusual-looking plants. They are not very colorful, but they have an arresting textural presence in the garden. Amethyst sea holly has spiny, pointed leaves and, in late summer, tight, cone-shaped clusters of tiny amethyst or steely blue flowers atop branched stems. It's not the flowers that get your attention, though; it's the spiny, metallic steely blue to silver-green bracts surrounding the stem immediately beneath them that stand out. The bracts look soft and feathery, but they're sharp.

Amethyst sea holly makes an interesting addition to a bed or border. It grows two to two and a half feet high. The bluish color is not as pronounced in southern gardens, perhaps due to the warmer nighttime temperatures.

Despite their name, not all sea hollies do well at the seashore, but this one does. Amethyst sea holly adapts to a range of soils, from ordinary garden soil to poor, sandy beach soils. With a long taproot that stretches deep underground in search of water, it is drought tolerant. It needs plenty of sun. Amethyst sea holly is evergreen in warm climates.

A wild species, sea holly eryngo (*Eryngium maritimum*), grows on sand dunes and beaches, and is sometimes available for gardens.

For an unusual, modernistic planting, you might combine sea holly with silver lavender cotton (*Santolina chamaecyparissus*) and artemisia, and bolder, more sculptural plants like yucca, agave, and phormium.

Eryngium amethystinum

Gaillardia × grandiflora
Blanketflower

Zones: 3–8
Exposure: Full sun
Salt Tolerance: Good
Drought Tolerance: Good
Deer Resistance: Good

This blanketflower is a hybrid species that can be short lived in the garden, but it's worth replanting every few years, if necessary, for its long blooming time and ease of care. Plants grow two to three feet high, with daisylike yellow flowers with a maroon central disk and a red band on the base of each petal-like ray. The lance-shaped leaves may be lobed, and are grayish green with toothed edges. Although the plants may not survive for many years, they do self-sow. And they bloom all summer into fall. Use blanketflower in beds and borders, along with perovskia, salvia, achillea (pictured), coreopsis, rudbeckia, and ornamental grasses.

Blanketflower needs lots of sun, and it can tolerate poor, sandy soils. Good drainage, in both summer and winter, is critical to its success. Blanketflower has good salt tolerance and will grow near the beach.

Another species, Indian blanket (*Gaillardia pulchella*), is an annual native to the prairie, growing one to two feet high. Its flowers may be yellow, red, or bicolor, single or double. Indian blanket also does well near the beach, withstanding fierce sun, salt, and very sandy soil.

RECOMMENDED CULTIVARS
- 'Baby Cole' — a dwarf just eight inches high; flowers are mostly deep red, with yellow tips
- 'Burgundy' — deep wine red flowers on plants to two feet high
- 'Goblin' (a.k.a. 'Kobold') — a dwarf 9 to 12 inches high, with yellow-tipped red flowers

Gaillardia 'Goblin' with *Achillea* 'Fanal'

Hemerocallis cultivars
Daylily

Zones: 3–9
Exposure: Full sun to partial shade
Salt Tolerance: Fair
Drought Tolerance: Fair
Deer Resistant: Poor

Daylilies are beautiful and versatile, among the most popular of all perennials. They are terrific in beds and borders, or planted in masses along a driveway, in front of a fence or wall, or on a slope. There are thousands of cultivars available, in practically every color except true blue. You can have daylilies in shades of yellow, peach, orange, red, pink, purple, white, even chartreuse and reddish brown. Some have a contrasting central eye, some have ruffled petals, others have narrow, spidery petals. Some daylilies repeat-bloom, and some, such as 'Stella de Oro', bloom all summer. There are early-, mid-, and late-season varieties that range in size from 10 inches to 6 feet high (although many are around 3 feet). Some daylilies are evergreen; these less-hardy varieties are good for southern gardens.

Hemerocallis 'Midnight Magic'

Each daylily flower lasts just a single day, but the plants produce many of them and they open in succession, so every plant flowers for several weeks. The best daylilies for seashore gardens, especially gardens near the beach, are those with shorter scapes (flower stems); the taller varieties are more likely to be damaged by strong winds. Daylilies can handle some salt, but do better behind a windbreak right near the beach. Good partners for daylilies include coreopsis, Siberian iris, phlox, aster, kniphofia, salvia, and many other perennials.

Daylilies will bloom in full sun to partial shade. They appreciate moist but well-drained soil, but they can tolerate some drought. Top-dress your daylilies with compost once a year, and give them a handful of balanced, all-purpose fertilizer in spring. If you have a really tough spot, with poor, dry soil, try growing tawny daylily (*Hemerocallis fulva*), the orange-flowered species that has naturalized along roadsides all over the eastern United States.

Daylilies do require some maintenance to keep them looking fresh and neat. Remove old flowers by twisting them off the plant with your thumb and forefinger. Be careful not to snap off nearby buds at the same time. After the plants have finished blooming, the foliage starts to look ratty. Reach into the mound of leaves to pull out withered and drying leaves. If you have lots of plants, you can use hedge shears to cut back all the leaves. New foliage will grow in by fall, so you won't be left with holes in the garden for a long time.

There are far too many daylily cultivars to even begin to recommend any here. Consult with gardening friends, your county Cooperative Extension office, and knowledgeable nursery personnel for suggestions regarding good varieties for your area.

Hibiscus moscheutos
Rose mallow

Zones: 5–10
Exposure: Full sun
Salt Tolerance: Fair
Drought Tolerance: Poor
Deer Resistance: Good

With its huge flowers, rose mallow looks like it belongs in the tropics. But it's a perfectly hardy perennial that grows with gusto and brings bold, late-season color to the garden.

Rose mallow forms an open, loose clump of thick stems five to eight feet tall with green, pointed-lobed leaves. In mid- to late summer there are huge, saucer-shaped flowers to eight inches across in shades of red, pink, and white.

Grow rose mallow in full sun, in moist soil of average fertility. It can tolerate some salt and does fine up on a bluff overlooking a bay, but it's not a good bet for an oceanfront garden unless it has wind protection and soil amended with compost. Plants will need water during dry weather.

Japanese beetles sometimes trouble rose mallow, but deer avoid it. Cut back the stout stems to a few inches above the ground in fall or spring. Plants are slow to get growing in spring, so be patient.

Hibiscus moscheutos

Hosta species and cultivars
Plantain lily

Zones: 3–9	
Exposure: Partial to full shade	
Salt Tolerance: Fair	
Drought Tolerance: Poor	
Deer Resistance: Poor	

Hostas are practically indispensable in shady gardens, even at the seashore. Although they're not good beachfront plants, they can manage if protected from salt spray and wind, and are fine in woodland or shade gardens away from the water.

Numerous species and hundreds of different cultivars are available, ranging from six-inch sprites to four-foot giants with huge, wide leaves. Those leaves can be narrow and lance shaped to broad and round; they may be smooth or puckered and quilted; in shades of green from golden to chartreuse to smoky blue-green; solid colored or streaked, edged, or striped in assorted combinations of green, gold, chartreuse, and creamy white.

In summer to fall, depending on variety, hostas send up stalks of trumpet-shaped white or lavender flowers that are fragrant in some species. Hostas mix beautifully with astilbes, foamflowers (*Tiarella cordifolia*), bleeding hearts (*Dicentra* species), ferns, snakeroots (*Cimicifuga* species), and other shade lovers.

If you have deer on your property, don't plant hostas; it's like setting a salad bar for them. But where deer are not a problem, hostas have myriad uses: large ones can anchor a bed or border, medium varieties can populate the middle ground, and small growers can work as edgers. You can plant hostas under trees or shrubs or mass them as ground covers. Large ones make impressive specimen plants.

Hostas grow best in soil that is moist but well drained and fertile, but they adapt to a range of conditions. When the clumps get too large, you can dig and divide them. Slugs love hostas as much as deer do, and voles can be pests, too, if you have them on your property.

There are hundreds, maybe thousands, of hosta varieties — too many to make recommen-

Hosta 'Blue Angel'

dations here. You'll be sure to find one you like if you visit local nurseries and peruse mail-order nursery catalogs.

Iberis sempervirens

Iberis sempervirens
Perennial candytuft

Zones: 3–8	
Exposure: Full sun	
Salt Tolerance: Fair	
Drought Tolerance: Poor	
Deer Resistance: Good	

Perennial candytuft is a low, sprawling, mat-forming plant that is often seen in rock gardens, and can be used at the front of beds and borders. It grows up to a foot high, with small, narrow, dark green, evergreen leaves and, in early spring, dome-shaped clusters of tiny white flowers. It is

lovely spilling over a wall or tucked into a soil pocket in a dry stone wall. Try it with tulips and daffodils, pansies, basket-of-gold (*Aurinia saxitilis*), and other early bloomers.

This is a plant that likes to bake in the sun in well-drained soil. But it also needs to be watered when the soil dries out. It has some tolerance for salt, but needs the protection of a windbreak near the beach. Amend very sandy soil with compost before planting, to improve fertility and boost humus content. To keep the plants looking neat, cut them back by about one third to a half when they finish blooming. Clubroot can be a problem. Perennial candytuft tends not to do as well in southern gardens as in northern ones.

Kniphofia cvs.
Red-hot poker, torch lily

Zones: 5–9
Exposure: Full sun
Salt Tolerance: Fair
Drought Tolerance: Good
Deer Resistance: Good

Red-hot poker grows as a clump of grassy, arching leaves 1½ to 5 feet high, with spikes of tiny, tubular flowers in shades of red, orange, yellow, pink, or cream on straight, slender stems in early summer. Flowers bloom from the bottom up, and some change color as they mature. Deadheading will keep the plants blooming longer, and some varieties rebloom in late summer or fall. The plants spread by rhizomes to form clumps.

Red-hot poker is a good choice for adding some vertical line to a bed or border. Good companions for it include coreopsis, salvia, gaillardia, nepeta, and Shasta daisy.

Give red-hot poker a place in full sun, with very well-drained soil that is moist in summer but dry in winter. Wet winter soil will surely kill it. Choose the location carefully; kniphofia does not like to be moved once it is established. As the flowers fade, cut back each flower stem to the ground.

RECOMMENDED CULTIVARS

- 'Alcazar' — three and a half feet high, salmon flowers, reblooms, very hardy
- 'Bressingham Comet' — one and a half feet high; orange flowers have red tips, yellow at the base
- 'Earliest of All' — two feet high, rosy coral flowers, reblooms, very hardy
- 'Gold Mine' — three feet high, golden flowers
- 'Green Jade' — five feet high, pale green flowers turn to cream, then white
- 'Primrose Beauty' — three feet high, soft yellow flowers, reblooms
- 'Royal Standard' — three feet high, scarlet buds open to bright yellow flowers, very hardy

Kniphofia 'Royal Standard'

Lavandula angustifolia
English lavender

Zones: 5–9
Exposure: Full sun
Salt Tolerance: Fair
Drought Tolerance: Good
Deer Resistance: Good

Lavender is loved by flower and herb gardeners alike for its beguiling fragrance. Actually a subshrub, not a true herbaceous perennial, lavender is part of many perennial and herb gardens. It can be used for edging or planted along a wall, or, since it takes shearing well, it can be a low hedge. Possible garden companions include coreopsis, dianthus, nepeta, evergreen candytuft (*Iberis sempervirens*, which blooms earlier but likes similar conditions), lavender cotton (*Santolina*), and thyme.

Plants grow one to two feet high and about two feet wide, with narrow, fragrant, gray-green leaves and wands of tiny, fragrant purple flowers in midsummer. Lavender loves the sun, and it must have well-drained soil, preferably with an alkaline pH, to thrive. It cannot tolerate heavy, wet soil in summer or winter. In fact, the two most common causes of lavender demise are wet soil and pruning in fall. Average to poor fertility suits it; wet soil does not. Lavender has some ability to tolerate salt, but it needs to be behind a windbreak when growing near the beach.

If you deadhead lavender, it may reward you with a second, less lavish, round of bloom in late summer. To deadhead, cut off individual flower stems or use hedge clippers. Any other pruning is best done in spring, when new growth has begun and you can see which plants are still viable. Don't prune in fall or plants will not have enough time to harden off before winter.

Every few years, cut back the plants to six to eight inches above the ground to keep them more compact and shapely. But take care not to cut back into very old, woody growth or the plant can be harmed.

Lavandula angustifolia

Limonium latifolium
Sea lavender

Zones: 4–9	
Exposure: Full sun	
Salt Tolerance: Good	
Drought Tolerance: Good	
Deer Resistance: Good	

Sea lavender looks a bit as though the ocean mist has descended into the garden. The plants take the form of a low basal rosette of leathery, dark green leaves. During mid- and late summer, branched clusters of tiny, papery, lavender-blue flowers bloom on thin stems two feet or more high. The effect in the garden is soft and misty. Grow sea lavender near the front of a bed or border. Because of its airy, delicate texture, you can also plant it as a scrim in front of the garden through which other plants are seen. It is also a good companion for lavender, germander, lavender cotton (*Santolina* species), and thyme. Sea lavender attains a spread of about two feet.

Sea lavender is a sun lover, and it thrives in very well-drained, sandy soil. It can handle salt and wind and generally does well near the beach, as well as farther inland. You can leave old flowers on the plants—they will dry in place. Instead of cutting back the plants in fall like most perennials, wait until the following spring.

RECOMMENDED CULTIVARS
- 'Blue Cloud'—mauve flowers
- 'Violetta'—deep violet blossoms

Limonium latifolium

Monarda didyma
Bee balm

Zones: 3–8	
Exposure: Full sun to partial shade	
Salt Tolerance: Fair	
Drought Tolerance: Poor	
Deer Resistance: Good	

Bee balm, or bergamot, native to the meadows of the eastern United States, is often found in herb gardens and is a traditional tea plant. These days it is often found in perennial gardens, too, where its shaggy flowers attract bees, butterflies, and hummingbirds. Plants grow two to four feet high, with oval, toothed leaves that have a fresh scent of citrus and mint. From mid- to late summer, the stems are crowned with whorls of tubular flowers surrounded by colorful bracts, in shades of red, pink, purple, and white. They can be three to four inches across. Possible companions include goldenrod and meadow rue (*Thalictrum*).

Monarda didyma

Bee balm grows in full sun to light shade, and needs moist, humusy soil of average fertility. It can't be allowed to dry out in summer. That wouldn't seem to describe a seashore plant, but bee balm does quite well away from the water. Over time, the plants spread to form clumps. Deadheading the plants keeps them blooming over many weeks. One problem that does trouble bee balm is mildew, and that susceptibility makes bee balm a gamble for many southern gardens. Allowing for good air circulation among plants helps minimize it, as does thinning out crowded stems. Mildew usually strikes when the plants are well along in their blooming, and if it becomes too severe, just cut back the plants close to the ground. New leaves will grow but bloom will be over for the season. There are some mildew-resistant cultivars, which are noted below.

RECOMMENDED CULTIVARS
- 'Cambridge Scarlet'—bright red
- 'Croftway Pink'—rosy pink
- 'Jacob Kline'—dark red, mildew resistant
- 'Marshall's Delight'—clear pink, mildew resistant
- 'Violet Queen'—red-violet, mildew resistant
- Another species, wild bergamot (*Monarda fistulosa*), is less showy, bearing pale lavender flowers with purple bracts, but it is more heat tolerant and mildew resistant than bee balm.

Nepeta × faassenii
Catmint

Zones: 4–8
Exposure: Full sun to partial shade; partial to light shade in southernmost gardens
Salt Tolerance: Fair
Drought Tolerance: Fair
Deer Resistance: Good

Catmint is among the easiest and most accommodating of perennials. Not a plant for formal gardens, it is floppy and lax, but its flowers are a soft shade of lavender-blue that goes beautifully with pinks or yellows, and they bloom for quite a few weeks in early to midsummer. Catmint can be charming in the front of a bed or border where it can spill over the edges of a path. It's a good underplanting for roses and a congenial companion for many summer perennials, such as coreopsis, daylilies, achillea, Shasta daisies, peonies, and artemisia.

Catmints are loose, spreading plants ranging from 10 inches to 3 feet high, with aromatic, oval, grayish green leaves with toothed edges. In early to midsummer, they produce loose spikes of lavender-blue flowers. When blooming slows, shear back the plants to promote a new, though spottier, round of flowers. In this case, shearing back the whole plant works better than dead-heading individual flowers to promote more bloom. It also helps keep the plants from flopping all over the place.

Give nepeta well-drained soil of average fertility; it can tolerate a range of soils but doesn't like soggy conditions. In northern gardens, catmint likes sun and will tolerate partial shade as well. In the South, a little shade is good for it. Catmint has some tolerance for salt, doing best behind a windbreak near the beach and thriving in many locations away from the water.

RECOMMENDED CULTIVARS

- 'Blue Wonder' — 12 inches high, greener leaves than most nepetas; flowers are larger than other types and bloom longer
- 'Dropmore Hybrid' — to 18 inches high, more upright and less floppy than other nepetas
- 'Six Hills Giant' — to three feet high and as wide, popular and widely planted, a better choice for moist conditions than other catmint varieties
- 'Souvenir d'Andre Chaudron' — 18 inches high, said to do well in southern coastal gardens

Nepeta × faassenii

Nipponanthemum nipponicum
Montauk daisy, Nippon chrysanthemum

Zones: 5–9
Exposure: Full sun
Salt Tolerance: Good
Drought Tolerance: Good
Deer Resistance: Good

Gardeners in either the North or the South in search of a durable, easy-to-grow plant that offers an alternative to autumn chrysanthemums should consider Montauk daisies. They don't always fit comfortably into beds and borders, although they can work with sedums, asters, and ornamental grasses. But in their brief few weeks of autumn glory, they make an impression when massed on a bank or slope.

Montauk daisy forms a clump of stems about three feet high (or taller, when not cut back), with fleshy, oblong leaves with scalloped edges. For a few weeks in fall, the plants bear classic yellow-centered white daisies.

This tough-as-nails plant needs sun but can grow in practically any well-drained soil, including poor, sandy ones. It tolerates drought and salt spray and can withstand a lot of neglect. One thing Montauk daisy does need is pruning, or the stems flop over, especially in a wet summer. Cut back the plants to a few inches from the ground every year in fall when plants finish blooming, or early the following spring. If plants are not cut back, they will become progressively woodier, and eventually you will end up with almost shrublike, unkempt bases with flowers blooming on new growth at the top of the gnarled woody parts. To keep the plants more compact and the stems less floppy, cut back the plants in late spring. Buds usually are not set until fall, so the pruning should not delay bloom.

Nipponanthemum nipponicum

Zones: Vary with species	
Exposure: Full sun	
Salt Tolerance: Moderate to good	
Drought Tolerance: Good	
Deer Resistance: Good	

This group of native wildflowers adds color to informal flower beds and borders. Their cup-shaped flowers bloom in early to mid-summer on sprawling plants. Although they tend to spread, they are valuable for their ability to grow in poor soils and tolerate drought. They do not thrive in wet, soggy conditions. Good companions in the garden are blue salvias, daylilies, nepeta, artemisia, and pennisetum.

Oenothera speciosa 'Siskiyou'

Oenothera drummondii
Beach evening primrose

If you can find it for sale, beach evening primrose is meant for seaside conditions. Hardy only in Zone 8 and south, it thrives in poor, sandy soil and has good tolerance for salt spray and wind. Plants have hairy, gray-green leaves and a sprawling, spreading form. The flowers are pale yellow.

Oenothera drummondii

Oenothera fruticosa
Sundrops

Hardy in Zones 4 to 8, sundrops grow from one to three feet high, with lance-shaped green leaves that turn reddish in cool fall weather. The summer flowers are bright, clear yellow. When the plants die back in fall, a low clump of evergreen leaves remains through the winter. Sundrops do best in soil of average fertility — it's a bit more demanding than the other types discussed here. The yellow flowers of the cultivar 'Fireworks' open from red buds. 'Summer Solstice' blooms practically all summer, and its leaves turn red in summer, deepening to burgundy in fall.

Oenothera fruticosa

Oenothera speciosa 'Rosea'
Showy evening primrose

Suited to Zones 5 to 8, showy evening primrose grows about a foot high, with narrow, toothed leaves on arching stems. The pretty flowers are light pink with deeper pink veining, and bloom for a long time in summer. The cultivar 'Siskiyou' has flowers of a richer pink. The plants spread by runners and can become a pest in small gardens. They have naturalized in parts of the South. Showy evening primrose does tolerate poor soil.

Perovskia atriplicifolia
Russian sage

Zones: 5–9
Exposure: Full sun
Salt Tolerance: Fair to good
Drought Tolerance: Good
Deer Resistance: Good

This lovely late-season perennial brings a soft haze of misty, lavender-blue flowers to the garden starting in midsummer and continuing into fall. It's a good addition to beds and borders and looks fine with black-eyed Susans (*Rudbeckia* species), salvia, coreopsis, sedum, heliopsis, and ornamental grasses.

Russian sage can grow as high as four feet, though it is often closer to two or three feet. The stems near the base of the plant are woody; it is actually a subshrub, like lavender, rather than a true herbaceous perennial. The aromatic leaves are silvery gray-green in color, finely divided and fernlike. In mid- to late summer, many tall, branched clusters of tiny purple-blue flowers grace the plants, and last for many weeks.

Give Russian sage a sunny spot and well-drained soil of average fertility. It is easy to grow and undemanding. Plants bloom for a long time. Some southern gardeners find that pruning back some of the spent flower stems promotes new growth and fresh bloom. It is generally best to let the plants stand through the winter and cut them back in spring, though you may want to trim them a bit when they finish blooming to give them a neater look. Plants can be slow to start growing in spring, so be patient with them.

Perovskia atriplicifolia with *Hibiscus moscheutos*

Phlox paniculata
Garden phlox

Zones: 4 to 8
Exposure: Full sun to partial shade
Salt Tolerance: Fair
Drought Tolerance: Poor
Deer Resistance: Poor

Garden phlox is actually a native of the eastern United States, found in the wild from New York to as far south as Georgia. Wild phlox is purple-pink or magenta in color, but garden varieties come in shades of pink, cherry red, salmon, and lilac to purple, as well as white. Plants grow from one and a half to about four feet tall, and if you deadhead them regularly to remove old flower heads, they'll bloom through much of the summer and into fall. The five-petaled flowers, which are fragrant in many varieties, are gathered into rounded or dome-shaped clusters atop tall, straight stems lined with oblong to lance-shaped leaves.

Although garden phlox has only a modest degree of salt tolerance, it flourishes in many seashore gardens. Grow it away from the water, or provide a good windbreak near the beach. The worst problem for garden phlox is a susceptibility to mildew. Seek out mildew-resistant varieties such as 'David', 'Laura', and 'Shortwood'. It is also a good idea to thin crowded clumps, removing some stems to promote better air circulation that can in turn help prevent disease.

Grow garden phlox in full sun to partial shade. Bluer varieties are said to do best with some shade because they tend to bleach out in strong sunlight. Moist, fertile soil is best, so enrich sandy soil with lots of compost, and water plants during dry weather. Tall varieties will need staking to stand up in windy seashore weather. Cut back the plants to the ground in late fall.

Phlox paniculata 'Laura'

Rudbeckia species

Zones: Vary with species
Exposure: Full sun
Salt Tolerance: Fair to good
Drought Tolerance: Good
Deer Resistance: Fair

The familiar black-eyed Susan is ubiquitous in seashore gardens in late summer. The golden, slightly orangey yellow daisy flowers have a dark center and bloom for many weeks, continuing into fall. Black-eyed Susan works best in an informal garden and can keep company with asters, sedums, boltonia, perovskia, and ornamental grasses.

The plants tolerate heat and drought, and grow in average soil. They are generally deer resistant, too, although I have seen them eaten in some gardens. In short, black-eyed Susan is about as foolproof as a perennial can be. It does, however, spread itself around. If you plant it, you will have more and more as years go by. Pull up unwanted seedlings, and dig up the plants when they spread beyond their boundaries. Plants are also sometimes susceptible to mildew. Make sure they get plenty of sun and good air circulation to minimize the risk of trouble. Deadhead the flowers after bloom, or leave the seed heads in the garden for winter interest or for birds to eat. Or cut back flowering stems near the ground after the plants finish blooming.

Rudbeckia fulgida

Rudbeckia fulgida

The parent of many varieties is *Rudbeckia fulgida*, hardy in Zones 3 to 9. It grows two to three feet high and about one and a half feet wide, with lance-shaped, hairy, rather coarse leaves and many flowers from late summer into autumn. The best-known variety is 'Goldsturm', which grows about two feet high.

Rudbeckia 'Herbstonne'

An imposing hybrid often categorized as a cultivar of shining coneflower, *Rudbeckia nitida*, is 'Herbstonne' or 'Autumn Sun'. This impressive plant grows to six feet high, with oblong leaves and many branched clusters of green-centered yellow flowers with down-curved rays atop the tall stems. 'Herbstonne' makes a dramatic statement in the back of the garden, but it will need staking in windy locations.

Rudbeckia hirta

The other most widely grown black-eyed Susan is *Rudbeckia hirta*, which is a short-lived perennial hardy in Zones 3 to 10 that is often grown as an annual. Plants are hairy, even bristly, with oblong to oval green leaves; they grow from one to three feet high. The Gloriosa Daisy group of cultivars comes from this species, with deep red, bronze, or red-brown coloration on their golden rays. Other cultivars are 'Goldilocks', two feet high, double or semidouble flowers; 'Irish Eyes', two to two and a half feet high, with bright yellow rays and a green center; and 'Rustic Dwarfs', to two feet high, with flowers of gold and mahogany.

Rudbeckia hirta

Rudbeckia 'Herbstonne'

Salvia species

Zones:	Vary with species
Exposure:	Full sun to partial shade
Salt Tolerance:	Fair
Drought Tolerance:	Poor
Deer Resistance:	Good

Salvias belong to the Mint family. This large genus includes culinary sages and both annual and perennial plants grown for their flowers. Those flowers are tubular and two lipped, and in most species they are gathered into slender spikes at the ends of the stems. Versatile and free blooming, salvias are excellent additions to beds and borders, and they do well in pots, too. Combine them in the garden with coreopsis, Shasta daisy, daylilies, nepeta, sea lavender (*Limonium latifolium*), and artemisia — they mix well with many other plants.

For the most part, salvias grow well in full sun to partial shade, in moist but well-drained soil of average fertility. They don't need constant moisture, but they can't tolerate extended dry spells, either. Deadhead the plants to prolong bloom, cutting back old flower stems to the next pair of leaves on the stem. Cut back the plants to a few inches above the ground in fall. Pests and diseases seldom cause problems.

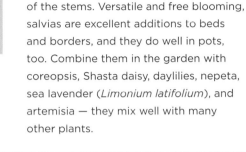

Salvia farinacea 'Victoria'

Salvia farinacea
Mealycup sage

A perennial for most parts of Zone 7 (although not on Long Island) to Zone 11, mealycup sage is grown as an annual farther north. The bushy plants grow two to three feet high, with oblong leaves and many spikes of blue-violet flowers all summer long and well into fall. The plant blooms like crazy and the flowers last — and they don't need constant deadheading.

RECOMMENDED CULTIVARS
- 'Blue Bedder' — like 'Victoria' but somewhat bigger
- 'Indigo Spires' — grows much taller, to four feet, with long flower spikes that curve and twist; it's like a supercharged version of 'Victoria'
- 'Victoria' — one and a half to two feet high, very floriferous and easy to grow

Salvia × sylvestris
'May Night'

Salvia × sylvestris 'May Night', or 'Mainacht', is hardy in Zones 5 to 9, growing about two feet high, with wrinkly dark green, lance-shaped leaves. Slender spikes of deep violet-blue flowers bloom all summer if deadheaded as they fade. This variety is one of the longest-blooming, most dependable plants in the perennial garden, and a fine addition to seashore beds and borders.

Salvia × sylvestris 'May Night'

Santolina chamaecyparissus

Santolina chamaecyparissus
Lavender cotton

Zones: 6–9	
Exposure: Full sun	
Salt Tolerance: Fair to good	
Drought Tolerance: Good	
Deer Resistance: Good	

This evergreen subshrub has a variety of uses in the garden. Santolina can be grown as a low hedge in an herbal knot garden or to outline geometric beds — it takes clipping well. In less formal settings, lavender cotton adds touches of silver-green that work especially well with pink, blue, and purple flowers. Plant lavender cotton behind a retaining wall, massed on a bank or slope, or in a rock garden.

Lavender cotton grows in a clump about two feet high and three feet wide, with aromatic, silvery leaves divided into tiny leaflets, and small, yellow button flowers that are somehow not terribly attractive, in early summer. A related species, *Santolina virens*, has bright green, needlelike foliage that has a less pronounced scent than that of lavender cotton. This species, too, has small yellow flowers on tall, slender stems in summer. It is aromatic and less salt tolerant than *Santolina chamaecyparissus*.

Lavender cotton is a sun lover that must have well-drained soil to survive. It does well in poor, sandy soil but cannot tolerate soggy conditions. Too much water and fertilizer will kill it. It is said not to like humidity, but it does beautifully in many coastal gardens, even near the beach and in the South. Lightly prune the plants after they bloom to keep them from getting leggy.

Scabiosa columbaria
Pincushion flower

Zones: 3 to 8	
Exposure: Full sun	
Salt Tolerance: Slight to moderate	
Drought Tolerance: Moderate	
Deer Resistance: Good	

There are both annual and perennial species of pincushion flower, all of which are long blooming. This perennial species will bloom all summer if you regularly remove brown, spent flowers. However, the plants may exhaust themselves and behave as biennials or live just a few years. Still, they have a light-hearted look to them that is a nice addition to a seashore garden.

Pincushion flower is not a plant for formal gardens or for gardeners who like a neat, controlled look. Its slender stems don't stand up straight but rather bend and weave through one another in a carefree mass. The purple-blue or pink flowers are composed of petal-like florets surrounding a central dome of smaller florets that resembles a pincushion. Bees and butterflies find the flowers attractive. The plants grow about two feet high, with a basal clump of narrow, deeply lobed, almost fernlike leaves.

Give pincushion flower a spot in full sun. It prefers well-drained soil of average fertility, with a neutral to mildly alkaline pH. If your soil is acidic, you will need to add lime. Good drainage is important for scabiosa in winter as well as in summer. If you live where winter usually brings lots of snow, this plant is probably not a good bet for your garden. Plants have some salt tolerance, but they often do well in seashore gardens when they are not near the water.

RECOMMENDED CULTIVARS
- 'Butterfly Blue'— lilac-blue flower heads
- 'Pink Mist'— has flowers of a slightly purplish shade of soft pink

Scabiosa columbaria

Sedum species

Zones: Vary with species
Exposure: Full sun
Salt Tolerance: Moderate
Drought Tolerance: Good
Deer Resistance: Fair

Sedums have succulent, fleshy leaves that tolerate dry soil quite well. They come in a range of sizes from low ground huggers to upright clumps of two-foot stems. Use small ones in the front of beds and borders and in rock gardens. Taller varieties can add late-season color to the middle ground of beds and borders. They will do fine in containers, too. Combine them with black-eyed Susans, asters, and ornamental grasses.

Give sedums full sun and well-drained soil of average or even rather poor fertility. Drainage is essential; the plants will not be happy with wet feet. Bees are drawn to sedum flowers like magnets.

Sedum 'Autumn Joy'

Sedum acre
Goldmoss sedum

Hardy in Zones 3 to 9, goldmoss sedum grows just two inches high. It forms a low, spreading mat of succulent, needlelike leaves and bears little star-shaped yellow flowers in late spring or summer.

Sedum acre

Sedum spathulifolium

Another diminutive species, *Sedum spathulifolium*, hardy in Zones 5 to 10, grows as a mat of gray-green leaves with starry yellow flowers in summer. This sedum will tolerate partial shade as well as full sun.

Sedum spathulifolium

Sedum 'Autumn Joy'

A real star of late-summer gardens, *Sedum 'Autumn Joy'* (or 'Herbstfreude') is a carefree, dependable plant that has real presence as summer eases into fall. Hardy in Zones 3 to 10, it forms a two-foot-tall clump of thick, upright stems lined with fleshy, oval leaves with toothed edges. In mid- to late summer, plants produce flat-topped clusters of tiny flowers resembling heads of broccoli. The flower heads start out light green, then, over a period of weeks, turn pink and then salmony bronze, deepen to russet, and eventually turn brown. The whole process unfolds over a couple of months. Many gardeners like to leave the old flower heads in place to add winter interest to the garden; others prefer to cut back the stems when the flowers have turned brown. Whatever approach you take, this plant is a standout. It combines beautifully with warm-colored chrysanthemums, purple asters, black-eyed Susans, and ornamental grasses.

Solidago species

Goldenrods are terrific in seaside gardens. In one of the gardens profiled in chapter 4 (see page 112), a meadow of goldenrod grew by itself when the ground was cleared. Goldenrod has good tolerance for salty winds. In fact, there's a species of goldenrod that grows right on the beach. Goldenrod's sprays of yellow flowers mark the end of summer and the beginning of fall. Besides being a fine plant for a meadow, or a wildflower or native plant garden, goldenrod has a place in an informal bed or border. It is at home with asters, boltonia, 'Autumn Joy' sedum, and ornamental grasses.

In the garden, goldenrods are adaptable and easy to grow. Most of them grow three to four feet high and up to two feet wide, with lance-shaped green leaves. In midsummer to early fall, goldenrods produce their arching sprays or wands of tiny golden flowers — they seem to shimmer in the softer light as the days grow shorter. Goldenrods grow well in sun to light shade, and they're not fussy about soil. They tolerate low-fertility soils with no problem, but they'll be weak and floppy in rich soil. Drought does not bother them.

The plants spread by means of both rhizomes and self-sown seeds. If you grow goldenrod in a bed or border, you will need to divide the plants every few years, in spring or fall, to keep them where they belong. Deadheading old flowers before the seeds mature will decrease the numbers of volunteer seedlings.

Solidago odora
Sweet goldenrod

This is an interesting species for gardens. Hardy in Zones 3 to 9, it grows three to four feet high, with licorice-scented leaves that can serve as a substitute for fresh tarragon in the kitchen. Branched clusters of flowers bloom in late summer.

Solidago odora

Solidago rugosa 'Fireworks'

An unusual variety, *Solidago rugosa* 'Fireworks' has flowers in a burst of arching, narrow sprays that really do resemble their namesake. The flowers bloom on three-foot plants from midsummer to early fall. 'Fireworks' is hardy in Zones 5 to 9.

Solidago sempervirens
Beach goldenrod

This species grows in salty sands along the coast from Long Island to Florida; you may find it blooming among clumps of beach grass in fall. Beach goldenrod is hardy in Zones 6 to 9, and has rather coarse-looking, thick, bright green leaves that are narrow and up to eight inches long. Clusters of bright yellow flowers bloom on four- to six-foot stems. As you'd expect, beach goldenrod has excellent tolerance for wind, sand, and salt spray.

Solidago rugosa 'Fireworks'

Solidago sempervirens

Stachys byzantina
Lamb's ears

Zones: 4–8
Exposure: Full sun
Salt Tolerance: Fair
Drought Tolerance: Fair to good
Deer Resistance: Good

The fuzzy, silvery leaves of lamb's ears serve as a softener or blender for strong flower color in beds and borders, and they bring some shimmer to a garden of soft pink, blue, and purple flowers. Lamb's ears have some tolerance for salt, but they need the protection of a windbreak close to the beach. The plant grows as a clump of thick, oblong, green leaves that are covered with soft white hairs. In midsummer a thick stem lined with small purple flowers arises from the middle of the clump. The flowers aren't very attractive; in fact, their appearance actually detracts from the overall look of the plant. In addition, the foliage starts to decline when the flower spike appears. Most gardeners cut off the flowering stems to preserve a better look for the plant.

The two most important environmental considerations for success with lamb's ears are well-drained soil and plenty of sun. Excellent drainage is absolutely critical — the plant will rot in wet or heavy soil. Lamb's ears don't like high humidity, and do not take well to life under overhead sprinklers, either. This would argue against its inclusion in southern gardens, but the cultivar 'Countess Helene von Stein' holds up better than other lamb's ears in heat and humidity.

Given the right growing conditions, lamb's ears don't need a lot of maintenance in the garden. You will want to cut off flower stems as they form, unless you grow the variety 'Silver Carpet', which does not bloom. Remove any leaves that rot or just start to look bad. It is better to wait until the following spring to clean up the plants for the season and remove all the old foliage, rather than doing it in fall.

RECOMMENDED CULTIVARS
- 'Countess Helene von Stein' — sometimes known as 'Big Ears', grows to 10 inches high, with larger leaves than those of the species
- 'Primrose Heron' — has yellow-gray leaves that are really interesting or sickly looking, depending on your point of view
- 'Silver Carpet' — does not bloom, and its leaves are very silver-white

Stachys byzantina

Teucrium chamaedrys
Germander

Zones: 4–9
Exposure: Full sun
Salt Tolerance: Fair
Drought Tolerance: Good
Deer Resistance: Good

Germander is familiar to herb gardeners as one of the plants used in the low hedges that create the patterns in knot gardens. It can also figure into rock gardens and beds and borders. Germander is quite drought tolerant, but it's not a plant for the beach — winter winds would burn the foliage. Away from the water, however, it can be a good choice.

Germander is a low, woody subshrub growing about a foot high and one to two feet wide, with small, glossy, dark green leaves. In summer it bears tiny pink or purple flowers. The plant must have very well-drained soil in order to thrive; it cannot abide soggy conditions. A neutral to mildly alkaline pH is ideal. Germander doesn't take well to very high humidity. Southern gardeners may prefer to grow a different species, the silver-leaved *Teucrium fruticans*, which is suited to Zones 8 to 10. This germander grows two to three feet high and spreads as wide, with light blue flowers in summer. Good companions for germander include santolina, lavender, sea lavender, African daisy (*Arctotis*), and thymes.

Germander takes clipping and shearing well. Shear back the plants to shape them, if you like, after they bloom, but do it by the end of summer so they have time to harden off before the onset of cold winter weather. In spring, cut back the plants to a few inches from the ground if you want to keep them compact, such as for a small hedge. Otherwise, just shear the plants lightly at this time to shape them and remove any stem tips that were damaged over the winter.

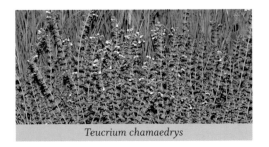
Teucrium chamaedrys

Yucca filamentosa
Adam's needle

Zones: 5–10	
Exposure: Full sun	
Salt Tolerance: Good to excellent	
Drought Tolerance: Good	
Deer Resistance: Good	

The stiff, sword-shaped leaves of Adam's needle make a bold, architectural statement in seashore gardens, both at the beach and farther inland. The leaves point to the sky and provide a strong vertical line that offers a good counterpoint to the softer, rounder forms of perennials or the lower cylindrical shapes of cacti. Yucca has excellent tolerance for salty wind, making it a candidate for inclusion in a windbreak or helping to control erosion on the dunes. In the garden it mixes well with other architectural plants such as palmetto, crested celosias, and New Zealand flax (*Phormium tenax*), along with sedums, sea holly (*Eryngium*), blue lyme grass (*Elymus*), and other ornamental grasses.

Adam's needle forms a clump of pointed evergreen leaves two to two and a half feet high, with curly threads along their edges. In summer a tall, thick stalk of bell-shaped white flowers shoots up from the center of the plant. If plants are not deadheaded, the flowers are followed in fall by nonornamental oblong fruits.

Yucca needs full sun and very well-drained soil. It will rot in wet conditions. The plants demand little in the way of care. They do look best if old flower stalks are cut down when blooming is finished (use lopping shears for the task).

RECOMMENDED CULTIVARS
- 'Bright Edge' — yellow-edged leaves
- 'Variegata' — blue-green leaves edged with white
- 'Color Guard' — leaves have a gold center and edges that turn pink in winter

Yucca filamentosa 'Garland Gold'

Annuals and Tender Perennials

Arctotis × hybrida
African daisy

Exposure:	Full sun
Salt Tolerance:	Moderate to good
Drought Tolerance:	Good
Deer Resistance:	Good

African daisies are native to dry, rocky soils in South Africa. They thrive in hot sun and handle drought with aplomb, which makes them prime candidates for adding color to seaside gardens. They are perennials that usually are grown as annuals in East Coast gardens, and they bloom heartily all summer and well into fall, often continuing beyond the first frost.

The rather sprawly plants grow from 8 to 12 inches high and about a foot wide, with a basal rosette of lobed, silvery green leaves covered with soft hairs, and daisy flowers 2 to 3 inches across, usually with dark-colored or blue centers, on long stems. Flowers come in a range of colors, including clear pink, rose-pink, burnt orange, bright pumpkin orange, soft apricot, gold, yellow, cream, white, burgundy, and purple. The blossoms of older varieties would close in the afternoon and during cloudy weather, but newer cultivars stay open longer.

Grow African daisies in garden beds or borders or in containers. They are good partners for blue lyme grass, blue oat grass, yarrow, catharanthus, lantana, nepeta, snow-in-summer, lavender, and portulaca. Give them a location in full sun with very well-drained soil. The plants will fail in soggy soil. Although they love heat, African daisies do not handle continual high humidity well, making them a better bet for northern gardens than southern ones.

Deadhead the plants regularly in summer to keep the plants producing lots of new flowers. Water only when the soil is dry an inch or two below the surface.

Arctotis × hybrida

Catharanthus roseus
Madagascar periwinkle

Exposure:	Full sun to partial shade
Salt Tolerance:	Some
Drought Tolerance:	Good
Deer Resistance:	Good

Madagascar periwinkle is a colorful little plant that doesn't look nearly as heat and drought tolerant as it is. It's pretty as an edging for a bed or border, and is an excellent source of summer-long color in pots and planters, where it works beautifully with lantana, Victoria salvia, geraniums, petunias, verbena, sweet potato vine, and vinca, among others.

Plants grow 6 to 12 inches high, with dark green oval leaves and flat-petaled flowers, resembling those of phlox, in tropical shades of magenta, pink, lilac, purple, salmon, and white, some with a contrasting eye.

Madagascar periwinkle loves sun, heat, and sandy soil, and it can tolerate drought. Do not plant it outdoors until all danger of frost is past in spring. Although it is a sun lover, it will bloom in partial shade, too. With some deadheading, the plants will bloom all summer.

RECOMMENDED CULTIVARS
- Cooler series — large flowers in a range of colors including pink, lavender, and white, some with a contrasting eye
- Pacifica series — includes a red, as well as several shades of pink, rose, lavender, and white
- 'Parasol' — grows eight inches high, with white flowers with a deep red eye
- 'Santa Fe Deep Salmon' — has salmon-pink flowers

Catharanthus roseus

Celosia argentea var. *cristata*

Exposure: Full sun
Salt Tolerance: Fair
Drought Tolerance: Poor
Deer Resistance: Poor

Celosias count among their number some of the weirdest-looking flowers in the plant world. They can be real conversation pieces, and make your garden look like a science project. For the less flamboyant souls among us, there are also celosias with plumelike flowers that work very well with other garden flowers. Try them with yuccas, phormium, and other spiky-leaved plants. Or combine them with round or daisylike flowers. They can also work in a garden with ornamental grasses in the background.

Celosias grow from eight inches to four feet high, depending on the variety, with oval to lance-shaped leaves. The flowers come in many warm colors — shades of red, rose, pink, orange, gold, yellow, and white.

They need full sun and warm temperatures; so do not plant them out until all danger of frost is past in spring and the soil has warmed. Celosias need well-drained soil but they don't like to get too dry; water during spells of dry weather. They stand up nicely to heat and humidity.

This is a confusing group of plants, taxonomically speaking. You may see variations in nomenclature in different places, but here are the main groupings.

Cristata Group

These are really oddball flowers — they can look like alien life-forms beamed in from across the galaxy. The flower heads resemble the combs of roosters, fans with ruffled edges, brains, or coral, or just impossible-to-describe curled and twisted things. The colors include lurid magentas and brilliant reds. Childsii Group is similar and sometimes included with this one.

RECOMMENDED CULTIVARS
- 'Big Chief Mix' — three feet high, twisted, rounded flower heads in red, pink, and yellow

Cristata Group

- Olympia series — dwarf, eight inches high, with fan-shaped flowers in shades of red and yellow

Plumosa Group

Plumosa Group has the most appealing (to my eye) varieties, with feathery, plumelike flowers.

RECOMMENDED CULTIVARS
- 'Apricot Brandy' — two feet high
- Castle series — 12 inches high, 8-inch-long, feathery plumes in several colors: pink, yellow, orange, and scarlet
- 'New Look' — to one and a half feet high, with reddish bronze leaves and deep scarlet flowers

Plumosa Group

Spicata Group

Spicata Group, also called wheat celosias, have narrow, plumy flower spikes on branched stems atop the plants.

RECOMMENDED CULTIVARS
- 'Flamingo Feather' — two to three feet high, pink flowers that fade to cream as they age
- 'Flamingo Purple' — three to four feet high, rosy purple flowers and purple leaves
- 'Pink Candle' — two to three feet high, rosy pink flowers

Spicata Group

Cosmos species

Exposure: Full sun	
Salt Tolerance: Fair	
Drought Tolerance: Good	
Deer Resistance: Poor	

Cosmos are charming additions to summer flower gardens and cottage gardens. The slender stems and finely cut leaves give the plants a rather willowy grace until late in the season, when they start to look weedy. The bowl-shaped flowers come in shades of pink, crimson, white, yellow, orange, and maroon. Sometimes they self-sow. In the garden, cosmos work well with annuals like celosia, lantana, and four-o'clocks, and with such perennials as heliopsis, daylilies, sea lavender, perovskia, salvia, and black-eyed Susan. They also do well in containers.

Give cosmos a location in full sun, with well-drained soil of average fertility. They grow well in sandy soils and can tolerate a fair amount of drought. Cosmos need some protection near the beach but are reasonably salt tolerant. Regular deadheading keeps the plants blooming, but they do begin to look straggly by fall.

Cosmos atrosanguineus

Cosmos atrosanguineus
Chocolate cosmos

Perennial in Zones 7 to 10, chocolate cosmos grows as an annual elsewhere. It gets to be about 2½ feet high, with divided, fernlike leaves and velvety maroon flowers with reddish brown centers. The flowers really do smell like chocolate.

Cosmos sulphureus

Cosmos bipinnatus

The most familiar type of cosmos, *C. bipinnatus* grows three to four or more feet high. The leaves are thin and threadlike, and flowers may be pink, rose, white, or crimson.

RECOMMENDED CULTIVARS
- 'Seashells' — petals are rolled into tubes
- 'Sensation' — grows three feet high, with large pink or white flowers
- 'Sonata' — shorter, one to two feet high, in red, pink, or white

Cosmos bipinnatus 'Sensation'

Cosmos sulphureus
Golden cosmos

This cosmos produces semidouble yellow or orange flowers on two- to three-foot plants.

RECOMMENDED CULTIVARS
- 'Bright Lights' — gold, red, and yellow
- Cosmic series — double flowers in orange, yellow, and gold
- Klondike series — one to one and a half feet high
- 'Lemon Twist' — soft yellow flowers, a different color for cosmos

Dahlia cultivars
Dahlia

Exposure: Full sun
Salt Tolerance: Good
Drought Tolerance: Poor
Deer Resistance: Poor

Dahlias are excellent additions to seashore flower gardens and containers. Use tall varieties near the back of the garden and shorter ones closer to the front. The plants bloom nonstop all summer until frost shuts them down; they reach their peak in many gardens in August and September. There's a range of warm colors avail-

Dahlia 'Jitterbug'

able: shades of red, rose, pink, yellow, orange, and white, and a variety of flower forms — from small, round pompoms to single and daisylike to slender petaled and spidery. The flowers come in many sizes, too, although the big dinner-plate types are hard to mix with other plants in the garden. Plants range in size from foot-high dwarfs to three- and four-footers. Use dwarf dahlias in the front of garden beds and borders or in pots. Taller varieties can go into the middle ground of a sunny bed or border, or you can combine them with other annuals in large containers. Dahlias combine well with daisylike flowers such as coreopsis, spiky blossoms like salvia and veronica, small-flowered baby's breath and *Verbena bonariensis,* and many other flowers.

Dahlias are not true annuals; they grow from tuberous roots that are tender — they must be dug and stored indoors over winter except in very warm climates where the ground does not freeze. Plants grow best in soil that is fertile and moist but well drained. Amend soil with compost in fall for planting the following spring. Good drainage is important; dahlias will rot in soggy soil.

If you are starting with tubers, plant them in the garden in spring, when the danger of heavy frost is over (a few weeks before the average last frost date in your area). Place the tubers deep enough that the "eyes," or growth buds, are two to four inches below the soil surface. Set in dahlia plants from the nursery outdoors when all danger of frost is past. Set plants in the garden at the same depth they were growing in their nursery pot.

As the plants grow, pinch off the stem tips when there are four sets of leaves on the stems; pinch back to the next set of leaves. Pinching will result in bushier plants with more flowers.

Like many annuals, dahlias are heavy feeders. Feed them every couple of weeks with a balanced, all-purpose fertilizer. Water plants during dry weather. Plants growing in containers may need daily watering during hot weather, depending on the size of the pot. Tall varieties may need staking.

To store dahlia tubers for replanting next year, dig them in fall after the first couple of light frosts. Cut back the stems to five or six inches, and when the soil is dry, brush it off the tubers. Store in a cool place indoors over winter, in peat moss.

There are far too many dahlia varieties to make recommendations here. Visiting local nurseries and investigating mail-order catalogs will give you numerous choices.

Euphorbia marginata
Snow-on-the-mountain

Exposure: Full sun to partial shade
Salt Tolerance: Moderate
Drought Tolerance: Good
Deer Resistance: Good

Snow-on-the-mountain, a relative of the poinsettia, is primarily a foliage plant. Its white-edged leaves, some of which are mostly white, can inject sparkle into a garden that contains lots of deep-colored flowers and dark green foliage.

The branched plants grow two to three feet high; pinching back the stem tips when plants are young promotes bushier growth. Tiny white flowers cluster in the leaf axils in late summer, but they are not particularly decorative. Plants may need staking in warm climates.

Give plants full sun and well-drained soil of average to poor fertility. Do not plant outdoors until frost danger is past. Plants don't need much except for some water during prolonged dry spells. The white sap in the leaves and stem is toxic when ingested and is a skin irritant for many people; wear gloves if needed.

Euphorbia marginata

Lantana cultivars
Lantana

Exposure: Full sun
Salt Tolerance: Good
Drought Tolerance: Good
Deer Resistance: Good

Lantana is a woody-stemmed perennial that is hardy in the warmest climates but is grown as an annual in most East Coast gardens. Plants grow one to three feet high and have dark green, rather coarse-textured, toothed, oblong leaves. Throughout the summer they bear many dome-shaped clusters of little flowers in warm shades of red, orange, gold, yellow, pink, lavender, and white. There are solid colors and bicolors. Some varieties change color as the flowers mature, so individual flower heads may be two or three different colors at once. The flowers attract butterflies.

Lantana cultivar

Use lantana in the front of an informal bed or border, or grow it in containers or window boxes where it can cascade over the edge. Good companions for lantana are verbena, salvia, coreopsis, achillea, geraniums, petunias, butterfly weed (*Asclepias tuberosa*), and nepeta.

Lantana needs full sun and adapts to a range of soils. It does best in well-drained soil but will tolerate moister conditions, too, as long as the soil is not continuously soggy. The best bloom usually occurs in sandy or gravelly soils that are low in nutrients. Plants will also tolerate partial shade. Lantana generally does well near the beach, and holds up well in summer heat. If lantana is hardy where you live, don't cut it back in fall; instead, wait until early the following spring. Aphids and whiteflies sometimes cause trouble for lantana.

RECOMMENDED CULTIVARS

- 'Alba' — white flowers on trailing stems to three feet
- 'Feston Rose' — pink and yellow flowers
- 'Gold Mound' — variegated yellow leaves, golden yellow flowers
- 'Patriot Rainbow' — multicolored flowers of red, orange, yellow, and purple; 'Confetti' is very similar
- 'Tangerine' — orange and yellow-orange flowers

Lobularia maritima
Sweet alyssum

Exposure: Full sun to partial shade
Salt Tolerance: Fair
Drought Tolerance: Poor
Deer Resistance: Good

These sweet little plants have many uses in the garden. They are classic edging plants, and are widely grown in pots, window boxes, and hanging baskets, where they can spill over the edges. Less common but quite delightful ways to use sweet alyssum are as a carpet under spring bulbs, taller perennials and annuals, or roses; between paving stones in a patio or path; and as an annual ground cover in an area that does not get foot traffic.

Sweet alyssum grows just 3 to 6 inches high and 8 to 12 inches wide, forming a low mat of small, oblong green leaves. The plants bear many clusters of small, white, honey-scented flowers. There are also pink- and purple-flowered varieties.

Sweet alyssum grows best in cool weather. It will bloom through the summer, too, although it does not like heat. If bloom slows and plants begin to look ragged in midsummer, shear then back to promote fresh growth and renewed bloom. In southern gardens, sweet alyssum is fine in winter and spring gardens, but doesn't do well in summer heat.

Give sweet alyssum well-drained soil of average fertility, in full sun or partial shade. Water during spells of dry weather. Sweet alyssum will self-sow if its location suits it.

RECOMMENDED CULTIVARS

- Easter Bonnet series — flowers in purple, lavender, violet, rose, and dark pink
- 'Rosie O'Day' — six inches high, with rose-pink flowers
- 'Snow Crystal' — six to nine inches high; white flowers are larger than those of most other varieties
- 'Violet Queen' — deep violet flowers

Lobularia maritima

Pelargonium × hortorum
Geranium

Exposure: Full sun
Salt Tolerance: Fair to good
Drought Tolerance: Poor
Deer Resistance: Good

Geraniums are the most widely grown annuals in American gardens, and they perform well in a variety of situations. At the seashore they grow happily even near the beach. A location behind the dunes or a windbreak is ideal if you are on the ocean, but I have seen them flourishing on the exposed upstairs deck of a house right behind the dunes. Away from the water, they just need a sunny spot.

Geraniums are most often grown in containers, where they are excellent for adding volume to pots. In a large container you can combine them with spiky Victoria salvia, dracaena or a small fountain grass (*Pennisetum*) for height; some smaller fillers such as calibrachoa or million bells, narrow-leaved zinnia, lobelia, and sweet alyssum; with trailing vinca, Wave petunias, or sweet potato vine to spill over the edges. Geraniums can work as bedding plants, too, in formal or informal gardens.

Geraniums have rounded to kidney-shaped, lobed leaves that may or may not have the dark purplish, orange, or yellow bands, or zones, that gave rise to the name "zonal geranium." The round flower heads come in a range of warm shades — red, scarlet, rose, pink, salmon, and white. The plants grow one to two feet tall, with an equal spread.

Geraniums need lots of sun to do their best. Give them moist but well-drained, fertile soil that is rich in organic matter. Deadhead regularly to keep the plants blooming — they will continue until frost shuts them down.

Geraniums are usually trouble-free, although virus diseases can afflict them, as can aphids and whiteflies. Mildew and rot can occur when soil is poorly drained or plants are overwatered.

RECOMMENDED GROUPS

- Americana series — vigorous, with medium green leaves and flowers in a range of colors; Eclipse series is similar, but the plants are smaller and the leaves more bronzy
- Candy series — dark green leaves and plants with names like 'Bubblegum' (single flowers combining magenta and deep pink), 'Cotton Candy' (semidouble salmon pink flowers), and 'Lollipop' (semidouble coral-red flowers)
- Orbit series — widely available and comes in 17 colors
- Tango series — has zoned leaves and flowers in deep red, red, orange, salmon, and violet

Orbit series pelargoniums

Petunia × *hybrida*
Petunia

Exposure:	Full sun to partial shade
Salt Tolerance:	Fair
Drought Tolerance:	Poor
Deer Resistance:	Good

Petunias are colorful and easy to grow, and they come in a broad range of colors and several different sizes and flower types. Colors include many shades of purple, rose, pink, salmon, red, and white, plus some yellows. True blue is hard to find; although numerous cultivars are called "blue," most of them, to my eye, are more violet.

Petunias are terrific in pots, planters, window boxes, and hanging baskets, and they are useful in the front of beds and borders, too. Trailing kinds can even serve as ground covers in areas that get no foot traffic. Probably the greatest drawback to petunias is that they take a pounding during heavy rain and can look bedraggled for days afterward.

The most familiar and widely grown petunias are cultivars of the hybrid species *Petunia × hybrida*. At the seashore, the smaller, single, multiflora types generally hold up better than the big, ruffly grandiflora varieties, which can look tattered and disheveled after doing battle with strong winds and heavy rains. The trailing Wave varieties are vigorous and free blooming, but they tend to peter out and look bad toward the end of summer. An old-fashioned trailing species, *Petunia integrifolia,* stays attractive and vigorous longer than the Wave varieties, at least in my experience. Its dark-eyed, purple-pink flowers continue blooming nicely into fall. Calibrachoa, or million bells, which is like a miniature petunia with a cascading habit, also does well at the seashore and is terrific in hanging baskets and pots.

Good companions for petunias are salvia, celosia, marigolds, marguerites (*Argyranthemum frutescens*), catharanthus, New Guinea impatiens, lantana, and tradescantia.

Plant petunias in full sun to partial shade, in well-drained soil. They will tolerate poor, sandy soils as long as you fertilize them regularly. Frequent deadheading will keep the plants blooming. In late summer, when the stems get long and floppy, especially on Wave petunias, start cutting them back by half, a few stems at a time, to promote fresh growth and renewed flowering.

Petunias may be attacked by botrytis or tobacco mosaic virus, aphids, and whiteflies.

RECOMMENDED GROUPS
- Carpet series — these multiflora types are especially heat tolerant and good for southern gardens
- Celebrity series — comes in more than 20 colors, including bicolors, flowers with contrasting veining, and some with a central star
- Supermagic series — larger than average plants, in a good range of flower colors
- Surprise series — low and mound forming, and good bloomers
- Wave petunias (which are actually multifloras) — bloom on long, vining stems in purple, magenta, pink, white, rose, or lilac

Wave petunias with purple tradescantia

Phormium tenax
New Zealand flax

Exposure: Full sun to partial shade
Salt Tolerance: Fair
Drought Tolerance: Poor
Deer Resistance: Good

New Zealand flax makes a great foliage accent where you want a vertical line and bold, spiky, sword-shaped leaves. It is hardy in Zones 8 and south, but everywhere else we grow it as an annual. The leaves of different cultivars come in various colors and combinations of colors. The leaves of some varieties are longitudinally striped or infused with pink, red, orange, yellow, or white. The most common sizes available seem to be two to three feet high, although there are varieties ranging from one to six feet. You can use phormium in beds and borders or large contain-ers. They lend a contemporary or tropical touch to the garden. Try them with hibiscus, cannas, castor bean (*Ricinus communis*), yucca, dahlias, celosia, or salvia.

Give New Zealand flax full sun to partial shade and moist but well-drained, humusy soil of average to good fertility. Shade is especially good for them in southern gardens where the strong sun can tend to fade the colors. The plants are easy to care for — they need no deadheading or staking. At the end of the season, you can bring them indoors in pots to a bright room to use as houseplants.

RECOMMENDED CULTIVARS

- 'Apricot Queen' — two to three feet high; leaves are infused with apricot-orange and striped in yellow and green
- 'Atropurpurea' — to six feet, with bronzy purple leaves
- 'Aureum' — green leaves striped with yellow
- 'Bronze Baby' — two to two and a half feet high, with bronze leaves
- 'Dazzler' — three feet high, arching leaves striped in orange, pink, and red
- 'Flamingo' — pink, green, and yellow leaves

Phormium tenax

Portulaca grandiflora
Rose moss

Portulaca grandiflora

Exposure: Full sun
Salt Tolerance: Good
Drought Tolerance: Good
Deer Resistance: Good

These tough little plants, with their warm-colored flowers, are at their best in the front of dry, sunny beds and borders. Good companions include lantana, smaller artemisias, dusty miller, coreopsis, yarrow, nepeta, perovskia, and African daisy. Rose moss is a low, sprawling plant to six or eight inches high, with succulent, fleshy, needle-like leaves and ruffly, cup-shaped flowers in many shades of red, rose, pink, orange, yellow, and white. The flowers close up at night and on rainy days.

Portulaca loves the sun, and withstands heat and drought with no problem. What it doesn't like is humidity, so it's not a great performer in southern gardens. Give it well-drained, sandy soil of average to poor fertility. It has good salt tolerance and will grow near the beach. In humid conditions, rose moss is prone to rot or disease, but otherwise it is generally trouble-free. Plants often self-sow in conditions to their liking.

RECOMMENDED CULTIVARS

- 'Calypso Mixed' — with double flowers in bright, hot colors
- Sundance hybrids — large, double flowers in many bright colors on semi-trailing plants; the flowers remain open into the evening
- Sundial series — varieties that perform better in cooler, cloudier conditions, with double flowers in a good range of colors

Salvia species

Exposure: Full sun to partial shade

Salt Tolerance: Fair

Drought Tolerance: Poor

Deer Resistance: Good

The two tender sages described here are both good choices for coastal gardens. Red-flowered varieties look best when planted by themselves as a group or combined with white flowers, foliage plants such as dusty miller and snow-on-the-mountain, or lots of green foliage to tone down their bright colors. Or you can use them sparingly as accents in beds and borders of softer-hued flowers. White-flowered sages can mix with many other annuals and perennials.

Salvia splendens

Salvia coccinea
Texas sage

A perennial in Zones 9 and south, Texas sage is an annual for the rest of us. The bushy plants grow one to two feet high, with oval green leaves and loose spikes of cherry red, coral or white flowers all summer. It looks similar to the very familiar scarlet sage, but the plants are bushier and more compact. A good plant for informal beds and borders, Texas sage attracts butterflies and sometimes hummingbirds.

Texas sage is easy to grow in full sun to partial shade in the North, with afternoon shade in the South, in almost any well-drained soil.

RECOMMENDED CULTIVARS

- 'Cherry Blossom' — bicolored flowers of salmon and white
- 'Coral Nymph' — red and white flowers
- 'Lady in Red' — flowers of brilliant scarlet
- 'Snow Nymph' — with white flowers

Salvia coccinea

Salvia splendens
Scarlet sage

This often-used sage figures into many municipal park and roadside plantings. The flaming scarlet flowers can be hard to mix comfortably with other colors in the garden, but surrounding it with lots of green and white helps tone it down. There are also varieties with pink, purple, and creamy white blossoms that are easier to work with. Plants grow six inches to two feet high, depending on variety, with dark green oval leaves.

Scarlet sage can fade in intense sun; planting in partial shade can help the flowers hold their color better. Give them moist but well-drained soil of good fertility. Pinch the stem tips of young plants to promote bushier growth.

RECOMMENDED CULTIVARS

- 'Blaze of Fire' — lighter green leaves, red flowers
- 'Bonfire' — two to three feet high, scarlet flowers
- Empire series — comes in purple, red, rose-pink, burgundy, salmon, and white
- 'Flare' — grows to one and a half feet and has tall scarlet-red spikes
- Sizzler series — flowers of red, burgundy, lavender, purple, salmon, white, and a salmon-and-white bicolor

Senecio cineraria
Dusty miller

Exposure:	Full sun to partial shade
Salt Tolerance:	Good
Drought Tolerance:	Good
Deer Resistance:	Good

What artemisias do for perennial gardens dusty miller does for annual beds and container plantings. The silvery white leaves soften color contrasts in the garden, tone down bright, hot colors, and blend mixtures of colors. Dusty miller is especially pretty with pink and blue flowers. Plants grow from about 10 inches to 2 feet high, with silver-white leaves whose edges are cut and filigreed.

Dusty miller thrives in full, baking sun, but it can also handle partial or even light shade. Too much shade, however, will cause the leaves to lose their whiteness and turn green. The plants have no trouble with heat and are quite drought tolerant. They don't hold up well in high humidity. They can withstand wind and salt spray and grow well near the beach. You can grow them in practically any soil, as long as it is not soggy. Pinch the stem tips when plants are young to encourage bushier growth. If the plants bloom, remove the yellow flowers to preserve the best foliage quality (the flowers aren't very ornamental). Plants sometimes winter over in southern gardens.

RECOMMENDED CULTIVARS
- 'Cirrus' — eight inches high, very white leaves
- 'New Look' — 8 to 10 inches high; very white, somewhat broader leaves
- 'Silver Dust' — 10 to 12 inches high, an old variety with silvery, deeply cut leaves
- 'Silver Lace' — to 15 inches high; leaves are finely cut and lacier than those of 'Silver Dust'

Senecio cineraria

Strobilanthes dyerianus
Persian shield

Strobilanthes dyerianus

Exposure:	Full sun to partial shade
Salt Tolerance:	Moderate
Drought Tolerance:	Poor
Deer Resistance:	Poor

Persian shield deserves to be better known. A shrubby plant in its native Burma, it is an annual or greenhouse plant for American gardeners. Grow this plant for its stunningly beautiful leaves. They are oval to lance shaped with toothed edges, and up to six inches long. The upper surface is a bronzy green but is covered in magenta-purple and overlaid with a silvery sheen — the effect is one of shimmering iridescence. On the underside, the leaves are a darker purple.

Over the course of a growing season the plants will grow tall — to three feet or even more. Pinching them while they are young will promote more branching, but the plants will still be upright rather than full and bushy. Use them as vertical accents in containers or in the middle ground of a bed or border. Persian shield produces tubular blue flowers in autumn when grown in a greenhouse, but you probably won't see them in a summer garden.

Persian shield does best away from the water or behind a windbreak, although it does have a reasonable degree of salt tolerance. It likes sun but appreciates some afternoon shade, especially in southern gardens. Give the plant moist but well-drained soil of reasonable fertility; feed it once a month if you grow it in a container. Persian shield does poorly in cool weather, so wait until the weather warms in spring before planting it outdoors.

Exposure: Full sun	
Salt Tolerance: Fair	
Drought Tolerance: Good	
Deer Resistance: Good	

Cheerful marigolds are garden stalwarts, with a role to play in beds and borders and containers. Marigolds look good with other red, orange, and yellow flowers such as coreopsis and gaillardia, and also with blue flowers like salvia and bachelor's buttons (*Centaurea cyanus*) or purples including verbena and petunias. They love the sun, although signet marigolds will also grow in partial shade. All three tolerate poor, well-drained soil, but signet marigold prefers even moisture while the other two like it drier. Rich, fertile soil is not recommended for any marigolds — it makes them floppy and weak, and they won't bloom as well. Deadhead often to keep the plants blooming and looking neat. There are three main types of marigolds, and many cultivars within those types.

Tagetes erecta
African marigold

This largest of the marigolds grows one to four feet high and has yellow, orange, or creamy white flowers two to four inches across. The leaves are dark green and deeply divided, with a strong aroma. The plants tend to grow as one or two straight stems unless you pinch them when they are young to encourage bushiness. Use the tallest ones in the back of the garden; smaller ones can go into the front of a bed or border, or in pots, tubs, or window boxes.

RECOMMENDED CULTIVARS

- Crush series — 10 to 15 inches high, large, double yellow or orange flowers
- Discovery series — 8 to 10 inches high, compact and heat tolerant, orange or golden yellow flowers need no deadheading
- Inca series — 14 inches high, orange, yellow, or gold double flowers, heat tolerant, hold up well in rain
- 'Snowball' and 'French Vanilla' — both are creamy white

Tagetes patula
French marigold

These are the smallest marigolds, growing 6 to 12 inches high. They sport 1- or 2-inch flowers in golden yellow, orange, or bicolors including brownish red. The plants are naturally bushy and need less pinching than African marigolds.

RECOMMENDED CULTIVARS

- Bonanza series — 10 to 12 inches high, double flowers, early blooming
- 'Bolero' — 12 inches high, gold-edged maroon petals
- Bounty series — 10 inches high, good for hot, humid climates; gold, orange, yellow, and bicolor flowers
- Disco series — 12 inches high, single flowers in various bicolor combinations

Tagetes tenuifolia
Signet marigold

Intermediate between the previous two is the signet marigold, which grows from 8 to 18 inches high but has the smallest flowers. The finely cut, feathery foliage has a pleasant, citrusy scent, and the yellow or orange flowers, if you grow them organically, are edible. The plants are looser and less rigidly upright in form than the other two types.

RECOMMENDED CULTIVARS

- 'Lemon Gem' — 6 to 12 inches high, single yellow flowers
- 'Tangerine Gem' — 6 to 12 inches high, single orange flowers
- 'Starfire Mix' — single, bicolor flowers in orange, red, and yellow

Tagetes 'Tangerine Gem'

Tropaeolum majus
Nasturtium

Exposure: Full sun

Salt Tolerance: Fair

Drought Tolerance: Poor

Deer Resistance: Good

Nasturtiums grow on long, sometimes trailing stems that can sprawl over the ground, spill over the side of a container, or scramble up a shrub (see photo at right). The bright, warm-colored flowers are delightful in informal flower beds and borders, in a cottage garden, or in a kitchen garden. They're edible, too, as are the round, blue-green leaves, which have a peppery tang similar to watercress, to which nasturtium is related. Flowers bloom in shades of red, rose, pink, orange, gold, creamy white, and mahogany.

Give nasturtiums a place in full sun in the North; in the South they do better with some afternoon shade. They need well-drained soil of average to poor fertility; in rich soil there will be few flowers. Nasturtiums may slow down and sulk in summer, but if you can keep them going, they will come roaring back in fall. The plants don't like to be disturbed, so sow seeds where you want the plants to grow, or transplant them with care.

RECOMMENDED CULTIVARS

- 'Alaska' — to 15 inches high, leaves splashed with white, flowers in various colors
- Climbing Hybrids Improved — to five feet, many colors
- 'Empress of India' — 12 inches high, with non-trailing, orangey red flowers
- Gleam series — trailing plants with double red or yellow flowers
- 'Jewel Mix' — 12 inches high and non-trailing, semidouble flowers in mixed colors
- 'Jewel of Africa' — similar to 'Alaska', but with trailing stems

Tropaeolum majus

Zinnia angustifolia

Zinnia angustifolia
Narrow-leaved zinnia

Exposure: Full sun

Salt Tolerance: Fair

Drought Tolerance: Good

Deer Resistance: Poor

Narrow-leaved zinnia is a smaller, less flashy plant than the more familiar common zinnia (*Zinnia elegans*). That makes it better able to withstand the heat, humidity, and drought it will encounter near the sea. It is less prone to the mildew and foliar diseases that disfigure its larger, showier relatives. Narrow-leaved zinnia grows 12 to 15 inches high, with slender leaves and small, single flowers of yellow, orange, or white. It's charming in the front of a bed or border and grows beautifully in pots and window boxes.

Give narrow-leaved zinnia full sun and well-drained, fertile soil. The small flowers need no deadheading; in general, the plants are easy to grow, and take to all kinds of climates.

Varieties include 'White Star' and 'Crystal White' (white flowers), 'Gold Star' (golden yellow), and 'Orange Star' (orange flowers).

Ornamental Grasses

Ammophila breviligulata
American beach grass

Zones: 3–9	
Exposure: Full sun	
Salt Tolerance: Excellent	
Drought Tolerance: Good	
Deer Resistance: Good	

This perennial native grass is the first line of defense in stabilizing dunes, and, in fact, that is how it is best used, although you can also plant it in very well-drained, sandy soil on a slope or a bank. Beach grass traps and holds sand on both the ocean side and the lee side of dunes. The plants spread widely from rhizomes. Interestingly, when the stands of grass have grown dense enough to hold the sand in place, the grass begins to lose its vigor. At that point, if the dunes are on your property and you are permitted to plant on them, you can begin to replace the beach grass with more permanent grasses or shrubs (or with new plugs of beach grass).

American beach grass grows one to three feet high, with narrow leaves that are green in spring and fade to brownish beige in winter in the North; in the Carolinas, the leaves often remain partially green in winter. In summer or fall, plants produce tall seed stalks, each bearing a slender seed spike 6 to 10 inches long.

Plant beach grass during cool weather. In the North, that means spring (March and April on Long Island, where I live). In the Carolinas, the best planting time is in winter, from November to March. If you're in doubt about when to plant, check with your local nursery — they'll usually have plugs of beach grass available at the proper time for planting in your area. Set the plugs upright in the sand about eight inches deep. It's all right to bury part of the leaf. Pack the sand firmly around each plug when you plant it.

Space the plugs 12 to 18 inches apart on center, in staggered rows 2 to 2½ feet apart. (If you have a large space to fill and use 1-foot spacing, plan on using about 1,000 grass plugs per 2,000 square feet.) Fertilize with a balanced or high-nitrogen fertilizer three times during the first year after planting (in early spring, late spring, and early fall). The second year fertilize twice, in spring and in fall. Thereafter, fertilize just once a year, in spring.

Ammophila breviligulata

Elymus arenarius 'Glauca'
Blue lyme grass

Zones: 4–10

Exposure: Full sun to light shade

Salt Tolerance: Good

Drought Tolerance: Good

Deer Resistance: Good

Elymus arenarius

Blue lyme grass has been grown in gardens for a hundred years, and it's a rugged, reliable plant in seascape gardens today. The plant forms a clump of blue-green leaves to ½ inch wide that grow to three feet long but arch over, so the visual height is closer to two feet. Spiky gray-green seed heads appear in summer, but they are not very ornamental — the leaves are the reason to grow this plant. Blue lyme grass is a spreader, but is less problematic in poor, sandy soils.

Given its vigorous nature, blue lyme grass is probably best used in poor soil, but it will grow practically anywhere. It can be planted to stabilize dunes or control erosion on slopes, and it will tolerate salt spray and salt-laden winds off the ocean. The gray-blue leaves look especially good with deep purple foliage, pink, rose, and lavender flowers, and silver foliage in beds and borders. Or you might just plant it by itself in a mass where you want to strike a cool note.

Cut back the plants in early spring, to a few inches above the ground. If they start to look ragged during the growing season, mow or trim them back to encourage fresh new growth. Pests and diseases don't attack this plant, and, like most ornamental grasses, it is deer resistant.

Helictotrichon sempervirens
Blue oat grass

Zones: 4–9

Exposure: Full sun

Salt Tolerance: Fair

Drought Tolerance: Good

Deer Resistance: Good

Blue oat grass grows as a clump of thin, metallic-blue leaves to two feet high and wide that are evergreen in warmer climates and semievergreen in cooler climates. In late summer, plants produce on stiff, upright, four-foot stems graceful clusters of flat seed heads resembling oats. They begin white and age to light beige as they dry. Plants do not always bloom in warm climates.

In seashore landscapes, blue oat grass makes an interesting accent in beds and borders or massed together.

Blue oat grass likes full sun for the most part, though it appreciates some shade in the southernmost gardens. It needs very well-drained soil with some fertility, but will adapt to a range of soil types. It does not tolerate heavy, soggy soils. Allow adequate air circulation between plants; otherwise they may suffer in very humid conditions.

Helictotrichon sempervirens

Miscanthus sinensis
Maiden grass, eulalia grass

Zones: 5–9
Exposure: Full sun to partial shade
Salt Tolerance: Fair to good
Drought Tolerance: Fair
Deer Resistance: Good

Miscanthus is among the most widely bred and planted of all ornamental grasses. A visit to a good nursery will show you cultivars ranging from two to seven feet high, with leaf blades varying from about an inch wide to thin and almost needlelike. The clump of arching, grassy leaves may be plain green, edged or striped in creamy white, or banded in gold. In late summer and fall, plants bear glistening, airy, fan-shaped seed heads that may be pinkish, coppery, or silvery. Seed heads turn beige or white as they age, as do the leaves. Where winter winds are not too fierce and snow and ice not too heavy, the seed plumes may stay on the plants through winter.

One problem with miscanthus is that it is vigorous and can become invasive in good growing conditions. To be safe, you might do best to plant it where its spread can be contained, such as in a built-in planter bed, in a large tub, or in an area bounded by pavement. And watch for unwanted seedlings that may come up where you don't want them; pull them when they are young.

Miscanthus will grow in full sun to partial shade. It thrives in moist but well-drained, reasonably fertile soil but will tolerate drier conditions, too, and even a fair degree of drought.

RECOMMENDED CULTIVARS
- 'Adagio' — two to four feet high, gray-green leaves; pink flower plumes age to white
- 'Gracillimus' — five to six feet high, has narrow leaves with a white midrib and bronze seed heads in fall
- 'Morning Light' — four to five feet high; has thin, white-edged leaves that appear luminous from a distance and coppery seed plumes that age to tan or beige

- 'Purpurascens' (flamegrass) — three to four feet high and less hardy than most varieties, turns purplish in the cool weather of fall except in very warm southern gardens; has silvery seed plumes in late summer
- 'Silver Feather' or 'Silberfeder' — to six feet high; has gracefully arching leaves and silvery to pinkish brown plumes
- 'Zebrinus' — five to seven feet high; has green leaves horizontally banded with yellow, and coppery seed heads in late summer

Miscanthus sinensis 'Zebrinus'

Panicum virgatum
Switchgrass

Zones: 5–9
Exposure: Full sun to partial shade
Salt Tolerance: Fair to good
Drought Tolerance: Good
Deer Resistance: Good

Switchgrass is native to the tallgrass prairies of the Midwest, and makes a fine addition to seashore gardens, too. It forms a clump of narrow, bluish green leaves. In late summer, plants produce delicate, airy, reddish brown seed clusters. The leaves turn golden or reddish in fall, fading gradually to beige.

Switchgrass is lovely in mixed beds and borders. You can use it as a background plant behind an informal flower garden, mix it with other grasses in a low-maintenance border, or plant it in groups or masses. Or plant tall varieties in a row on a berm or alongside a deck or patio for a summer privacy screen.

Not fussy about soil, switchgrass will grow in a range of soils from wet to dry and sandy. It does best in full sun but tolerates partial shade. Plants can withstand a fair degree of drought (they curl in their leaf edges when it's very dry), but they appreciate water during prolonged periods of hot, dry weather. Cut back plants to a few inches above the ground in early spring to remove old foliage and encourage new growth.

RECOMMENDED CULTIVARS
- 'Cloud Nine' — six feet high, bluish green
- 'Haense Herms' — three to four feet high; turns red in fall with silvery seed heads
- 'Heavy Metal' — narrow, upright clump of metallic-blue leaves to four feet high

Panicum virgatum

Pennisetum species

Zones: Vary with species	
Exposure: Full sun to partial shade	
Salt Tolerance: Fair to good	
Drought Tolerance: Good	
Deer Resistance: Good	

Fountain grasses are valued for their handsome bottlebrush flowers in late summer and their gracefully arching leaves. They vary in their hardiness and cultural requirements, so be sure to read the descriptions below for more information.

Fountain grasses are lovely in beds and borders, massed or grouped with other ornamental grasses, and even in pots. They can handle salt and are attractive near the beach or alongside a garden pool. They will grow in full sun to partial shade, and prefer well-drained soil with varying degrees of moisture. Like other ornamental grasses, fountain grass is not troubled by pests or diseases, and deer don't eat it.

Pennisetum alopecuroides 'Moudry'

Pennisetum alopecuroides

This is the hardiest species familiar to gardeners, growing well in Zones 6 to 9. It grows actively in warm weather and forms a clump of bright green leaves two to three feet high. In midsummer, stiff bottlebrush flowers begin to bloom, starting out creamy white or beige and maturing to coppery-red. They remain in good shape until fall, when the flower heads shatter and drop their seeds. These may take root and grow into new plants, so pull up any unwanted seedlings. This species prefers moist but well-drained soil, but once established it is generally drought tolerant in cooler climates.

RECOMMENDED CULTIVARS

- 'Hameln' — one and a half to two feet high, with narrower, deeper green leaves than the species form and earlier blooming flowers; grows best where winters are cold, and can struggle in Zones 8 and 9
- 'Little Bunny' — a dwarf just eight inches high, for the front of the garden, a rock garden, or containers
- 'Moudry' — black-flowered pennisetum, grows about two and a half feet high with reddish–purple-tinged leaves and dark brown-black flower heads; foliage turns yellow to orange in fall; a prolific self-sower, so be warned

Pennisetum villosum Feathertop

This is another warm-climate fountain grass grown as an annual north of Zone 9. It grows one and a half to two feet high, with narrow, bright green leaves. In midsummer, plants bear fuzzy-looking, arching seed plumes of creamy white. Feathertop is extremely drought tolerant, and will grow in almost pure sand. It's a good bet near the beach. The plants are striking in a mass and as individuals in pots or at the front of a garden bed.

Pennisetum villosum

Pennisetum setaceum 'Rubrum' Purple fountain grass

Mostly grown as an annual north of Zone 9, purple fountain grass grows to three feet high. Its narrow leaves are a striking deep purplish red. The bottlebrush flowers are red-purple and beige. It prefers moist but well-drained soil and generally does well in sandy coastal soils. Once established, it is somewhat drought tolerant. One thing it won't tolerate, though is heavy, wet soil.

Pennisetum setaceum 'Rubrum'

Spartina pectinata
Cordgrass

Spartina pectinata

Zones: 4–9	
Exposure: Full sun	
Salt Tolerance: Good	
Drought Tolerance: Good	
Deer Resistance: Good	

Cordgrass is native to the eastern half of the United States and is found both in marshes and on prairies. It grows as a clump of arching leaves about ½ inch wide and three to six feet high. In midsummer, plants produce narrow flower spikes that start out green and mature to a brownish color. The leaves turn yellow in fall. The plants spread by means of rhizomes (underground stems).

Cordgrass is very drought tolerant once it is established, and it grows well in sand. Plants spread aggressively in moist soils but are better behaved in dry conditions. Dig up rhizomes around the edges of a clump of plants to help contain their spread if you find them getting out of bounds. They can handle plenty of wind and a range of soils but will get floppy if planted in the shade.

Use cordgrass on the back of dunes, to cover ground in difficult locations, or massed alongside a pond or pool. It also grows well in containers.

The cultivar 'Aureomarginata' has a thin yellow edge along its leaves.

Uniola paniculata
Sea oats

Zones: 7–10	
Exposure: Full sun	
Salt Tolerance: Excellent	
Drought Tolerance: Good	
Deer Resistance: Good	

Sea oats is native to coastal areas from Virginia to Florida and along the Gulf Coast. It is the predominant dune grass in the Southeast. But it is an endangered species now and is protected by law in many places. The plants grow three or more feet high, with tough, narrow, light green leaves; in late summer to early fall, brownish seed heads top long, arching stems. The plants spread by means of long rhizomes and root to form colonies in the sand. Sea oats is excellent for holding sand dunes, and unlike American beach grass, it continues to thrive after the sand is stabilized. It is illegal to dig plants from the wild, but you may be able to find plants available commercially. Contact the county Cooperative Extension office in your area to see what the regulations are locally, and if plants are available from approved sources.

If you have existing plants on your property, you may be able to divide them to get more. Make sure each division has a piece of the rhizome attached. Replant the divisions at least one foot deep — it's all right to partially bury the leaves. Water well after planting and fertilize with a high-nitrogen or balanced fertilizer three times during the first year after planting (early spring, late spring, and early fall). The second year, fertilize in spring and fall. Thereafter fertilize once a year, in spring.

Uniola paniculata

Vines and Ground Covers

Ajuga reptans
Bugleweed

Zones: 3–10	
Exposure: Partial to full shade	
Salt Tolerance: Fair	
Drought Tolerance: Poor	
Deer Resistance: Good	

Bugleweed is a familiar, easy-to-grow ground cover that adapts to a variety of situations. The oblong evergreen leaves sit close to the ground and may be deep green, bronze, purple-red, or multicolored, depending on the variety. In late spring or early summer, the plants bear small, upright spikes of deep lavender-blue flowers. Bugleweed spreads well but is not generally invasive, although if planted next to a lawn, it will spread into the grass.

Bugleweed does well in partial to light shade in northern gardens, but in the South it is best in light to full shade. The leaves will scorch under full, blazing sun. The plants adapt to a range of soils, tolerating most types except for very wet and very dry soils. Bugleweed grows even in poor, sandy soil, although it can die if allowed to dry out too much. Water it during spells of dry weather.

RECOMMENDED CULTIVARS
- 'Braunherz' — deep burgundy leaves and lavender flowers
- 'Burgundy Glow' — flushed leaves with burgundy, violet-blue flowers
- 'Catlin's Giant' — large, bronze-purple leaves and eight-inch violet flower spikes
- 'Jungle Beauty' — gold- and purple-splotched leaves, violet-blue flowers
- 'Multicolor' or 'Rainbow' — deep bronzy green leaves splashed with cream and purple and suffused with pink
- 'Pink Surprise' — bronze leaves and pink flowers

Ajuga reptans

Arctostaphylos uva-ursi
Bearberry

Zones: 2–6	
Exposure: Full sun to partial shade	
Salt Tolerance: Excellent	
Drought Tolerance: Good	
Deer Resistance: Good	

Bearberry is a low, mat-forming evergreen shrub with small, rounded, leathery, glossy dark green leaves that may take on a bronze tone in winter. In spring it bears clusters of small, pinkish white flowers, and in late summer or fall there are bright scarlet-red berrylike fruits. Bearberry grows just four to six inches tall and spreads to form a wide mat several feet across.

Extremely tough and durable, bearberry makes a superb ground cover for seaside gardens. It thrives in well-drained, sandy soil with an acidic pH, but it will adapt to beach sand — you can grow it practically down to the dunes.

Space plants one to two feet apart. Once established, they need little or no fertilizer. Plants are sometimes prone to leaf diseases, but resistant varieties are available, including 'Massachusetts' and 'Vancouver Jade'.

Arctostaphylos uva-ursi

Campsis radicans
Trumpet creeper

Zones: 5–9
Exposure: Full sun to light shade
Salt Tolerance: Fair
Drought Tolerance: Fair
Deer Resistance: Good

Trumpet creeper is a familiar late-summer sight in seashore towns along the East Coast. The bright red-orange trumpet flowers can be seen on fences and sturdy trellises, and trained over arbors. You can let trumpet vine climb a tall, sturdy tree trunk or use it as a ground cover to hold soil on a slope or a bank. In many places the vines grow wild, along roadsides and clambering over trees and shrubs. A tough, vigorous vine, trumpet creeper has become rampant in parts of the South.

Trumpet creeper is a woody, clinging vine that can grow to 40 feet long climbing by sticky aerial rootlets. Its pinnate leaves are divided into pairs of oblong, deep green leaflets. In late summer the clusters of tubular, trumpet-shaped blossoms burst forth. They are red-orange in the species, and there are orange- and yellow-flowered forms, too. Hummingbirds are drawn to the flowers, especially the redder ones.

Trumpet vine has a long taproot that goes deep into the ground, giving the plant good tolerance for drought. The vine blooms best in full sun, but it will also grow in partial to light shade, and afternoon shade is helpful in southern gardens. The ideal soil is fertile, moist, and well drained, but given its vigor, it is probably best to plant it in leaner, less-fertile ground. Trumpet creeper has a fair degree of tolerance for salt and wind. At the beach it generally does best behind the dunes. It may take a few years for young vines to bloom after they are planted, so be patient.

Prune the plants severely in spring to keep them from getting out of hand. A hybrid, *Campsis × tagliabuana* 'Mme. Galen', is less rampant, with clusters of apricot-orange flowers.

Campsis radicans

Ceratostigma plumbaginoides
Plumbago

Zones: 6–9
Exposure: Full sun to partial shade
Salt Tolerance: Fair
Drought Tolerance: Fair
Deer Resistance: Good

Plumbago's greatest assets are the clusters of electric blue flowers that bloom in abundance from late summer into fall. When the weather turns cool in fall, the oblong, dark green leaves develop a reddish tinge, further accentuating the flowers.

The plants stay close to the ground, growing no taller than 1½ feet (and usually considerably less than that, in my experience). They spread by means of rhizomes and make a handsome ground cover in low-traffic areas. You can also use them in the front of beds and borders. Ceratostigma can be paired in the garden with daylilies (*Hemerocallis*), asters, black-eyed Susan (*Rudbeckia*), salvia, nepeta, and sedum, among other plants. It is also a good companion for crocuses, small narcissus, grape hyacinth (*Muscari*), crested iris (*Iris cristata*), and other small spring bulbs — it will grow in around them and camouflage their maturing leaves.

Plumbago is a familiar sight in southern gardens, where it is semievergreen. It prefers full sun in the North, but is better with some afternoon shade in the South. Moist but well-drained soil of average fertility suits plumbago well. Near the beach, plant it behind a windbreak or in a sheltered location. It can tolerate some drought but will need watering during prolonged dry spells. The plants are slow to send out new leaves in spring, so don't give up on them.

Ceratostigma plumbaginoides

Clematis species and cultivars

Zones: Vary with species
Exposure: Full sun to light shade
Salt Tolerance: Fair
Drought Tolerance: Poor, except sweet autumn clematis
Deer Resistance: Good

Clematis are among the most beloved of woody vines, and for good reason. They offer an array of flower sizes, forms, and colors, and blooming times from spring to fall. Most gardeners are familiar with the large-flowered hybrids that bloom in late spring or summer, but there are also lovely species clematis that flower at other times of the year. One that does quite well in seaside gardens is sweet autumn clematis (*Clematis terniflora*). Clematis comes in a spectrum of colors that is weighted toward the purple to pink range. There are no real oranges and only a few yellows, but there are a host of other colors to choose from: purples ranging from palest lavender to rich, deep violet, and also several shades of blue; pinks from soft blush to bright magenta, vibrant crimson, and wine red; and white, rounding out the palette.

All vining clematis are tendriled and climb by twisting their leafstalks around a support. The vines can grow to 5 to 20 feet long, depending on the species or variety. Many are quite hardy, growing as far north as Zone 3 and south to Zone 8 or 9. They have some tolerance for salt, but need the protection of a good windbreak near the beach. They can be challenging in southern seaside gardens.

Clematis are lovely on a lamppost, trellis, or lattice panel, or clambering over a shrub. They weave their stems among the branches of the host shrub, and decorate it with their blossoms like ornaments on a Christmas tree. A clematis can make an evergreen tree appear to bloom. They are classic companions for roses, too. They can be planted in the ground or in a large tub to decorate a patio or deck. Vigorous sweet autumn clematis is excellent for camouflage; this species will envelop fences and walls in a blanket of greenery that in late August to early September is spangled with fragrant white stars.

Large-flowered clematis hybrids are often divided into three groups, according to their flowering habit. Mature clematis can benefit from pruning, but the time and manner of pruning depends upon the flowering habit. The Patens Group bloom in spring on old wood. Prune them lightly after they bloom, and only if necessary to keep them under control or to remove damaged growth. Cultivars in this group include 'Barbara Jackman', 'Bees Jubilee', 'Guiding Star', 'Lasurstern', 'Miss Bateman', 'Mrs. Spencer Castle', and 'President'.

The Florida Group hybrids bloom in summer on old wood. They need only light pruning, if any. Prune after flowering. 'Belle of Woking', 'Dr. Ruppel', 'Duchess of Edinburgh', 'Enchantress', and 'Nelly Moser' belong to this group.

The Jackmanii Group bloom in summer and autumn on new wood. You can prune them all the way back to the ground when they are dormant. These hybrids are more cold tolerant than the other two groups. Jackmanii hybrids include 'Ascotiensis', 'Comtesse de Bouchard', 'Crimson King', 'Duchess of Albany', 'Elsa Späth', 'Ernest Markham', 'Etoile Violette', 'Hagley', 'Lady Betty Balfour', 'Minuet', 'Prins Hendrik', 'Ramona', 'Ville de Lyon', and 'W. E. Gladstone'.

Clematis appreciate a fertile, loamy soil that is light and well drained. Amend sandy soil with compost and topsoil before planting. The ideal pH is neutral to mildly alkaline; if your soil is acidic, add lime or crushed seashells to raise the pH.

Keep the soil evenly moist for the first few weeks after planting clematis to let the plants settle in. Thereafter, water when the soil dries out an inch below the surface. To encourage bushier growth, cut back the long stems by half their length during their first year in the garden. It takes two or three years for clematis to begin producing its full complement of mature growth; if your plants look a little spindly their first year or two, be patient.

Install the supports when you plant clematis, and begin guiding or attaching the vines to them as soon as they are long enough; the stems are slender and stiff, and likely to break in strong wind if not secured. Clematis benefits from a good layer of mulch to help conserve moisture and keep the roots cool. An old gardening saying is to plant clematis with its head in the sun and its feet in the shade.

Clematis 'Elsa Späth'

Gelsemium sempervirens
Carolina jessamine

Zones: 7–9	
Exposure: Full sun to light shade	
Salt Resistance: Fair	
Drought Tolerance: Poor	
Deer Resistance: Good	

This classic southern vine, the state flower of South Carolina, has a multiplicity of uses in the garden. It is lovely trained on a fence or trellis, allowed to climb small trees, trailing from containers, or spilling over the ground. You can use it to prevent erosion on slopes or banks.

Jessamine will twine and climb to 15 to 20 feet, or, used as a sprawling ground cover, the stems will form roots where they touch the ground. The small, waxy, dark green leaves are evergreen, pointed, and narrowly oblong, taking on a purplish tone in winter. Masses of small, fragrant, bright yellow flowers bloom in spring, and may appear again in smaller numbers in fall. The cultivar 'Pride of Augusta' has double flowers. The flowers, leaves, and roots are poisonous, so avoid planting Carolina jessamine where young children or nibbling pets are present.

Native from Virginia to Florida and westward, jessamine will grow in sun or shade, but blooms best in a sunny location. At the seashore, it needs a location protected from salt winds. It grows quickest in moist but well-drained soil of good fertility, but it will tolerate dry, sandy conditions. Prune plants, if needed, within a month after they finish blooming in spring.

Gelsemium sempervirens

Liriope muscari
Lilyturf

Zones: 6–10	
Exposure: Partial to full shade	
Salt Tolerance: Fair	
Drought Tolerance: Good	
Deer Resistance: Poor	

Lilyturf is a tough but graceful plant with a clump of narrow, grasslike, evergreen leaves about a foot high that remain in good shape through much of the winter. In autumn, plants send up slender spikes of tiny, round violet flowers that are followed by small black berries. Another species, *Liriope spicata,* is quite similar, and hardier, but it is a very vigorous spreader that can turn into an invasive nuisance. *L. muscari* spreads, but not aggressively, and is easily divided to fill new space.

The plants grow well in partial to medium shade. In the North they can take full sun, but not in the South or the foliage will burn. But they can handle full shade in southern gardens. Plants are adaptable and will grow in practically any soil. They don't have problems with pests or diseases, though deer may eat them. By late winter the leaves start to look ragged, so cut back the plants in early spring to make room for new growth.

RECOMMENDED CULTIVARS

- 'Big Blue' — 8 to 10 inches high, violet-blue flowers
- 'Majestic' — tall spikes of rich violet flowers
- 'Monroe White' — white flowers
- 'PeeDee Ingot' — yellow-green leaves that make a striking combination with red- or purple-leaved plants
- 'Variegata' — leaves edged in ivory, violet flowers

Liriope muscari

Lonicera species
Honeysuckle

Zones: Vary with species	
Exposure: Full sun to partial shade	
Salt Tolerance: Fair	
Drought Tolerance: Fair	
Deer Resistance: Good	

Honeysuckles are a group of vines with trumpet-shaped or two-lipped flowers in white, yellow, orange, pink, or red. They can be lovely covering a fence or rambling about a hillside, and some offer the bonus of sweet fragrance in their flowers. As a group, honeysuckles are easy to grow and need little in the way of maintenance. Where space is limited, prune them to control growth. Some honeysuckles, however, grow too well and can easily become invasive pests. Chief among these is Japanese or Hall's honeysuckle (*Lonicera japonica* 'Halliana'), which is still widely sold and planted along the East Coast for its ability to survive in tough seaside locations. It is best to avoid planting this honeysuckle on your property. The species described here are better behaved and very beautiful, although they will need the protection of a windbreak near the beach.

Everblooming honeysuckle (*Lonicera × heckrottii* 'Goldflame') has lovely flowers that begin as carmine-red buds and then open into fragrant blossoms that are yellow inside and rose-red on the outside. The flowers gradually fade to pink as they age. Everblooming honeysuckle flowers profusely in early summer and continues sporadically into fall. The vines twine and climb, reaching about 15 feet in height. It is hardy in Zones 6 to 9.

Trumpet honeysuckle (*Lonicera sempervirens*), native to the eastern United States, is hardy in Zones 4 to 9 and good for screening. Its stems are typically about 12 to 15 feet long, and are dressed in oval to oblong leaves that are evergreen in southern gardens. From late spring to late summer, the plant sends forth clusters of trumpet-shaped orange, scarlet, or yellow flowers. The flowers are not fragrant, but they do attract hummingbirds. A number of cultivars are

Lonicera sempervirens

available, including 'Cedar Lane', with dark red flowers; 'Magnifica' and 'Superba', with scarlet flowers; and 'Sulphurea', with yellow blossoms.

Honeysuckles take to a range of soils, as long as they are well drained. The plants do not need pruning, but over time they tend to grow into tangled thickets of stems that bloom only at the ends. Pruning after they finish blooming keeps the plants neater. Cut away all the dead old growth from underneath the younger stems with hedge clippers.

Ophiopogon japonicus
Mondo grass

Zones: 6–10	
Exposure: Partial to full shade	
Salt Tolerance: Fair	
Drought Tolerance: Good	
Deer Resistance: Poor	

Mondo grass is very similar to lilyturf (*Liriope* species), and is grown in many southern gardens. The two groups of plants are often confused, but liriope has violet flowers while those of mondo grass are white. Both plants are ideal for edging a sidewalk, path, or driveway. Or you can use them as ground covers, or for a leafy accent in a mixed container planting. Mondo grass is hardy in Zones 7 to 10, grows 8 to 12 inches high, and has white flowers.

Gardeners in Zones 6 to 10 can plant *Ophiopogon planiscapus* 'Nigrescens' or 'Ebony Knight'. This is a showstopper, about eight inches high, with very dark, nearly black leaves.

RECOMMENDED CULTIVARS
- 'Kyoto Dwarf' — grows just four inches high, with purple-black leaves.
- 'Silver Dragon' — grows to 12 inches, with white-variegated leaves

Ophiopogon planiscapus 'Nigrescens'

Parthenocissus species
Virginia creeper, Boston ivy

Zones: Virginia creeper, 3–9; Boston ivy, 4–8
Exposure: Sun or shade
Salt Tolerance: Fair to good
Drought Tolerance: Good
Deer Resistance: Good

Virginia creeper and Boston ivy are two tough, adaptable vines that are salt resistant and wind tolerant. Both are clingers that will hold on to a wall or tree trunk with no help from the gardener. They will also climb an arbor, trellis, or fence. You can use these vines for screening or camouflage, or as ground covers on a slope or a bank. Virginia creeper will also grow on the back side of a dune and can be useful for erosion control. Both vines are at their best in fall, when the foliage turns rich red, although the color may not be as bright in southern gardens.

Virginia creeper is native to eastern North America and can be found growing wild in woodlands and along roadsides up and down the coast. Its compound leaves are composed of five toothed, oblong leaflets radiating from a central point. The leaves turn fiery scarlet or red in fall. In late summer the plants bear dark blue-black berries that birds enjoy. The vines can grow to 30 feet or more.

Boston ivy is the plant from which the Ivy League universities got that name. It can grow to 50 feet, with lobed leaves somewhat resembling maple leaves that turn dark red in autumn. In late summer the plants produce blue-black berries attractive to birds. Numerous cultivars are available, including 'Lowii' and 'Veitchii', whose small leaves are purplish when young; 'Minutifolia', which also has small leaves; 'Purpurea', with dark purple leaves; and 'Robusta', which is exceptionally vigorous.

Both plants grow well in either sun or shade, although they need sun to produce fruit. They tolerate just about any kind of soil, including dry, sandy, and alkaline soils. They don't really need maintenance, except to trim them to keep the vines away from windows and rain gutters if you let them climb the walls of a building. To use the vines as ground cover, space plants about four feet apart. Set them closer together to grow vertically up a wall.

Parthenocissus tricuspidata

Thymus species
Woolly thyme, creeping thyme

Zones: 5–9
Exposure: Full sun
Salt Tolerance: Good
Drought Tolerance: Good
Deer Resistance: Good

Thymes are well known to cooks and herb gardeners, of course, but they make good ground covers too, especially the creeping kinds. These small-leaved plants spread slowly to form low mats. On hot, sunny days, and when stepped upon, the foliage is wonderfully aromatic. Thymes are delightful growing in spaces left between paving stones in a path or patio, tumbling out of pockets in a dry stone wall, or hugging the ground in a dry, sunny spot. They are also fine in rock gardens and in containers.

Woolly thyme grows just a couple of inches high, with tiny, fuzzy, silver-gray leaves and clusters of little rose-pink flowers in summer.

Creeping thyme, or mother of thyme, grows to 10 inches high and forms a mat 1½ feet across. It has tiny, hairy leaves and clusters of minute purple flowers in summer.

All thymes need full sun and light, porous, very well-drained soil. In wet conditions they will rot. A near neutral to mildly alkaline pH is ideal. Average to poor fertility is fine; they don't take well to rich soil. Thyme doesn't always do well in southern gardens due to the high humidity.

RECOMMENDED CULTIVARS
- 'Annie Hall' — light purplish pink flowers
- 'Carol Ann' — yellow-variegated leaves, lavender flowers
- 'Minimus' and 'Minor' — both very compact, just a few inches high
- 'Snowdrift' — white flowers

Thymus serpyllum 'Snowdrift'

Vinca species
Greater periwinkle, common periwinkle

Vinca minor

Zones: Greater periwinkle, 7–11; common periwinkle, 4–9	
Exposure: Sun or shade	
Salt Tolerance: Fair	
Drought Tolerance: Poor	
Deer Resistance: Good	

Periwinkles are easy-to-grow vines that are popular ground covers and container plants. Greater periwinkle (*V. major*) has rounded leaves, edged in cream in the variety 'Variegata', and in spring bears funnel-shaped lilac-purple flowers. Gardeners in the South can use it as a ground cover, but in the North it is strictly a container annual, spilling over the sides of window boxes everywhere. Greater periwinkle does best with at least some sun in the North.

Common periwinkle (*V. minor*) has smaller, oval leaves of deep, glossy green, and purple flowers in early spring. It is seemingly everywhere as a ground cover, and in fact has escaped from cultivation and can be seen weaving its way through woodlands in many parts of the Northeast. In the seaside garden it is tough and dependable, and has much better salt tolerance than does large periwinkle.

Both plants will grow in partial to light shade. Greater periwinkle needs some sun in the North but can take full shade in the South. Common periwinkle can also take full shade. Greater periwinkle is best in moist, fertile soil, while common periwinkle is less fussy and can tolerate drier conditions. Both are best with the protection of a windbreak near the beach.

Trachelospermum jasminoides
Confederate jasmine

Zones: 8–10	
Exposure: Full sun to partial shade	
Salt Tolerance: Good	
Drought Tolerance: Poor	
Deer Resistance: Poor	

An evergreen vine from China, Confederate jasmine got its common name from its long history in southeastern gardens. Confederate jasmine is a vigorous twiner that grows quickly to 15 feet or more. It has small, oblong to elliptical evergreen leaves that are dark green and glossy. In spring and early summer, the plant bears clusters of intensely fragrant, star-shaped, tubular-throated flowers of creamy white. The cultivar 'Variegatum' has green-and-white variegated leaves, and 'Japonicum' has leaves veined in white and turning bronze in autumn.

Confederate jasmine is excellent for screening or covering a trellis. Locate it where you can enjoy the fragrance when the plants are blooming. You can also plant it as a ground cover and let it sprawl over a slope.

The ideal location for Confederate jasmine is sunny or partially shaded, with moist but well-drained soil. Plants may take two or three years to become established, so give them time. Prune as needed to keep Confederate jasmine under control.

Trachelospermum jasminoides

Wisteria species
Wisteria

Zones: Japanese wisteria, 4–9; Chinese wisteria, 5–10	
Exposure: Full sun to partial shade	
Salt Tolerance: Fair	
Drought Tolerance: Poor	
Deer Resistance: Good	

The fragrant flowers of wisteria are pure delight in mid- to late spring. It's too bad the vines that produce them can get so out of control. If you intend to grow wisteria, plan on pruning every year to keep it under control. Southern gardeners, especially, should beware the rampant habit of wisteria, and prune regularly. For those of us who love the sweet-scented flowers, the extra work is well worth it.

Wisteria is lovely trained on an arbor or pergola, on a fence, or on a sturdy trellis. It is dense enough to use for screening. It will also climb a tree trunk and even the wall of a building. For a formal treatment, you can, over a period of years, train wisteria to take the form of a tree. Allow one main stem to develop, and support it with stakes until it is sturdy enough to stand by itself. Careful pruning and training of lateral stems will allow you to develop a canopy of foliage and flowers atop the main trunk. Over time, the stems of wisteria become thick, woody, and interestingly gnarled and twisted.

There are numerous native wisteria species, but the two most often grown for ornamental purposes are both from Asia. They are twining vines whose deciduous leaves consist of pairs of oval leaflets. The leaves turn an attractive yellow in autumn before they drop. The vines bear long, drooping flower clusters in spring.

Japanese wisteria (*W. floribunda*) grows to 25 feet, twining its stems in a clockwise direction, and is the hardier of the two. It also has the longer and more fragrant flower clusters. The species has pealike flowers of a light violet color, but there are cultivars with white, pink, red, or deeper violet flowers. The flowers of both wisterias are followed by flat, velvety seedpods in summer.

Chinese wisteria (*W. sinensis*) grows to 30 feet long, twines in a counterclockwise direction, and blooms a week or two ahead of the Japanese species. Its lightly fragrant, blue-violet flowers come in clusters 8 to 12 inches long. There are cultivars with white, and deeper violet-purple, flowers.

Wisteria flowers best in full sun but can also take partial to light shade. It enjoys fertile soil, but will tolerate poor, dry soils once established. Even moisture is important during the plant's first year in the garden. Transplant wisteria with care; like all legumes, its roots resent being disturbed. Fasten the young stems to their support until the vines are able to twine on their own.

Amend very sandy soil with compost before planting, and top-dress with fresh compost every fall. Young plants may take up to 10 years to bloom, so be patient when planting them.

The vines need regular pruning to keep them in bounds and looking their best. In summer, prune the long, straggly stems that develop, except for the ones the vine needs to climb. Also one third to half their length, to produce the best flowers. In late winter, while plants are still dormant, you can prune again, cutting back the previously pruned shoots to two or three buds. Cut back to six inches any long shoots that developed after last summer's pruning.

Wisteria floribunda

WHEN WISTERIA WON'T BLOOM

If your wisteria doesn't flower, ask yourself:

Is the plant old enough? Wisteria often takes six or seven, or more, years to produce its first flowers.

Is the soil too rich? Very fertile soil, especially soil rich in nitrogen, causes lavish foliage growth but no flowers. As a remedy, try digging a trench around the base of the plant and working in superphosphate or another phosphorus fertilizer to balance the excess of nitrogen. A more labor-intensive way to stimulate bloom is to prune the roots. Push a sharp spade into the soil in a circle around the base of the plant, 1½ feet out from the trunk, to cut the roots. Severely pruning long stems (back to two or three buds) may also help.

Is there enough light? Wisteria needs a sunny location.

Was last winter too cold? Low temperatures may kill flower buds. If you are in a very exposed location or northern Zone 4 or 5, try removing the vines from their support and laying them out on the ground in late fall. Cover with a foot-deep layer of leaves, hay, or evergreen boughs over winter.

Acknowledgments

WITHOUT THE HELP OF A NUMBER OF people, this book could not have come together. Special thanks to the homeowners, gardeners, garden designers, and landscape architects who so generously shared their time to talk with me about the gardens profiled in chapter 4. They are:

Cynthia Hosmer, in Maine; Tony Elliott, landscape gardener and owner of Snug Harbor Farm, in Kennebunk, Maine; Geraldine King, in Massachusetts; James van Sweden, founding partner, and Sheila Brady, partner, Oehme, van Sweden & Associates, Inc., in Washington, D.C.; Robbie Hutchison, designer, Donaroma's Nursery & Landscape Services, in Edgartown, Massachusetts; John Hill, head gardener, in East Hampton, New York; Edwina von Gal, Edwina von Gal and Company, East Hampton, New York; Mario Nievera, Mario Nievera Design, in Palm Beach, Florida; Meredith Marshall, in Delaware; and Clyde Timmons, senior designer, DesignWorks, in Charleston, South Carolina.

Many thanks also to Kevin Coffey, of Marders, in Bridgehampton, New York, for sharing his knowledge of coastal trees and shrubs; to Tom Stubelek, of Southampton, New York, for sharing his insights and experience gained in more than 20 years of gardening on oceanfront property; and to geologist Thomas Moyer, PhD (also my brother), for reviewing the coastline information in chapter 1.

Finally, thanks to my editor, Carleen Perkins, and to everyone else at Storey Publishing for their support of this book.

— *Anne Halpin*

THIS BOOK WOULD NOT HAVE BEEN possible without the generosity of people who love gardens. Whether it's digging in the dirt, designing a landscape on a bluff above the Atlantic, or sitting beside a marsh under a lichen-speckled olive tree, garden folks want to share their beautiful world with others. Photographing this book, I was the lucky beneficiary of this phenomenon. People shared their homes and gardens, hours of their day, years of their accumulated knowledge, and, of course, plants for my fledgling garden back home. It was my privilege and pleasure to spend time with each of these contributors in their beautiful gardens.

In Maine, Tony Elliott, at Snug Harbor Farm in Kennebunk, spent a day zipping me around to a collection of rock-strewn seascapes, and created a bold sunny border against the sea when Mother Nature wasn't accommodating our timetable. After the sun set on Cynthia and Calvin Hosmer's garden, they wouldn't let me go home without supper. Thanks also to Ed Lowrie, the Molsons, the Sahins, and Frank and Brook Todd.

On the Massachusetts coast, Deborah and Hart Peterson were indispensable. This project wouldn't exist without their vision and their introduction to the gardens around them. Thanks also to the Flannerys, the Goldensons, the Kings, the MacLeods, the McBratneys, and the Michauds.

On a rugged spit of land on Narragansett Bay in Rhode Island, Oehme, van Sweden & Associates shared a landscape that resembles a lucky accident until you spy a plant tag hiding in a thicket.

My friend and frequent garden collaborator, Jane Berger, hosted me and introduced me to the talent of Robbie Hutchison on Martha's Vineyard. Robbie lined up exquisite gardens designed by her and Mike Donaroma's staff at Donaroma's Nursery & Landscape Service. Many thanks also to the Eberstadts, John Glendon, Claudia Miller, the Point Way, and the Shanes.

Once again, I'm indebted to Mac Griswold, who pointed me toward gardens in the Hamptons, New York, that ranged from a series of wistful garden rooms, created by Ryan Gainey, to a spare contemporary meadow, designed by Edwina von Gal. At short notice, David Seeler, at The Bayberry in Amagansett, offered up an array of seaside garden retreats tucked among the dunes and beside the marshes. Thanks also to Susan Calhoun, John Hill, Mark Perlbinder, Steve Perlbinder, the Raphaels, the Rayners, the Rosenbergs, and Barbara Slifka.

At the Delaware beaches, thanks to Meredith and James Marshall, whose beachfront garden, designed by Mario Nievera, unwinds from the dunes into a formal garden.

In Maryland, Jim van Sweden invited me to his retreat on the Eastern Shore — a bold meadow that floats above the Chesapeake Bay. He cooked meals, discussed the landscape value of hackberry trees, and offered me the guestroom next to the pond, where the frogs serenaded me to sleep at night. Thanks also to the Brillembourgs.

In South Carolina, Clyde Timmons at DesignWorks made sure I had plenty of beautiful and inventive gardens to choose from, including a Japanese garden and another that rose out of the pink-tinged marshes. Thanks to the Ackermans, Peter Bartlett, Howell Beach at Robert Marvin/Howell Beach & Associates, the Dursts, Roger Good at Cloverleaf, Kiawah Development Partners, the Luries, and the Pennells.

Many thanks to Anne Halpin for bringing her vast experience in gardening and garden-book writing to this project, and to all those at Storey Publishing: Gwen Steege, for believing I was the "right" person to capture the drama of gardens shaped by wind and sea; Kent Lew and Vicky Vaughn in the art department, for their crisp, elegant design style; my editor, Carleen Perkins, whose calm professionalism guided the project; and the president, Pam Art, who said the words any garden photographer loves to hear: "We take every step to make sure the photographs look as beautiful on the page as they did when you took them."

— *Roger Foley*

ADDITIONAL PHOTO CREDITS

© Henry W. Art: 160 left, 164 right, 205 right; © Joseph DeSciose:140 left, 155 left, 178 right; © Global Book Publishing Photo Library/James Young: 139 top and bottom left, 141 left, 142 left, 146, 148 bottom right, 149, 150 top, 154 left, 156, 157, 161, 163, 168 left, 176 left, 177 bottom, 182 center, 184 left, 189, 193 bottom, 196 left, 197, 210 bottom, 211 bottom, 212 left; © Saxon Holt: 204 bottom right, 205 left; © Macore, Inc.; 143 bottom, 152 right, 153 bottom, 155 right, 158 left, 162 left, 167 left and bottom, 169 right, 170 bottom left, 173 right, 180 center and right, 181 bottom, 183 left, 184 right, 187 bottom, 190, 191 left and center, 194, 198 left, 199, 206; © Adam Mastoon: 70; New England Wild Flower Society, Garden in the Woods, Framingham, Massachusetts (508-877-7630, www.newenglandwildflower.org). © New England Wild Flower Society/Catherine Heffron: 147 top, © New England Wild Flower Society/William Cullina: 166 top, 171 left, 186 center, © New England Wild Flower Society/ John Lynch: 186 right; © Raintree Nursery: 144 bottom

GARDEN DESIGN CREDITS

Anthony Elliot, Snug Harbor Farm: 5, 55 (top), 92–95; Calvin and Cynthia Hosmer: 88–91; Clyde Timmons, DesignWorks: 35, 124–131; Edwina von Gal: 85, 112–115; Frank Todd & Associates: 87, 133; Geraldine King: 68, 96–98; James van Sweden, Oehme, van Sweden & Associates: 120–123; Mario Nievera Designs: 2, 24, 25, 66, 69, 116–119; Robbie Hutchison, Donaroma's Nursery: 104–107; Ryan Gainey: 26, 30, 40 (right), 82, 108–110; Sheila Brady, Oehme, van Sweden & Associates: 6, 40 (left), 52, 100–103

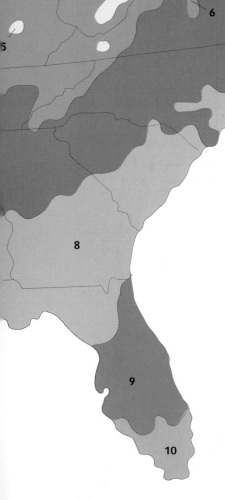

USDA Plant Hardiness Zone Map

THE UNITED STATES DEPARTMENT OF Agriculture (USDA) created this map to give gardeners a helpful tool for selecting and cultivating plants. The map divides North America into 11 zones based on each area's average minimum winter temperature. Zone 1 is the coldest and Zone 11 the warmest. Once you determine your zone, you can use that information to select plants that are most likely to thrive in your climate.

Range of Average Annual Minimum Temperatures for Each Zone

Zone 2	-50° to -40°F	
Zone 3	-40° to -30°F	
Zone 4	-30° to -20°F	
Zone 5	-20° to -10°F	
Zone 6	-10° to 0°F	
Zone 7	0° to 10°F	
Zone 8	10° to 20°F	
Zone 9	20° to 30°F	
Zone 10	30° to 40°F	

Index

Page references in *italics* indicate photos or illustrations.

M

Madagascar periwinkle. See *Catharanthus roseus*

Magnolia, 91

    grandiflora, 122, 130

    virginiana (southern magnolia), 19

maiden grass. *See Miscanthus sinensis*

Malva (lavender mallow), *27*

marguerite, 50

Mario Nievera Designs, 116

Marshall, Meredith, 116–19

marsh cordgrass. *See Spartina patens*

meadow, *102*, 112–13, *120*

mealycup sage. *See Salvia farinacea*

memorial rose. *See Rosa wichuraiana*

microclimates, 56

Milorganite, 88

Miscanthus sinensis (maiden grass, eulalia grass), 112, 115, 203

Monarda, 93

    didyma (beebalm), 35, *107, 178*

mondo grass. *See Ophiopogon*

Montauk daisy. See *Nipponanthemum nipponicum*

moon gate, *91, 105*

mugo pine. *See Pinus mugo*

Muhlenbergia filipes (native sweetgrass), 127, 131

mulch, 68-70, 99

muscadine grape. *See Vitis rotundifolia*

Myrica, 135, 152

    cerifera (wax myrtle), 19, 120, 124, 129–30, 152

    pensylvanica (northern bayberry), 17, 19, 52, *152*

N

narrow-leaved zinnia. *See Zinnia angustifolia*

nasturtium. *See Tropaeolum majus*

needle palm. See *Rhapidophyllum hystrix*

nepeta, *78, 97, 118*

Nepeta × *faassenii*, 179

Nerium oleander (oleander), 153

New England aster. *See Aster novae-angliae*

New Zealand flax. *See Phormium tenax*

nicotiana, *118*

Nievera, Mario, 116–19

Nipponanthemum nipponicum (Montauk daisy), 14, 179

northern bayberry. *See Myrica pensylvanica*

Norway spruce. *See Picea abies*

Nyssa sylvatica (black tupelo), 153

O

Oehme, Wolfgang, 122

Oehme, van Sweden and Associates, 100–103, 120–23

Oenothera, 93, 180

    drummondii (beach evening primrose), *180*

    fruticosa (sundrops), *180*

    speciosa (showy evening primrose), *180*

oleander. *See Nerium oleander*

Ophipogon

    japonicus (mondo grass), 124, 125, 210

    planiscapus (black mondo grass), *210*

organic matter, 48–49

ornamental grasses, *18, 128,* 201–5

outdoor living, 39

Oxydendrum arboreum, 122

P

Panicum virgatum (switchgrass), 122, 203

Parthenocissus, 211

    quinquefolia (Virginia creeper), 25, 211

    tricuspidata, 211

passionflowers, *92, 95*

path, *113, 122,* 129

pavement. *See* hardscaping

Pelargonium, 29, 37

    × *hortorum* (geranium), *194*

Pennisetum, 115, 204

    alopecuroides, 103, 204

    setaceum (purple fountain grass), *96, 204*

    villosum (feathertop), 204

perennial candytuft. *See Iberis sempervirens*

perennials, 168–88

    border, *93, 95, 107, 110*

    deadheading, 71–72

    fertilizer, 67

    planting guidelines, *60*

perilla, *94*

Perovskia atriplicifolia (Russian sage), 52, 103, 181

Persea borbonia (redbay), 130

Persian shield. *See Strobilanthes dyerianus*

pest control, 76–80, 161

Petasites japonicus (butterbur), 122

Petunia, 50

    × *hybrida* (petunia), *195*

    integrifolia (petunia, trailing), *195*

Phlox, 118

    paniculata (garden phlox), *181*

Phormium tenax (New Zealand flax), *196*

Picea

    abies (Norway spruce), *154*

    pungens (blue spruce), 97, *154*

pincushion flower. *See Scabiosa columbaria*

Pinus, 155–57

    bungeana (lacebark pine), 155

    leucodermis (Bosnian pine), 155

    mugo (mugo pine), 155, *156*

    nigra (Austrian pine), *156*

    parviflora (Japanese red pine), 155

    rigida (pitch pine), 155, *157*

    strobus (white pine), 155

    taeda (loblolly pine), 129, *130,* 155, 157

    thunbergii (Japanese black pine), 155

pitch pine. *See Pinus rigida*

Pittosporum tobira (Japanese pittosporum), *157*

plantain lily. *See Hosta*

planters, *127, 128, 131*

planting guidelines, 58–60

plant(s)

    adaptations, seashore, 19

    attributes to avoid, 53

    avoidance of, 54

    choice, 50–53

    crown exposed, 69

    deer-resistant, 77

    drought-tolerant, *56, 63*

    flood-tolerant, 22

    formal, 33

    fragrant, 116, 118

    hardiness zone map, *216*

    informal, 32

    invasive, 54

    native, 35, 65, *123,* 127, 129, 135

    naturalistic garden, 34

    protection from elements, 111

    salt-tolerant, 21, 84, 115

    tough, 99, 123

Other Storey Titles You Will Enjoy

Grasses
by Nancy J. Ondra. Here is a complete introduction to using ornamental grasses in combination with perennials, annuals, shrubs, and other garden plants. Beautiful full-color photos illuminate complete plans for 24 gardens featuring grasses. 144 pages. Paperback with French flaps. ISBN 1-58017-423-X.

The Weather-Resilient Garden
by Charles W.G. Smith. Plant a garden that is beautiful but tough enough to withstand almost anything nature delivers. Smith's encyclopedia of 100 hardy plants helps you garden defensively and includes detailed advice on what to do when a weather disaster strikes your garden. 416 pages. Paperback. ISBN 1-58017-516-3.

The Perennial Gardener's Design Primer
by Stephanie Cohen and Nancy J. Ondra. Learn how to create stunning perennial gardens using basic design principles for putting plants together in pleasing and practical ways. 320 pages. Paperback. ISBN 1-58017-543-0.

Shell Chic
by Marlene Hurley Marshall. Capturing the romance of the beach and a lush eccentricity, *Shell Chic* features creative works from today's shell artisans and tells you how to bring their decorative flair into your home. Gorgeous photography, design ideas, and practical instructions for shell art make this book a beautiful memento from a beach vacation and an inspiring book of craft projects. 160 pages. Hardcover; jacketed. ISBN 1-58017-440-X.

Garden Stone
by Barbara Pleasant. Practical information and more than 250 inspiring photographs explain how to use stone and plants together to create contrasting textures and colors in the garden. 240 pages. Paperback. ISBN 1-58017-544-9.

The Complete Houseplant Survival Manual
by Barbara Pleasant. This friendly approach to selecting and caring for indoor plants — with personality profiles, growing needs, and troubleshooting tips for 160 blooming and foliage varieties — helps guarantee that you'll never kill another houseplant. Whether you're looking for a hip flamingo flower, a delicate orchid, or a sturdy Swedish ivy, you'll find it here. 384 pages. Flexibind. ISBN 1-58017-569-4.

The Flower Gardener's Bible
by Lewis and Nancy Hill. All the inspiration and advice you need on flower gardening is gathered here in a single volume with basic plant information, design ideas and theme gardens, and a photographic encyclopedia of more than 400 plants. 384 pages. Paperback. ISBN 1-58017-462-0.

The Gardener's A–Z Guide to Growing Flowers from Seed to Bloom
by Eileen Powell. This encyclopedia of 576 annuals, perennials, and bulbs includes information on sowing, regional suitability, transplanting, flowering schedule, propagation, and general care for each plant listed. 528 pages. Paperback. ISBN 1-58017-517-1.